GCSE
Religious Studies

Complete Revision and Practice

Covering Christianity (including Mark's Gospel), Judaism and Islam

Contents

Contents

Key to Symbols and Bible / Qur'an References:

(1) The boxes in Section 1 tell you whether the page covers:

CHRISTIANITY — the Christian view...   JUDAISM — ...the Jewish view...   ISLAM — ...the Muslim view...

GENERAL — ... or general views that everyone doing a perspectives option needs to learn.

(2) In Section 2 there's also a box to tell you you've reached the stuff about Mark's Gospel.
You might not need that stuff, even if you do need the rest of the section.   GOSPEL

(3) References from the Bible always go in the order: *Book Chapter:Verse(s)*. So whenever you see something like:
Mark 3:5-6, it means it's from the book of **Mark**, **Chapter 3**, **verses 5-6**.
Similarly, references from the Qur'an are shown with the *Surah (Chapter)* followed by the *Ayat (Verse)*.

Published by Coordination Group Publications Ltd.

Editors:
Sharon Keeley, Alan Rix.

Contributors:
Stewart Bates-Treloar, Toria Forsyth-Moser, Jill Hudson, Simon Little, Tim Major, Hugh Mascetti, John Nichols, Andy Park, Duncan Raynor, Glenn Rogers, Paul D. Smith, Ami Snelling, Nigel Thomas, Claire Thompson, Julie Wakeling, Sharon Watson

With thanks to Glennis Atkinson for the proofreading.

AQA material is reproduced by kind permission of the Assessment and Qualifications Alliance.

Edexcel examination questions are reproduced by permission of Edexcel Ltd.

OCR examination questions are reproduced by kind permission of OCR.

ISBN-10: 1 84146 387 6
ISBN-13: 978 1 84146 387 2

Website: www.cgpbooks.co.uk
Printed by Elanders Hindson Ltd, Newcastle upon Tyne.
Clipart from CorelDRAW®
With thanks to Enid Thompson for some of the church photos.

Spirituality

Here we go then, with a really tricky page. What a way to start.

Spirituality isn't necessarily to do with religion

There are a couple of ways of defining spirituality:

a) Concern with anything relating primarily to the spirit (or soul): this isn't necessarily to do with religion. Someone whose mind or emotions work on a 'higher plane' may be described as a spiritual person.

b) An expression of faith: anything relating to the way in which a religious person demonstrates his or her spiritual side — something which is built up through religious practice.

Spirituality is hard to put your finger on

1) An important part of spirituality for many people (whether it's religious or not) is the search for the meaning of life. This may involve thinking about questions such as "where did I come from?" and "why am I here?" — questions that are difficult to find answers to.

2) A spiritual person might also be described as someone who's more aware of things that aren't simply physical — they feel there's another dimension to life.

3) It's about feelings of awe and wonder, or a sense of inner peace. Some people might get these kinds of feelings from a beautiful sunset, a wild sea or a rugged mountain range.

4) Spirituality could also be described as being self-aware — aware of your actions and their effects on others, or having a deeper understanding of your self-worth or purpose in life.

5) This might lead to a more refined recognition of the value of the world, of our place within it, and of those we share the planet with. A less selfish world-view perhaps.

6) For religious believers, spirituality is linked strongly to their beliefs in God. Others say that although they don't believe in God as such, and don't belong to a specific faith, they do believe in 'something'.

There are different ways of expressing spirituality

1) Many ways of expressing spirituality are religious, but certainly not all of them.

2) Religious symbolism can express spirituality, like an ichthus (Christian fish symbol) on the back of your car, or a kippah (a small round cap worn by Jewish men). Your actions might also demonstrate spirituality — e.g. meditating, praying, leading a disciplined life, or belonging to a faith community. A faith community can range from a monastic lifestyle to taking part in community-based activities.

3) For those who have no specific faith, support or membership of a voluntary organisation (and the reasons for that support) would demonstrate spirituality.

4) But people can also explore their spirituality in a number of other ways. This could be through art, literature or music, or some other creative area. These activities allow people to explore their emotions in an attempt to produce work of beauty and meaning.

Spirituality doesn't have to be about religion...

Hmmm — a page about spirituality to get the book going. Not the easiest thing in the world to get your head round... but interesting. You definitely shouldn't be put off by this 'heavy' opening page. This is a cracking subject, and a whole lot more interesting than maths. Read on...

The Nature of Truth

There are different kinds of truth, and they all have their problems. Yep, I know... tricky.

There are **four** main kinds of **truth**

① SCIENTIFIC TRUTH:

This is what people often mean by 'truth'. Scientists test their theories by observing things or performing experiments. But even if the same thing happens every time, does that necessarily mean their theory is true... A more accurate measurement or more sophisticated experiment might give a different result.

② HISTORICAL TRUTH:

We work out what happened in the past by looking at historical evidence (e.g. eyewitness accounts, archaeological evidence). But an eyewitness account might be biased. And other kinds of evidence can be misinterpreted, so it's difficult to say for sure that we know what went on.

③ MORAL TRUTH:

A person's idea of moral truth is what they believe to be morally right or wrong. They might arrive at this conclusion through thinking about life, watching or talking to people, or perhaps through thinking about what their religion teaches. For example, one person might think, *"It's always wrong to lie,"* whereas another person might think, *"It's generally wrong to lie, but if a lie will stop someone getting hurt unnecessarily, then it's okay."*

④ SPIRITUAL / RELIGIOUS TRUTH:

Two different Christians (for example) might interpret the Bible in different ways, and each could claim that their interpretation comes from God — their versions of the truth are different. This kind of truth is a matter of faith and conscience — it's not the kind of thing that can be proved. But does that mean it isn't true...

Many people believe it's impossible to find absolute truth — certainly none of these 4 kinds of truth is infallible.

Evidence isn't the same as *proof*

1) Evidence is a reason to believe a theory, and the more evidence you have for something, the more likely it is to be true. And with enough evidence, you might be able to persuade someone that something is true.
2) But even if you could persuade people of something, does that make it true...
3) Also, people might interpret a piece of evidence in a different way — they may argue that the evidence actually points to something else being true.
4) Proof, on the other hand, is something which definitely shows truth and can't be disputed.

People look for **religious truth** in different places

Religious people look in various places to find the 'truth' about the nature of God, or what God wants.

SACRED WRITINGS Believers most commonly look to sacred writings (e.g. the Bible, the Qur'an or the Torah) for religious truth. But some people will claim that the Bible should be interpreted to suit the times, whereas others argue that it's the Word of God and must be taken literally. Who can really know exactly what God intended...

RELIGIOUS LEADERS Religious people may also look to religious leaders (e.g. the Pope), institutions (e.g. the Church) or their religious traditions to find truth. But religious leaders are human, and humans have failings — do they really speak on behalf of God... The same goes for members of the Church — present and past. And the Church and its traditions were founded by humans — so the same argument could be used.

CONSCIENCE You might also believe that inner truth comes from your conscience — that little voice in your head telling you what's right or wrong. Some people argue that this is the voice of God. Others say that people's ideas of what's right and wrong depend on their personal circumstances — e.g. your parents or your environment could influence what you think is morally right.

Everything on this page is true — trust me...

Religion is a matter of faith — believers will believe certain things to be true regardless of whether there is any evidence. That's the nature of the thing. Now go back and make sure you know the truth.

Believing in God

Millions of people worldwide believe in some kind of <u>divine being</u> or '<u>god</u>'. They believe for various reasons — for some people, it's based on <u>personal religious experience</u>, for others it's more <u>indirect</u>. For many, the fact that they're <u>brought up</u> in a religious environment leads to or supports belief in a god.

*It can start with your **upbringing** or a **search for meaning***

1) If you were brought up by <u>religious parents</u> and your <u>upbringing</u> itself was based on <u>religious teaching</u>, it seems <u>more likely</u> that you would <u>believe</u> in a god. The same would apply if you grew up in a <u>religious community</u> where life was based on faith in one particular religion.

2) The presence of <u>religion in the world</u> may also have an influence. It could be that you are influenced by the <u>good work</u> that religion does in the world — whether it be for <u>individuals</u>, <u>communities</u> or those who are experiencing <u>suffering</u>.

3) You may also be drawn to the <u>purpose</u> and <u>structure</u> it provides — or simply to the desire to have <u>something to believe in</u>.

4) The <u>search for meaning</u> is a major reason for people becoming interested in a particular religion. People want to find <u>answers</u> or find out why life is as it is, and they might believe religion can help. Becoming a follower of God in this way is called <u>conversion</u>.

5) This desire to find out <u>why we are here</u> or <u>why bad things happen</u> in the world might also <u>explain</u> why some people <u>move from one religion</u> to another.

*Someone **must have** **designed** the **planet***

1) Many people are convinced by what might be termed '<u>design</u>' arguments. The idea here is that the <u>intricate workings</u> of the <u>Universe</u> (or of <u>life</u>) <u>can't</u> have come about by <u>random chance</u>. There must have been some kind of <u>designer</u> and this designer was <u>God</u>.

2) Isaac Newton's <u>thumb theory</u> (*because every <u>thumbprint</u> is intricate and <u>unique</u>, there must be a God*) and William Paley's watchmaker theory (*you <u>wouldn't think</u> an <u>intricate watch</u> you found was made by <u>chance</u> — so why believe the <u>world was</u>*) are both design arguments.

Einstein

3) Even Albert Einstein, one of the most prominent scientists of the twentieth century (and an agnostic), said:

"When I see all the glories of the cosmos, I can't help but believe that there is a <u>divine hand</u> behind it all."

4) Einstein might have been talking about design, but this might also be interpreted as a reference to a '<u>numinous</u>' experience — something which <u>inspires awe and wonder</u> at God's creation (see page 4).

5) <u>Miracles</u> and the <u>power of prayer</u> might also lead someone to believe in God, but these are <u>directly religious</u> reasons which we'll look at later.

6) However, some of the <u>non-religious ideas</u> about the origin of the world might lead some people to become <u>agnostic</u> (to believe it's <u>impossible to know</u> whether there's a god or not) or <u>atheist</u> (to <u>reject completely</u> the idea of a divine being).

7) These ideas might include the theory of <u>evolution</u> (often called <u>Darwinism</u>) and the <u>Big Bang theory</u> (<u>cosmology</u>). (More about that on page 12.) <u>Miracles</u> can also be <u>explained</u> by using <u>science</u> and this too <u>may convince</u> some that there is <u>no god</u>.

Darwin

Looks like the jury's still out on this one...

Basically, religion's a personal thing — Bob believes cos his mum does, Al doesn't believe at all. Learn all these reasons for believing (or not) — you get marks for including them in your answers.

Religious Experiences

There are <u>lots of ways</u> people claim to <u>experience God</u>. These experiences allow people to 'know'
God as he reveals himself to them. A <u>key concern</u> for <u>nonbelievers</u> is whether the experiences are real.
Some might claim they're <u>just illusions</u> brought on by <u>religious hysteria</u> or a <u>desire to believe</u>.

Revelation — God **reveals** his presence

God can reveal his presence in <u>different ways</u>...

1) **NUMINOUS**

   This word describes an <u>experience</u> which <u>inspires awe and wonder</u> and might allow someone to <u>feel God's</u>
   <u>presence</u>. For example, a <u>butterfly's wing</u> might convince you there must be a creator.

2) **MIRACLES**

   <u>Jesus</u> was renowned for his miracles — <u>amazing events</u> which <u>couldn't be explained</u> by the laws of <u>nature</u> or
   <u>science</u>. People claim miracles still occur (miracles of <u>healing</u> at <u>Lourdes</u>, for example)
   and bring people to God. Miracles are said to <u>show God's power</u> and presence.

3) **PRAYER**

   Revelation can also come in the form of <u>prayer</u> (talking with God) — a person might feel that a prayer was
   <u>answered</u> (e.g. by an ill person being miraculously cured), or they might simply be filled with a sense of <u>deep</u>
   <u>inner peace</u> or <u>wonder</u>.

4) **RELIGIOUS SCRIPTURE**

   People can read <u>religious scripture</u> (e.g. the Bible, the Qur'an or the Torah), and feel that the nature
   of <u>God</u> has been <u>revealed</u>.

5) **CHARISMATIC PHENOMENA (or Charismatic Worship)**

   Following conversion, a <u>Christian believer</u> may claim to have been <u>touched by the Holy Spirit</u> (p.8) and
   may demonstrate <u>spiritual gifts</u>. These range from singing, dancing, shaking or crying during worship to
   '<u>speaking in tongues</u>' (unknown languages), having <u>visions</u> or <u>prophesying</u> (predicting the future).

6) **SACRAMENTAL RITUAL (see page 78)**

   For example, <u>Holy Communion</u> is an act of sacramental worship. In the Roman Catholic
   Church, the <u>bread and wine</u> are <u>believed</u> to actually <u>become</u> Christ's body and blood
   (called <u>transubstantiation</u>) and this reveals the presence of God.

7) **MEDITATION**

   <u>Focusing mental energies</u> on God may bring about <u>visions</u> or <u>voices</u>. These could be inspired by <u>prayer</u>,
   <u>reading scripture</u> or <u>fasting</u>. It doesn't need to be in a place of worship — you can <u>meditate anywhere</u>.

> <u>CONVERSION</u> refers to the <u>first time</u> a person <u>becomes a follower</u> of God (although it can also be
> used when someone <u>changes their faith</u>). They might say they've been '<u>saved</u>' or '<u>born again</u>'.

Revelation can be **general** (for **everyone**) or **special** (a **personal** visit)

<u>General revelation</u> refers to <u>experiences</u>
which are <u>available to everyone</u>, including:
- acts of nature, conscience and morality,
- religious scripture,
- the work of religious leaders.

Special revelation describes experiences of <u>God revealing</u>
<u>himself directly</u> to an <u>individual</u> or to a <u>select group</u>, e.g.:
- visions,
- dreams,
- prophecies.

1) Some religious believers would <u>argue</u> that <u>general revelation is enough</u> for us to know God,
   while <u>others</u> would say that <u>God must reveal himself</u> in a new, <u>special way</u> for <u>each generation</u>.

2) Many <u>believers</u> would argue that a <u>balance of general and special</u> revelation is required.

Believers can have many different kinds of religious experience

Revelations, eh... Wow. I mean, just imagine. It's just <u>mind-blowing</u>...

The Nature of God

What's God like? — the debate continues

The question of <u>what God is like</u> has occupied religious thinkers for <u>hundreds of years</u>.
There are three main issues:

> 1) Is God a kind of '<u>person</u>' or a kind of '<u>force</u>'?
> 2) Is God <u>within or outside</u> the Universe?
> 3) Is there just <u>one god</u> or are there <u>many gods</u>?

None of these ideas are without problems, however, and many
people would argue that God is actually a combination of them all.

Is God a 'person'?

1) The term '<u>personal god</u>' refers to God as a '<u>person</u>' — albeit an almighty and <u>divine person</u>.
God would be someone that <u>supports and cares</u> for us <u>as a friend</u> would, with <u>human emotions</u>.
In this case, <u>prayer</u> would become part of our individual relationship — a '<u>conversation' with God</u>.

2) The problem with this is that God is meant to be <u>omnipresent</u>
(everywhere at once) — which poses the question of <u>how</u> a
<u>personal god</u> can be <u>everywhere at once</u>.

3) The term '<u>impersonal god</u>' refers to God as a <u>concept</u>, a <u>force</u> or an
<u>idea</u> of <u>goodness and light</u>. The '<u>prime number</u>' theory is often used to
represent this idea of God — something that <u>can't be divided</u> or reduced.

4) The <u>obvious problem</u> here is how you can have a <u>relationship</u> with a <u>force</u> or an <u>idea</u>.

Where is God?

1) An '<u>immanent</u>' God is a God who is <u>in the world</u> with us — a God who has taken an <u>active role</u> in the
progress of <u>human history</u> and <u>continues</u> to do so.

2) The <u>problem</u> here is that an immanent God may appear <u>small</u> and <u>fallible</u>.

3) On the other hand, a '<u>transcendent</u>' God is <u>outside the world</u> and <u>doesn't directly act</u> in human history.

4) This view of God makes him <u>remote</u> and <u>separate</u> from our experience on Earth.
However, <u>Christians</u> who see God as transcendent might argue that it is <u>they</u> who
<u>do the work</u> of God and that he is working <u>through them</u>.

5) Unfortunately, this definition is a bit <u>too abstract</u> for a lot of people to understand.

6) Religious believers (and Christians in particular) often try <u>not</u> to deal with <u>extremes</u> of any of these ideas,
preferring instead to draw on <u>different aspects</u> for different occasions. Many would argue that God needs
to be a <u>blend</u> of all of the above.

How many gods are there?

1) <u>Monotheism</u> is the idea of <u>one God</u>.
This exists in <u>Christianity</u>, <u>Judaism</u> and <u>Islam</u>.

2) <u>Polytheism</u> is the belief in <u>more than one</u> god,
e.g. in Classical Greek and Roman civilisations,
and some forms of Hinduism.

> Although Christianity is monotheistic,
> there is a belief that God is actually three
> in one (the Trinity, see p.8) — the Father,
> the Son (Jesus) and the Holy Spirit.

These questions have been worrying <u>loads</u> of people for <u>ages</u>...

But, tricky or not, you'll have to understand all these arguments to do well in your GCSE.

Warm-Up and Worked Exam Question

Warm-up Questions

1) What is meant by a belief that God is "omnipresent"?
2) What is an agnostic?
3) Describe two non-religious experiences which would usually be described as spiritual?
4) Name three sources from which religious people believe they can find the truth about the nature of God or what He wants.
5) Name two world religions that are monotheistic.

Worked Exam Question

Read through this worked example carefully, then have a go at the practice exam questions on the next page. Even though this is an "opinion" question, you need to give both sides of the argument — just ranting about one point of view won't get you the marks.

1   "People who say that they are spiritual without believing in God are kidding themselves." Do you agree? Give reasons for your answer showing you have thought about more than one religious point of view.

This statement suggests that you cannot really be spiritual if you do not believe in God, yet millions of people who follow religions such as Hinduism and Buddhism do not believe in "God" in the sense of a single all-powerful God. Despite this, they are clearly spiritual. Furthermore, people who do not have any formal religion can still think deeply about non-material things and may still believe in "something".

On the other hand, the word "spiritual" starts to lose its meaning if it is just used to mean "good". An atheist and a religious person might be equally good, but it seems odd to call the atheist "spiritual" if he or she does not believe in any kind of soul or spirit.

I feel that if people are truly spiritual, they will express it somehow. This may be by practising a religion, working for a voluntary organisation or producing creative work, through art or music. Believing in God is just one aspect of spirituality. Therefore, I disagree with the statement above.

This is just one possible answer. You get marks for how good your argument is, not for your particular opinion. You do need to give an opinion though — if you don't, you haven't answered the question.

(5 marks)

Exam Questions

2   a)   Explain what is meant by a "personal God."

(2 marks)

     b)   According to the Christian view of Jesus' incarnation on Earth, was he an example of a transcendent or an immanent God?

         Explain your answer.

(2 marks)

3   Truth can be found in many different forms.

     a)   What is meant by scientific truth?

(4 marks)

     b)   Explain the difference between evidence in favour of a theory and proof of it.

(3 marks)

     c)   Explain why some religious people say it is a good thing to believe in God without evidence.

(3 marks)

4   Name a famous thinker who has used the "design" argument to support the existence of a Creator.

     Briefly describe the argument he or she used.

(3 marks)

5   a)   What is the difference between special and general revelation?

(2 marks)

     b)   What does it mean "to experience the numinous"?

(2 marks)

     c)   State THREE other ways in which religious people believe God reveals his presence.

(3 marks)

| CHRISTIANITY & JUDAISM | # Christian and Jewish Teaching on God |

Judaism and *Christianity* say *Similar* Things about *God*...

1) As Christianity grew directly from Judaism, the two faiths share the same basic concept of God.

2) The Judaeo-Christian God is usually seen as male (referred to as He or Father) although nowadays many religious believers would argue that this is simply because when these religions were founded society was male-dominated, and that God is actually neither male nor female.

3) Both faiths share the ideas that God is omnipotent (all-powerful), omnipresent (everywhere) and omniscient (all-knowing), that God is divine, supreme, totally good and totally perfect, and that God has given us free will.

However, some Jews and Christians believe that our lives are predestined — we control individual actions, but not the ultimate outcome of our lives.

...but there are some **big differences**

4) The biggest difference is the Christian belief in the Trinity. Jews never believed Christ was the Son of God.

5) Another key difference between Jewish and Christian teaching is that Jews are forbidden to draw or make images of God.

The **Trinity** is explained in the **Nicene Creed**

1) The Christian idea of the Trinity is perhaps best expressed in the Nicene Creed:

> *"We believe in one God, the Father, the almighty, maker of heaven and earth... We believe in one Lord, Jesus Christ, the only son of God... Of one being with the Father... We believe in the Holy Spirit... The giver of life... Who proceeds from the Father and the Son..."*

2) God the Father might be described as the transcendent part of God, the Son as the immanent and personal part, and the Holy Spirit the immanent yet impersonal (see page 5).

3) Similarly, Christians might describe the Father as the creator and judge, the Son (Jesus) as the human incarnation of God (and the Messiah, or saviour), and the Holy Spirit as the force of God — inspiring, guiding and comforting them.

See page 58 for more about this stuff.

The Jewish **Shema Prayer** talks about just **one God**

> *"Hear, O Israel: the Lord our God, the Lord is one."*   **Deuteronomy 6:4**

1) This passage is contained in the Shema — one of the most important prayers in Judaism. The Jewish God is, therefore, quite clearly seen as one.

2) Maimonides, a twelfth-century Jewish thinker, came up with a set of principles of Jewish faith. These principles contain many of Judaism's key teachings on God (see page 92).

Christianity says there's a **Devil** — **Judaism** says there **isn't**

1) Judaism has no concept of a devil fighting against God and tempting people into doing evil deeds. It is believed that God created all — and that includes both good and evil.

Satan is mentioned in the Hebrew Bible (particularly the Book of Job), but this concept isn't really part of modern Judaism.

2) Some (but not all) Christians do believe in an evil, spiritual force known as the Devil or Satan who is working against God, bringing evil and suffering to humanity. E.g. in one of St. Paul's letters to the Ephesians, he says:

> *"Put on the full armour of God, so that you can take your stand against the Devil's schemes."*   **Ephesians 6:11**

Muslim Teaching on God

The *Muslim* name for God is *Allah*

1) For Muslims, God is called <u>Allah</u> — and the word '<u>Islam</u>' can be translated as meaning '<u>submission</u>' or '<u>surrender</u>' <u>to Allah</u>.

2) According to Islamic teaching, <u>Allah</u> is the <u>creator</u> of everything.

3) He is referred to by <u>ninety-nine names</u> in the Qur'an — these names tell you what <u>Muslims believe</u> about Allah and his power. They include: <u>Ar-Rahim</u> — The <u>Compassionate</u>, <u>Ar-Rahman</u> — The <u>Merciful</u>, <u>Ar-Aziz</u> — The <u>Almighty</u>. He is also called The <u>Provider</u>, The <u>Just</u>, The <u>Maintainer</u>, The <u>Hearer</u> and The <u>Real Truth</u>.

"He is *Allah, The One*, Allah is *Eternal* and *Absolute*"

1) This passage is taken from **Surah 112** and describes the <u>basic principle</u> that <u>Allah is one</u>. Islam is a <u>monotheistic</u> religion (see page 5) and this belief in the oneness or the <u>unity of Allah</u> (called <u>Tawhid</u>) is a <u>fundamental</u> principle of Islam.

2) The ninety-nine names sum up much of the nature of Allah. He is <u>loving</u> and <u>compassionate</u>, he is the <u>creator</u> and <u>judge</u> of all humans, and knows <u>everything</u> they do.

3) Allah cannot be thought of in human terms — he is the Supreme Being and has no equal.

4) To Muslims, Allah is <u>both immanent</u> and <u>transcendent</u> (see page 5). He is <u>transcendent</u> in that he is the <u>power behind the Universe</u> and is <u>outside</u>, above or beyond both <u>his creation</u> and <u>time</u> itself. His <u>immanence</u> is demonstrated in this passage:

> "We created man and We <u>know</u> what his <u>soul</u> whispers to him, and We are nearer to him than his <u>jugular vein</u>." **Surah 50:16**

(In this passage 'We' refers to Allah and 'him' or 'his' refers to humankind.)

5) Human lives are <u>planned</u> by Allah — but humans do have <u>free will</u> (see page 17).

There are *five* main ways to *know Allah*

1) Muslims believe that Allah has <u>intervened</u> in <u>human history</u> and that this is one way of <u>knowing</u> him and <u>his power</u>. His message was delivered by the <u>prophets</u>, of whom twenty-five are mentioned in the Qur'an. These include <u>Musa</u> (<u>Moses</u>) and '<u>Isa</u> (<u>Jesus</u>). The last was the Prophet <u>Muhammad</u>, who <u>brought Allah's message</u> to the people.

2) Allah has also performed <u>miracles</u>.

3) The <u>Five Pillars of Islam</u> (see pages 119-120) also provide opportunities to know and be close to Allah. These are: Shahadah (a statement of <u>belief</u>), Salah (<u>prayer</u>), Zakah (<u>charitable</u> duty), Sawm (<u>fasting</u>), Hajj (<u>pilgrimage</u>).

A Muslim prayer ritual

4) The <u>Qur'an</u> itself, being the <u>word of Allah</u>, allows humans to know him. Many Muslims learn it off by heart, and all try to live according to the guidelines found within it.

5) Allah is good and kind. However, there is a belief in a <u>devil</u> (called <u>Iblis</u> or <u>Shaytan</u>) who was <u>cast out by Allah</u> and tries to <u>lead people away</u> from him. <u>Some</u> Muslims would argue that Allah <u>allows Shaytan</u> to use this power to <u>test and tempt</u> us — we have the <u>free will to resist</u>.

Immanent AND transcendent — tricky to get your head round...

At the end of the day, it seems Christians, Jews and Muslims all agree on the fundamentals — that God/Allah is <u>divine</u>, <u>supreme</u>, <u>all-powerful</u> and <u>all-knowing</u>, that our lives are <u>planned</u> and that we have <u>free will</u>.

CHRISTIANITY & GENERAL

Evil and Suffering

Loads of bad things happen in the world. People suffer from terrible <u>illnesses</u> and die in <u>pain</u>. Some people commit horrible <u>crimes</u> and other people <u>suffer</u> as a result. These issues often cause people to ask <u>why</u>. For religious people, the bigger question is: *"Why is <u>God</u> <u>letting</u> this happen?"*

Evil can be either **human-made** or **natural**

Evil and suffering can be divided into <u>two types</u>:

HUMAN-MADE (OR MORAL) EVIL

1) This is when suffering is brought about by the <u>cruel</u> actions of <u>people</u>.
2) This includes things like murder, war, rape and torture.
3) The person causing the evil is able to make a <u>choice</u> about what is morally <u>right or wrong</u>.

NATURAL EVIL

1) This kind of evil, and the suffering that comes with it, is <u>caused by the world</u> in which we live and is <u>no one's 'fault'</u>.
2) This includes things like floods, earthquakes and hurricanes.
3) However, many <u>recent natural disasters</u> may have been caused by <u>human interference</u> in the natural world, raising the question of whether that makes those events human-made.

Evil can lead people to **question** their **faith**

1) <u>Evil</u> and <u>suffering</u> may lead some people to <u>question</u> their belief in God — or even to <u>reject</u> their faith.
2) This might be because they can't believe that a God who is <u>good</u> would <u>allow</u> such things to happen, or because they feel that their <u>prayers</u> are not being <u>answered</u> (i.e. they think God <u>could</u> help, but <u>doesn't</u>).
3) Other people might argue that God can't be very <u>powerful</u> if he is <u>unable</u> to prevent suffering (i.e. God <u>can't</u> help, even if he wanted to).

Many people have tried to define evil and work out what it is or where it comes from. Some have argued that human-made evil is a psychological phenomenon that some people are more prone to than others.

4) People often argue that we <u>can't</u> know <u>why</u> there is suffering in the world — only <u>God</u> knows that. Suffering is often seen as a <u>test of faith</u> — God will have his <u>reasons</u> (even if we <u>don't know</u> what they are).
5) <u>Praying</u> for and <u>helping</u> those who suffer is often seen as a key part of various <u>faiths</u>.

The **Christian** View — **Adam & Eve**, **Satan**, a **test of faith**

1) <u>Christianity</u> and <u>Judaism</u> teach that evil <u>entered</u> the world as a result of <u>Adam and Eve</u> giving in to <u>temptation</u> in the Garden of Eden — this switch from a perfect world to one containing evil is known as '<u>The Fall</u>'.
2) After the Fall, every human being was born with a <u>flawed</u> nature — this is the idea of <u>original sin</u>.
3) Christians believe God created humans with <u>free will</u> — it's up to us to <u>choose</u> whether we perform evil deeds or not — just as it was up to <u>Adam and Eve</u> whether to give in to temptation or not.

Christianity and Judaism differ in that Christians believe Jesus was put on Earth to pay for the sins of all humankind.

4) Christianity has also <u>personified</u> evil as <u>Satan</u> or the <u>Devil</u> — a <u>supernatural</u> evil force over which we have no control. Satan was one of God's <u>archangels</u> but was <u>thrown out</u> of heaven.
5) Christians might refer to someone who has performed evil deeds as being <u>possessed by the Devil</u>, although this isn't really a part of <u>modern</u> Christian teaching.

Not the cheeriest page in the book for sure...

You need to learn the distinction between human-made evil and natural evil, and the effect that any kind of evil can have on religious people and their faith. If you're studying Christianity, learn those last five points as well.

Judaism and Islam — Evil and Suffering

The problem of evil, why people suffer, and how to deal with it. It's the sort of thing religion was invented for.

Islam and Judaism also say we have the choice...

1) Both Islam and Judaism teach that humankind was created with free will.
2) Therefore, people can choose to follow God, or choose to do wrong.
3) Islam and Judaism also have similar perspectives on how to deal with suffering and evil.

Judaism says suffering can have positive results

1) The Book of Job in the Hebrew Scriptures contains a key Jewish idea on evil and suffering. Job endures terrible suffering of all kinds and he questions God. In the end Job comes to the conclusion that God is all-powerful and knows what he is doing — and that suffering must be accepted because we can't really understand the world or God's plan.
2) Judaism teaches that we have free will and are able to choose what we do (like Adam and Eve — see page 10). But we are prone to making mistakes which could lead to suffering.
3) Like many Christians, Jews may also respond to suffering and evil through prayer.
4) The Jewish approach to suffering often stresses the idea that good can come out of terrible suffering. Suffering can bring people closer to each other and closer to God. It also allows people to make sacrifices for other people and draw on their inner strength.
5) The following passage is from taken from the Midrash (a collection of Rabbinical commentaries on the Tenakh or Jewish Bible): "Not to have known suffering is not to be truly human." It suggests that suffering is simply a part of the human experience and, therefore, must be accepted.

Although Satan isn't a part of modern Judaism, he does give Job a hard time.

The Qur'an says "Surely We shall test you"

1) Muslims believe that evil is a test of humanity's free will. Allah allows Shaytan (the Devil) to tempt humankind — we have free will so can choose whether to give in to temptation or not. It's a test of faith.
2) Islam teaches that if we choose to act against the will of Allah we will have to answer for that wrongdoing on the Day of Judgement.
3) The following passage is taken from **Surah 2:155-6**

— "Surely We shall test you with something of fear and hunger, and loss of wealth and lives and crops... but give glad tidings to the steadfast who say when misfortune strikes: we are Allah's and to Him we are returning."

 This is remarkably similar to the moral of the Book of Job, when you think about it.

4) The idea here is that suffering should be accepted. Muslims believe that, despite suffering in this life, there will be joy in the next as Allah is compassionate.
5) Prayer is one way of coping with evil and suffering. If people pray for forgiveness when they have done wrong they will be forgiven. One of the ninety-nine names of Allah is Al-Ghaffar — The Forgiver (see page 9).
6) Muslims believe that those who are suffering should be treated compassionately by others. Many Muslims work to help those who are suffering.

Christianity, Judaism and Islam see suffering as a test of faith...
Three different religions, but pretty similar ideas about this stuff: 1) Suffering is mostly seen as a test from God/Allah. 2) You should always try to help others who are suffering. 3) Evil is wrong and against God/Allah, but if you pray for forgiveness after doing something wrong, God/Allah will be merciful and forgive you.

The Origin of the World

No one saw exactly how the Earth came to be like it is... but science and religion still think they know.

Scientific arguments — there are two main types

COSMOLOGICAL THEORIES — How the Universe came into being

Chief amongst these is the Big Bang theory. Scientists argue that the Universe began in an explosion of matter and energy. Matter from this explosion eventually formed stars, planets and everything else. The Universe still seems to be expanding today — important evidence for this theory.

EVOLUTIONARY THEORIES — How living things came to be as they are today

In 1859, Charles Darwin published 'The Origin of Species'. In this book he argued that all life on the planet originated from simple cells. Life evolved over millions of years into a huge variety of forms. According to this theory, we evolved from apes — not from Adam and Eve.

These theories are at odds with many religious arguments. However, if you don't take everything written in the Bible or the Torah literally, scientific and religious ideas can exist in harmony. Science tells us how, religion tells us why.

Religions have their own ideas about all this...

Christian ideas

1) Christian and Jewish ideas about Creation come from the same scriptures, and so are quite similar.

2) Christian thinking is based on the idea that God created everything. If the Bible is taken literally the process took six days, and humankind didn't evolve from apes but descended from Adam and Eve.

3) However, if it's viewed as a symbolic description of a more gradual evolution, then it's possible to believe both in the Bible and science.

For example, the Bible says things were created in the following order — the heavens (i.e. space) and Earth, the atmosphere, land and sea, and then plants, animals and people. This is pretty much the same order as scientists believe things appeared. So the timescale is different (millions of years rather than six days), but the general idea is the same.

4) In 1996 the Roman Catholic Church accepted the Big Bang theory — definitely a significant acceptance of science.

Jewish ideas

1) Orthodox Jews, who see the Torah as the word of God and so literally true, would find it difficult to accept scientific arguments about creation. God is believed to have created the world in six days. And humanity is believed to have started with Adam and Eve.

"In the beginning God created the heavens and the earth." **Genesis 1:1**

2) Progressive or Liberal Jews might argue that Creation as described in the Torah is more a way for us to understand, not an explanation of how it happened.

Islamic ideas

1) Muslims believe that Allah created the world and everything in it.

2) However, unlike Christianity and Judaism, descriptions of creation in the Qur'an are not entirely at odds with science. Islam does not really have a problem competing with the Big Bang theory or Darwinism. In fact, scientific theories are supported by passages such as this.

"Have not those who disbelieve known that the heavens and the earth were of one piece, then We parted them, and We made every living thing of water?" **Surah 21:31-2**

This is a key question in the science vs. religion debate...

Albert Einstein once said that if you see something beautiful or amazing, you are seeing the work of God. But whether the Universe came to be this way through chance (Big Bang) or design is a big question.

Warm-Up and Worked Exam Question

Warm-up Questions

1) According to the Book of Genesis in the Bible, how long did it take to create the world?
2) What are the Five Pillars of Islam?
3) Of Jews, Christians and Muslims, which believe in the Trinity?
4) What is the Muslim name for the Devil?
5) Give one example of natural evil and one example of human-made evil.
6) What is the name of the Jewish prayer that begins with the words, "Hear, O Israel: the Lord our God, the Lord is one"?

Worked Exam Question

Okay, it's exam question time, and I've done the first one for you. Have a go at answering the question yourself and compare your answer with the one given. Then turn over and try the questions on page 14.

1 a) What is the difference between natural and moral evil?

Natural evil causes suffering without being anybody's fault. An example is a tsunami. Moral evil is caused by someone's choice to sin.

(2 marks)

b) Give a brief outline of the Biblical account of how evil first came into the world.

Adam and Eve lived lives of perfect innocence and obedience in the Garden of Eden. They were tempted by Satan in the form of a serpent to disobey God by eating forbidden fruit. They gave into temptation and were expelled from the Garden of Eden. After this, every human was born with a flawed nature.

You get marks for the "quality of your written communication" as well as what you actually say.   *(4 marks)*

c) Natural disasters can kill or harm innocent people.

Explain how some people use this to argue that Christians, Jews and Muslims are all wrong about the nature of God.

Many people argue that if God lets the innocent suffer or die then it shows either that he cannot help them or that he can help but refuses to. This appears to contradict the idea, shared by all three religions, that God is both good and all-powerful.   The question mentions Christianity, Judaism and Islam, so make sure you refer to all three in your answer.

Some claim that the only other explanation is that God does not exist. This argument clearly contradicts the beliefs of Christianity, Judaism and Islam.

(5 marks)

Exam Questions

2   a)   Describe what ONE religion you have studied teaches about suffering.

(8 marks)

      b)   "If only good things happened in the world our lives would be meaningless."

         Do you agree? Give reasons for your opinion, showing that you have considered another point of view. In your answer you should refer to religious ideas.

(5 marks)

3   Read the following dialogue and then answer the questions.

      a)   Is Andy's argument an example of: A – a cosmological theory; B – an evolutionary theory; C – an argument from design; D – an argument from scripture?

(1 mark)

      b)   Nguyet refers to evolution. Explain why some Christians believe in evolution but others do not.

(4 marks)

      c)   Tara refers to the Big Bang. This is the explosion of matter and energy that cosmologists believe began the Universe.

         Give ONE reason to either agree or disagree with Tara's argument.

(2 marks)

4   a)   Which of the Persons in the Trinity is described as "The giver of life... Who proceeds from the Father and the Son"?

(1 mark)

      b)   In which Christian statement of faith does the statement in part (a) appear?

(2 marks)

      c)   The Shema prayer describes the Jewish view of the nature of God.
         How does this compare to the Christian view of the nature of God?

(2 marks)

      d)   Is the Muslim principle of Tawhid closer to the Jewish or the Christian view of the nature of God? Explain your answer.

(2 marks)

Life After Death

Every religion in the world has got something to say about <u>death</u> — and what they say can have quite an effect. What people believe will happen to them in death can influence the way they <u>live</u> their lives.

Life after death — some people **believe**, others don't

1 Some people believe that when you die, you're dead <u>forever</u> — that's it, your body will decay and you cease to <u>exist</u>.

2 Others believe that, although your <u>body</u> may die and decay, your <u>soul</u> can live on — in other words, you move on to a different kind of existence. This is the basic idea of <u>life after death</u>.

3 But it's not always easy to say exactly when someone's dead anyway. Are those on a life-support machine, who will <u>probably</u> never regain consciousness, really <u>alive</u>... It's not always easy...

Near-death experiences and the paranormal

There are many reasons why people <u>believe</u> (or <u>don't believe</u>) in life after death.

1) Certain <u>religions</u> teach that we all move on to an <u>afterlife</u> of some kind. For some people, this will be enough to make them believe in life after death — they have <u>faith</u> in what their religion teaches.

2) Other people use the example of <u>near-death experiences</u> (NDEs) to argue that a soul exists after death. A near-death experience usually involves someone having an out-of-body experience when they are close to death. While apparently physically dead, they may have glimpsed what they believe to be an afterlife or <u>Heaven</u>, or spoken to long-dead family members.

3) Not everyone thinks of near-death experiences as proof of life after death. Some people believe that the visions are a result of <u>chemical</u> activity in the <u>brain</u> when it is short of oxygen.

4) The <u>paranormal</u> (things that science can't explain, e.g. ghosts) is sometimes used as evidence of life after death. Some people claim they can talk to the dead 'beyond the grave', and use this as proof of an afterlife.

5) Other people say that events we call paranormal have a <u>scientific</u> explanation — maybe we don't know what that explanation is yet, but there <u>will</u> be one. And some people don't believe that these events happen in the first place.

Christian teaching — Heaven and Hell

1) Christianity teaches that the <u>soul</u> lives on after death (<u>immortality</u> of the soul). After death, your soul will go either to <u>Heaven</u>, or to <u>Hell</u> — depending on how you lived your life on Earth.

2) Heaven is often portrayed as a place of great beauty and serenity, a <u>paradise</u> where you will spend eternity with God — as long as you've lived a good life and followed the teachings of <u>Jesus</u>, that is. Those in Heaven are said to belong to the <u>Communion of Saints</u>.

3) Hell, on the other hand, is a place of <u>torment</u> and <u>pain</u> — the final destination of <u>nonbelievers</u> and those who have led <u>bad</u> lives.

4) However, not all Christians believe that these are <u>real</u> places — many Christians see Heaven and Hell as <u>states of mind</u>. In Heaven you'll be <u>happy</u>, and know God — in Hell you'll be <u>unable</u> to know God's love.

5) Some believe those who God finds unacceptable will be <u>annihilated</u>. They had no interest in spiritual things when they were <u>alive</u>, therefore their spirits were never awakened and cannot survive death.

6) Roman Catholics also believe in a place called <u>Purgatory</u>. Here <u>sins</u> are punished before the soul is able to move on to Heaven. This concept isn't in the Bible, so Protestants reject it.

7) Some Christians believe even those who led sinful lives may find <u>salvation</u> thanks to God's saving power.

Get ready to do some soul searching...

There are some complex moral questions to do with death. When is someone dead exactly... If someone could be kept alive by using a life-support machine but with minimal <u>quality of life</u>, would it be better to say they're incapable of independent life, and therefore dead... Dunno. It's one for your <u>own conscience</u>.

JUDAISM | Jewish Beliefs About Life After Death

It should come as no surprise at all to learn that Judaism has something to say about death as well.

Sheol — the shadowy destination of the dead

1) When the earliest Jewish scriptures were written, it was believed that after death everyone would go to a place called Sheol — where the dead lived as shadows.

2) Sheol was believed to be dark and damp, and your soul would stay there for eternity.

3) However, Jews later began to believe in an afterlife spent in places called Heaven and Hell — God would judge people after death, and send them to the place they deserved.

4) If you have lived a good life and performed worthy deeds, you will spend eternity with God in Heaven.

5) Those who have failed to lead good lives will go to Hell — a place of suffering and punishment.

6) Note that Judaism teaches that the body and soul stay together after death, and that Heaven and Hell are open to both Jews and non-Jews.

> "Many of those that sleep in the dust will awake, some to eternal life, others to reproaches, to everlasting abhorrence." **Daniel 12:2**.

Your behaviour during your life is judged

> "Our fathers sinned and are no more, and we bear their punishment." **Lamentations 5:7**

1) Originally, there was a belief amongst Jews that you would be punished for the sins of parents or grandparents.

2) However, this view eventually changed and it was believed that it was how you lived your own life that mattered.

Three kinds of Judaism means three different views

Although most of these beliefs are held by all Jews, there are a few important differences between the different traditions.

ORTHODOX JEWS believe that the physical body will be resurrected, intact, at the end of the Messianic Age. Because of this, the body should not be cut after death (autopsies are frowned upon) and cremation is forbidden. A Jewish cemetery is called the 'House of Life' (Bet ha-Hayyim) and this also reaffirms the opinion that the body will be resurrected.

The Messianic Age is the period after the Messiah (the future leader of the Jewish people) is on Earth — Jews do not believe Jesus was the Messiah.

LIBERAL JEWS believe that the body is simply a vessel for the soul, and it is the soul that will be judged by God. This is why some liberal Jews are now not so strongly against cremation.

See page 95 for more about different Jewish traditions.

REFORM JEWS are more concerned with the earthly life than with the afterlife. Their attitude is summed up by this phrase from a Reform prayer book: "What can we know of death, we who cannot understand life."

The three Jewish traditions have quite different views about death...

Not all Jews hold the same beliefs about what will happen to a person when they die — make sure you know the difference between the ideas of orthodox, liberal and reform Jews...

Muslim Beliefs About Life After Death

Islam, like other religions, has very definite teachings when it comes to life after death.

Akhirah — life after death

1) Muslims call life after death <u>Akhirah</u> — it's one of the key Islamic beliefs.
   Not to have a belief in life after death would make <u>this</u> life meaningless for a Muslim.

2) Islam teaches that nothing that happens to us during our earthly lives is <u>accidental</u> —
   Muslims believe we are being <u>tested</u>, and that the way we act in life will determine
   what happens to us after we die.

3) A key teaching of Islam is that we remain in the grave after death until the <u>Day of Judgement</u>
   (called <u>Yawmuddin</u>). On this day, Allah will judge <u>everyone</u> — not just Muslims.

Yawmuddin is the Day of Judgement

1) Although the <u>earthly</u> life is short compared with the eternal, Muslims believe it's still very important.
   It's in this life that Allah <u>tests</u> us. At <u>Yawmuddin</u>, it's <u>too late</u> to beg forgiveness for any wrongdoing.

2) Islam teaches we are judged on:

   ① our <u>character</u>,
   ② our <u>reactions</u> to good and bad events in life,
   ③ our <u>way of life</u>.

3) Muslims believe everything is the <u>will of Allah</u> — so there's no point <u>moaning</u> about your
   circumstances. We cannot know <u>why</u> things happen, or what Allah wishes us to learn from it.
   The important thing is that we react to it the <u>right</u> way.

4) The reward for those who have followed Allah will be entry into <u>Paradise</u> — this is a place of peace,
   happiness and beauty. In fact, the Qur'an refers to Paradise as '<u>gardens of delight</u>', filled with
   flowers and birdsong.

5) For those who don't <u>believe</u> in Allah, or have committed bad
   deeds, the reward is <u>Jahannam</u> (or <u>Hell</u>). The Qur'an describes
   Jahannam as a place of scorching <u>fire</u>, hot <u>winds</u> and black
   <u>smoke</u>. Here, those who have ignored Allah's teaching and
   failed to act righteously will be <u>punished</u> for eternity.

*Allah is merciful and compassionate, but at the
same time, he's a tough judge. Basically, if you're a
good Muslim, you'll go to Paradise.
But if you're a bad Muslim or a non-Muslim, you
deserve Hell, but you might get lucky and be sent
by Allah to Paradise if he's feeling merciful.*

6) But Allah is also <u>merciful</u>, so many of those who
   have lived <u>sinful</u> lives may not be sent to Jahannam.

The soul is the real person

1) Muslims believe human beings are Allah's <u>greatest</u> physical
   creation. They also believe that humans are different from
   other animals, because we know we will <u>die</u>.

It's <u>free will</u> that makes human
beings different from <u>angels</u> —
angels obey him <u>perfectly</u>.

2) Islam teaches that every <u>soul</u> (<u>ruh</u>) is unique and has <u>free will</u>.

3) At Yawmuddin, it is the soul that will be <u>judged</u>, as it is the
   soul that is our <u>consciousness</u>. Our body is thought of as a
   kind of 'vehicle for the soul'.

*Muslims believe in predestination — Al-Qadar.
Although we have free will, Islam teaches we
cannot do everything we want — God is still in
control. In recognition of this, Muslims will
often say "insh' Allah" (if God is willing).*

Akhirah and Yawmuddin are important Islamic beliefs...

The concepts of a soul and life after death are fundamental beliefs for Muslims — the whole point of living a
good life, by following the teachings of the Qur'an, is the ultimate goal of entering Paradise when you die...

Warm-Up and Worked Exam Question

Warm-up Questions

1) What is the Muslim name for the Day of Judgement?
2) What does the "Communion of Saints" mean to Christians?
3) What do Muslims say makes humans different from animals?
4) What is Purgatory and which Christian denomination believes in it?
5) Give an example of a paranormal phenomenon.
6) What do Orthodox Jews believe will happen to the body at the end of the Messianic Age?

Worked Exam Question

It's very important that you understand what questions are asking for, so study this worked example, then try the questions on the opposite page.

1 a) How would an atheist explain the visions some people say they have seen during a near-death experience?

   An atheist would say that the visions have purely physical causes, e.g. a shortage of oxygen causing chemical activity in the brain.

   Make sure you learn the terminology. An atheist is someone who doesn't believe in God.   *(1 mark)*

   b) What do Christians mean by the "immortality of the soul"?

   The belief that even when a person's body dies a part of them called the soul lives on forever.

   (2 marks)

   c) According to Christian belief, when does someone become a member of the Communion of Saints?

   When they die and go to Heaven.

   (1 mark)

   d) Christians have different beliefs about the nature of Hell. Describe some of these beliefs.

   Some Christians believe that Hell exists literally as a place of eternal torment. Others believe that Hell is a state of separation from God. Some Christians do not believe in Hell at all — they believe that those who have rejected God will be annihilated.

   There are three marks for this question, so make sure you give three good points.   *(3 marks)*

Exam Questions

2 a) What do Muslims mean by "Akirah"?

(1 mark)

   b) What do Muslims believe is the purpose of the events we face in our earthly life?

(1 mark)

   c) "A provision shall they have of fruits; and honoured shall they be in the gardens of delight, upon couches face to face. A cup shall be borne round among them from a fountain."

   What is being described in this passage from the Qur'an?

(1 mark)

   d) Where does Islam say that the dead are now?

(1 mark)

   e) According to Islamic teaching, what will happen to body and soul on Yawmuddin?

(4 marks)

3 a) Why is a Jewish cemetery called "the House of Life"?

(2 marks)

   b) What was the earliest Jewish belief about the afterlife, still held by some Jews today?

(2 marks)

   c) Describe the belief about the afterlife that is held by most Jews today.

(2 marks)

   d) Describe how Jewish teaching about how the sins of your ancestors affect you has changed.

(2 marks)

   e) "Be not like servants who serve the master on condition that they receive a reward."

   This quotation from the Talmud refers to life after death. How might a Reform Jew interpret it?

(3 marks)

4 What do Roman Catholics believe about what happens after death?

(6 marks)

Life & Death and the Christian View

CHRISTIANITY & GENERAL

Abortion and contraception are subjects that people often hold very strong views about.
And as you'd probably expect, religions have strong views about them too.

Abortion — *terminating a pregnancy*

1) Abortion is when a foetus is removed prematurely from the womb, before it is able to survive.

2) Abortion has been legal in England, Scotland and Wales since 1967. It can take place up till the 24th week of pregnancy, as long as two doctors agree that it's required. They must consider the quality of life of the woman, the unborn child, and any children the mother may already have.

There are complicated arguments for and against abortion...

i) The 'pro-choice' argument says that a woman has a right to choose what happens to her body (and since the foetus isn't independent of the woman, this argument says it must be considered part of the woman).

ii) But is it right to consider the foetus part of the mother when it's genetically different?

iii) Although many people are generally against abortion (seeing it as the taking of a life) they will agree that in certain circumstances, abortion should be permitted, e.g. if the mother's or child's health is at risk, if a woman has become pregnant through rape, or if a mother is too young to cope with a child.

iv) The question of when life actually begins is important here, too. Is it at conception (as the Roman Catholic Church says)? Or at birth? And is a foetus an actual person, or just a potential person?

3) Abortion is a very complicated and emotional issue, but generally speaking, Christianity teaches that abortion is undesirable. However, the Roman Catholic Church goes so far as to say that abortion is wrong.

"Abortion has been considered murder since the first centuries of the Church, and nothing permits it to be considered otherwise." — Pope Paul VI (Leader of Roman Catholic Church, 1970)

4) Not all Christian churches see it in such 'black-and-white' terms. The Church of England believes that abortion is permissible in certain circumstances, while the Religious Society of Friends (the Quakers) argues that the life of the unborn child cannot be valued above that of the woman.

5) Indeed, many Christians argue that allowing a woman to choose is a way of showing Christian compassion — whether they agree with the choice made or not.

Contraception — *preventing a pregnancy*

1) Contraception (or birth control) is anything which aims to prevent a woman from becoming pregnant.

2) The Roman Catholic Church believes that preventing conception is against 'natural law'. Indeed, it teaches that humans have an obligation to 'be fruitful and increase in number'. Many individual Roman Catholics disagree with this.

3) The Anglican Church suggests that contraception allows parents to plan their family in a more responsible way.

The *'sanctity of life'* argument

Probably the most important biblical passage regarding the Sanctity of Life argument is the sixth of the Ten Commandments, *"You shall not murder."* — **Exodus 20:13**

1) Because the Bible says we were created in the image of God and given the gift of life, many Christians believe that we do not have the right to interfere with when life ends, or to prevent the beginning of a new life.

2) Although the Bible doesn't actually mention abortion, other Christian writings (e.g. the Didache, a 2nd century manual of Christian teaching) are quite specifically against it.

It's tricky, emotional stuff...

There are no easy answers. So learn the stuff on the page, and be ready to give both sides of the argument.

Life & Death and the Christian View

Another couple of very complicated subjects...

Euthanasia is often called *mercy killing*

Euthanasia means killing someone painlessly to relieve suffering, especially from an incurable illness. It's often called mercy killing.

1) There are two forms of euthanasia — voluntary euthanasia and involuntary euthanasia.

2) Voluntary euthanasia is when an ill person actively requests assistance to die, or refuses treatment which is keeping them alive, i.e. the person decides that they want to die and seeks help to achieve this.

3) Involuntary euthanasia is when the patient is unable to make such a request, and the decision is made by someone else — usually doctors and family members.

4) Suicide is when someone takes their own life — usually because of depression or illness. Attempted suicide used to be a crime in the UK, although it's now seen as a sign that someone needs help.

Euthanasia is *illegal* in the UK

1) Euthanasia is illegal in the UK, but it is allowed in certain circumstances in the Netherlands and in parts of Australia, as long as two doctors agree.

2) Many people want euthanasia legalised in the UK. The Voluntary Euthanasia Society (EXIT) believes that many people would be grateful of 'the mercy of a painless death'.

3) Legalisation would mean that scarce medical resources could be saved for people who could be cured.

4) Many doctors have even admitted helping patients to die, sometimes by giving a patient an excess of painkillers, which ease suffering but can also lead to eventual death — this is known as 'double effect'.

5) However, there is a concern that if euthanasia were legalised, the elderly may feel under pressure to end their life, even if they don't want to.

"Your body is a *temple* of the *Holy Spirit*"

1) The passage in the subheading (from **1 Corinthians**) suggests that God lives within each of us. Life is seen as a sacred gift, and so both euthanasia and suicide are seen as wrong by many Christians (see page 20 — the 'Sanctity of Life' argument).

2) Roman Catholics are the most strongly opposed to euthanasia. They believe that anything which intentionally causes death is 'a grave violation of the law of God'.

3) However, many Christians suggest that the easing of suffering is a way of demonstrating Christian compassion, and that the use of 'extraordinary treatment' (e.g. life-support machines) to keep a person alive is not always the best approach.

4) Most Anglican denominations agree that terrible distress should not be suffered at all costs, and that death may be considered a blessing. They argue that the quality of life must also be considered.

5) Local churches often have links with hospices. A hospice is a place where terminally ill people can be cared for, and can discuss any fears they may have about death.

I told you it was complicated...

Some specifications also need you to know about assisted suicide. Euthanasia and assisted suicide are pretty similar — it all depends on who performs the last act of someone's life. If the doctor gives a lethal injection, it's euthanasia. But if a patient takes a fatal dose of pills provided by a doctor for that purpose, it's assisted suicide.

JUDAISM | Life & Death in Judaism

There are no black and whites in any of this — only shades of grey...
But this is abortion and contraception we're dealing with.

Abortion *and* contraception — *generally seen as* bad

1) As a general rule, Judaism is opposed to abortion, contraception and euthanasia
   — the passages below are often used to support this view.

> *"Be fruitful and increase in number... fill the Earth."* **Genesis 1:28**

> *"There is no god besides me. I put to death and I bring to life."* **Deuteronomy 32:39**

2) Judaism traditionally teaches that a child is a gift from God, and contraception interferes with God's plans to bless couples with children. However, most Jews are happy with the use of contraception for family planning, or if a woman could be physically or psychologically harmed by pregnancy. (Having said that, not wanting to have children isn't a good enough reason to use contraception for many Orthodox Jews.)

3) Sex should still be as natural as possible, though, so condoms are generally frowned upon. But their use may be encouraged by some as a means of preventing the spread of HIV and other STIs (sexually transmitted infections).

4) Abortion is generally seen by Jews as being worse than contraception, because a potential life is being denied existence. However, Judaism does not believe that the life of an unborn child is more valuable than that of the mother.

5) Many Jews accept that, in certain cases, abortion should be allowed. Some rabbis allow abortion if pregnancy becomes physically or mentally dangerous for the woman concerned, or if the child is likely to be severely disabled and unable to lead a full life. But it cannot simply be carried out for convenience.

6) The later in the pregnancy abortion is requested, the more difficult it becomes for Judaism to allow it.

Only God *can* decide *when we* die

1) Jewish teaching is, generally, opposed to the practice of euthanasia — life is seen as a gift from God and is therefore sacred. We do not have the right to decide when a life should end.

2) The same thing applies to suicide — it is seen as such a great sin that those who take their own lives are not buried in the same part of the cemetery as other Jews.

3) However, the relief of pain and suffering is a key part of Jewish teaching. So although euthanasia is seen as wrong if it involves actively doing something to cause someone's death, it may be possible to withhold treatment, if this treatment was causing further distress.

4) The words of Rabbi Moses Isserles are sometimes used to argue that it may be reasonable to switch off a life-support machine that's keeping someone alive.

> "If there is anything which causes a hindrance to the departure of the soul... then it is permissible to remove it."

You need to learn all the arguments...

I mean, in maths, things are true or false, right or wrong, black or white... But like I said, with this it's all shades of grey. And that makes it harder in the Exam, since you have to be aware of lots of different points of view on the same subject. But on the bright side, you don't need to know anything about algebra...

Life & Death in Islam

It's all very tricky...

Islam teaches the life is a **sacred gift** from **Allah**

1) Muslims believe that Allah created the world and everything in it. Our lives are sacred, and only Allah can decide when a life may end or when it may begin.

2) This means that abortion, contraception and euthanasia are all generally seen as wrong.

3) In **Surah 3:145**, the Qur'an says,
   "No soul can ever die except by Allah's leave — and at a term appointed."

*Slay **not** your children*

1) The passage on the right sums up Islamic teaching on both abortion and contraception. Neither is particularly welcomed, although there are circumstances in which such practices are permissible.

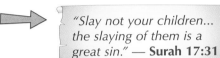

"Slay not your children... the slaying of them is a great sin." — **Surah 17:31**

2) When the mother's life is in danger, abortion is seen as lawful. The potential life in the womb is not as important as the actual life of the mother.

3) Some Muslim women argue that they should be free to choose what happens to their bodies. Those that disagree claim that in the Qur'an it says that unborn children will want to know why they were killed.

4) Muslims believe that conception is the will of Allah, so contraception is unwelcome (although Muhammad never forbade it). But if it is used, only 'reversible' methods are to be used — permanent sterilisation and vasectomies are frowned upon.

"He bestows male and female children... and He makes barren whom he wills." — **Surah 42:49-50**

Contraception is permitted if:
① there's a threat to the mother's health,
② it could help a woman who already has children,
③ there is a greater than average chance of the child being born with disabilities,
④ the family is too poor to raise a child.

See page 20 for more general arguments about abortion.

*Allah knows **why** we **suffer***

1) Euthanasia is seen as wrong by most Muslims — because Allah gave us life, our lives are sacred.

2) Muslims believe that Allah has a plan for every living person — he has decided how long each of us will live on this Earth and we do not have the right to interfere with that plan.

3) Islam teaches that life on Earth is a test. Allah knows why we suffer, and we do not have good reason to end our own lives, no matter how bad that suffering becomes.

4) Instead, those who are suffering should turn to Allah, pray and 'patiently persevere' — Allah is merciful, and all will be revealed on the Day of Judgement.

Not all members of a religion believe the same thing...

People interpret their religion's teaching in different ways, so it's difficult to give a clear-cut overview of what a religion teaches. The best you can do is usually to say that 'Some people believe...' or 'Many people believe...', but hardly ever, 'Every person believes...'. These are very human topics and people are all very different.

GENERAL

Fertility Treatment

There are many similarities in the opinions of Christians, Muslims and Jews towards fertility treatment. All believe that a child is a gift, and therefore all allow some methods of fertility treatment.

Infertility *means the inability to* conceive *a child*

Nowadays, there are various kinds of fertility treatment that can be used to help.

Artificial Insemination by the Husband (AIH) — sperm from the husband is injected into the wife's ovum.

Artificial Insemination by Donor (AID) — sperm from a donor is used.

In Vitro Fertilisation (IVF) — eggs are fertilised in a test tube and (up to 3) implanted in the mother's womb.

Egg Donation — where eggs from a different woman are used. ← *In Britain, any extra embryos can legally be used in experiments until they are 14 days old — at this time they must be destroyed.*

Christianity *sees children as a* blessing from God

1) Most Christian Churches believe that it's okay for science to assist childless couples to conceive — as long as the process doesn't involve anyone else.

2) For this reason, artificial insemination using the husband's sperm (AIH) is permissible. The couple can be blessed with a child — and as no 'third party' is involved, the sanctity of marriage is not interfered with.

3) Artificial insemination using donated sperm (AID) is a less favourable method in the eyes of the Church, as the sperm is not that of the husband.

4) The Roman Catholic Church is particularly opposed to IVF, as it can lead to the creation of 'spare' embryos. These can be used for experimentation or simply thrown away. Many Catholics argue that life begins at fertilisation, and that even an embryo has rights.

Muslim *views are along the* same lines

1) Again, scientific methods are permissible — as long as no 'third party' is involved, and all other natural methods of conceiving have failed.

2) AIH and IVF are both believed to be reasonable, as the sperm of the husband is used.

3) However, AID is not acceptable as the sperm is donated. Many Muslims see this as a sin comparable with adultery, as the woman has become pregnant using the sperm of a man other than her husband.

4) There are also concerns about diseases that may be inherited from an anonymous donor.

Jewish *attitudes are* similar *too*

1) In Jewish teaching, there's an emphasis on having a family.

2) Because of this, it's left to individual married couples to decide whether they need to turn to scientific methods of conception.

"Be fruitful and increase in number... fill the Earth." **Genesis 1:28**

3) A Jewish couple might seek advice on the matter from their rabbi (religious leader).

4) AIH is usually permitted, but not AID, as the use of donated sperm might be seen as a form of adultery.

5) IVF is generally approved of — as long as the egg and the sperm are from the married couple involved.

6) Egg donation is seen as okay, though the couple will often prefer the egg to come from a Jewish woman.

AID *isn't generally permitted...*

Not being able to have children can be heartbreaking for a couple. If the technology exists to have a child, but their religion is against using it, what should they do... tricky.

Warm-Up and Worked Exam Question

Warm-up Questions

1) In medical emergencies where it is a choice between a woman dying or her unborn child dying, which life would Jews choose to save?

2) State two circumstances in which contraception is permitted in Islam.

3) When does the Roman Catholic Church believe that human life begins?

4) State the commandment that many Christians see as forbidding euthanasia and abortion.

5) Does the Church of England permit contraception?

6) What is the difference between voluntary and involuntary euthanasia?

Worked Exam Question

This stuff is all pretty serious. Make sure you know and understand both sides of any argument, and are able to describe the opinions of different religions. This worked exam question is a good example to take a look at.

1 a) Briefly describe why an incurably ill person might think it best to kill themselves.

In order to avoid pointless suffering. *This isn't the only answer —
e.g. they might not want to
be a burden to their family.*

(1 mark)

b) Name ONE country where euthanasia is legal.

The Netherlands

(1 mark)

c) Outline the teachings of ONE religion you have studied regarding euthanasia.

*Judaism teaches that since life is the gift of God we do not have
the right to decide when it should end. Actively causing a patient's
death is forbidden. However, Judaism also teaches that suffering
should be relieved, so withholding treatment may be allowed if the
treatment is causing pain.*

(4 marks)

d) Why is involuntary euthanasia more strongly opposed than voluntary euthanasia?

*Because with voluntary euthanasia, at least people can be sure the
patient really wants to die. When the decision is taken by another
(for instance because the patient is unconscious) we cannot know
what he or she would have wanted. There is also more danger of
greedy relatives pressing for euthanasia in order to inherit the
patient's money.*

*Euthanasia is a very controversial topic. Make sure you can support both
sides of the argument, and back it up with relevant points.*

(3 marks)

Exam Questions

2   a)   Briefly describe two types of medical procedure that can help a couple have a baby who could not before.

(4 marks)

    b)   Name one procedure that could help a couple have a baby that is biologically the child of both of them. Your answer can be the same as one of your answers to part (a) above.

(1 mark)

    c)   Why would AIH be acceptable to a Muslim but AID unacceptable?

(2 marks)

    d)   Why is it a problem to some Christians that in some fertility procedures more embryos are created than can be put into the mother's womb?

(2 marks)

3

Suzie   Ellen

    a)   What might Suzie say to explain why she is "pro-choice" on the issue of abortion?

(1 mark)

    b)   What might Ellen say to explain why she is "pro-life" on the issue of abortion?

(1 mark)

    c)   "It's crazy that the law says a foetus is a person at 24 weeks but not at 23 weeks! Life begins at conception."

    Do you agree? Refer to at least one religion in your answer and show that you have considered more than one point of view.

(8 marks)

4   Read the following dialogue and answer the questions below.

    Melanie: "Children are a gift from God. It is a sin to deliberately reject God's gift by using contraception."

    Enrico: "People should be encouraged to prevent unwanted children being brought into the world."

    a)   What is contraception?

(1 mark)

    b)   Look at Melanie's statement. Explain why similar statements could be made by some believers in TWO religions you have studied.

(6 marks)

    c)   Do you agree with what Enrico said? Refer to at least one religion in your answer.

(6 marks)

Marriage in Christianity

Marriage — a pretty big thing in anyone's life. Including yours if you get a question about it in the Exam.

Marriage in the UK — times are changing

1) The number of marriages in the UK has been decreasing for at least 30 years.

2) At the same time, it's become more popular (and acceptable) for couples to cohabit (i.e. live together) — either instead of getting married, or as a 'trial marriage' before doing it for real. (However, government statistics seem to show that a marriage is more likely to break down if the couple lived together first.)

3) Despite fewer weddings taking place, 90% of women and 80% of men are still married by the age of 30. But there are also signs that things are changing, and that marriage is becoming more popular again.

Christians say marriage should be forever

1) The Christian faith values marriage very highly — the joining of husband and wife in holy matrimony reflects the union of Jesus with his followers.

2) Jesus taught that marriage should be a lifelong union — marriage is seen as a covenant or contract between two people, involving commitment and responsibility. Christianity teaches that the purpose of marriage is for two people to offer mutual support and have children.

3) But the Church recognises that not everyone is called to marriage, and from these people it demands celibacy.

> "...a man will leave his father and mother and be united with his wife, and the two will become one flesh."
> **Mark 10:7**
>
> "You shall not commit adultery"
> **Exodus 20:14**

In **Ephesians 5:21-33**, wives are encouraged to submit to their husbands, and husbands to love their wives, laying down their lives for them as Christ layed down his.

BIBLICAL TEACHING ON MARRIAGE:
1) Marriage must be faithful.
2) Marriage must be worked at — you have to keep on forgiving.
3) Marriage reflects Christ's love for his followers, and involves submission.

Sex and marriage

1) The Christian Church teaches that the total giving of self in sex shouldn't be treated casually — self-control and sexual restraint are considered important.

2) Christians are urged to keep sex within marriage for positive reasons more than negative ones — marriage is believed to give sex a special status.

A Christian wedding has legal, social and religious features

Most Christian weddings take place in church. The details will vary according to tradition and denomination, but all combine legal, social and religious features.

1) **Hymns**

2) **Opening statement** (saying what marriage is about)

3) **Declaration** (couple and witnesses must state there is no reason why the couple can't marry)

4) **Vows**

5) **Giving of ring(s)**

6) **Proclamation** (that the couple are now married)

7) **Prayers** (and usually a sermon)

8) **Signing of the register** (to make it legal)

9) **Closing worship**

In an Orthodox wedding, crowns are placed on the heads of the bride and groom.

A Roman Catholic wedding will also include a nuptial mass.

Marriage is about commitment...

Although the percentage of Britain's population that gets married is falling, it is still something that most people will do sometime in their lives — so make sure you learn this stuff about the Christian view on marriage...

CHRISTIANITY The Christian Church and Divorce

Times change, and the old 'married with two kids' kind of family isn't as common as it used to be.

Family life in the UK is changing

1) There used to be two basic types of family that 'society' and the Christian Church considered 'ideal' — the nuclear family, and the extended family.

2) A nuclear family consists of parents and children.
An extended family is where three or more generations live together or as close neighbours.

3) In reality, families can have very different structures — e.g. single-parent families and reconstituted families (where divorcees remarry, or find new partners).

4) Family life is changing in the UK — and one of the most important changes in the past 30 years has been the growth of single-parent (or 'lone-parent') families. This is partly due to more children now being born outside marriage, but it's also because 1 in 3 marriages now end in divorce.

Christian Churches have different attitudes to divorce

1) Family life is seen as very important by most Christians — it's believed to be better for a child to have a father and a mother present (ideally the child's biological parents), so that he or she grows up with one role model of each sex.

2) Ideally, a stable family can give a child a sense of identity, a feeling of security, teach him or her how to behave in different social situations, and how to give and receive love.

3) The breakdown of a marriage is seen by all Christians as a tragedy. However not all Christians agree about whether divorce is permissible, or even possible.

The Roman Catholic Church states that it is actually impossible to divorce. Marriage is a sacrament — God has made the couple into one flesh, and this cannot be undone. However, a marriage can be annulled — annulment means that it was never a true marriage in the first place. This can happen if:
  i) either partner did not consent to the marriage or didn't understand what marriage is about,
  ii) the couple didn't or couldn't have sex, or one partner refused to have children.

Nonconformist Churches (e.g. Baptists and Methodists) will generally remarry divorcees, but an individual minister can refuse to do so if this goes against his or her own conscience.

The Church of England says that divorce is acceptable, but that divorced people can only remarry in church if they can find a minister willing to marry them. This doesn't satisfy every member of the Church of England.

Jesus talked about divorce in the Gospels

There are different attitudes to divorce among Christians — maybe because Jesus himself was anti-divorce, but pro-forgiveness.

In Mark 10:2-12 Jesus says that Moses allowed divorce because of people's 'hardness of heart'. But he says that at the Creation of mankind marriages were meant to last for life, and if a divorcee remarries it's the same as committing adultery.

Matthew 5:31-32 and 19:8-9 say the same thing — except that divorce is permitted to someone whose partner has already been unfaithful.

In John 8:1-11, Jesus freely forgives a woman caught in the act of adultery. But he tells her, 'Go, and do not sin again'.

Christians have different views about divorce...

One of the things you mustn't do with a 'Perspectives' question is just rant on and on, giving your own personal opinions and nothing else. You need to know what the different religions teach about the various moral issues, and why. And a bit of 'background' (e.g. how family life is changing) is dead useful too.

Marriage in Judaism

Traditionally all Jews have been <u>expected</u> to marry and have at least 2 children — a boy and a girl.

Marriage matters in Judaism

1) To Jews, marriage is an <u>emotional</u>, <u>intellectual</u> and <u>spiritual</u> union. It is seen as the proper context for <u>sex</u> (which is seen as natural and God-given), but is also for <u>companionship</u>.

2) <u>Family life</u> is also important, as it's through the family that the Jewish religion and customs are passed on.

3) It's the Jewish custom for parents to arrange for their children to meet suitable partners. To help in this it was common to use a 'shadchan', or <u>matchmaker</u> (and it still is among the ultra-Orthodox).

Nowadays there are shadchan services available via the <u>Internet</u>.

4) Although 40% of UK Jews 'marry out' (i.e. marry non-Jews), those who take their religion seriously find this <u>worrying</u> — children of 'mixed marriages' are less likely to be brought up as <u>observant</u> Jews. Many Jews see this as a threat to Judaism's survival, and even a 'posthumous victory to Hitler' (see page 94).

Kiddushin — the Marriage Ceremony

Different Jewish communities celebrate marriage in different ways, but there are some <u>common features</u>.

1) The groom gives the bride a <u>valuable</u> object, usually a ring.

2) The <u>ketubah</u> (marriage contract) is read out. This sets out the woman's right to be <u>cared for</u> by her husband. The text dates back to the 2nd century BCE.

3) There must be at least two eligible <u>witnesses</u> to observe the ceremony.

4) The ceremony takes place beneath a <u>huppah</u> (or <u>chuppah</u>), a wedding <u>canopy</u> — this is a piece of cloth supported by four poles. It is thought the cloth represents <u>privacy</u>, and the open sides <u>hospitality</u>.

5) <u>Blessings</u> are said over the couple — normally by a rabbi, who usually conducts the service.

6) The groom <u>breaks</u> a glass with his foot in memory of the destruction of the <u>Temple</u> in 70 CE (see page 91). It's said that there can never be complete joy for the Jewish people until the Temple is restored — this is why it's remembered.

7) After the service there will be a festive meal and dancing, and shouts of 'mazel tov!' (good luck, best wishes). Among some Orthodox Jews, the men and women dance <u>separately</u>.

Divorce is a last resort

1) Adultery is specifically forbidden in the <u>7th Commandment</u> — it's regarded as the <u>betrayal</u> of a covenant.

2) Judaism does allow for divorce ('<u>get</u>' in Hebrew) — but only as a very <u>last resort</u> after all attempts at <u>reconciliation</u> have failed. A woman cannot <u>initiate</u> divorce, but a divorce does require the wife's <u>consent</u>.

3) In Reform synagogues, if the husband will not grant his wife a 'get', the <u>Bet Din</u> (Jewish court) can do so, freeing her to remarry. In Orthodox synagogues, women who want a divorce but whose husbands will not grant one are known as '<u>agunot</u>' — chained women.

Marriage is a union of mind and body...

Christian, Jewish and Muslim teachings about marriage and morality have a lot in common. This isn't so surprising — all three religions share the same Near Eastern background. And can I just say how nice it is to have a few happy pages after some of the previous ones in this section. (Apart from the divorce bits, that is.)

Marriage in Islam

Marriage is very important in Islam. Muslims are advised to marry, and Muhammad himself was married.

Marriage is **recommended** for **four reasons**

1) The sexual instinct is very strong and needs to be carefully channelled.

2) Marriage provides companionship.

3) Marriage provides a secure environment for bringing up children as practising Muslims.

4) A stable family life teaches us all to be kind, considerate and affectionate towards others.

See the next page for more about marriage in Islam.

"Whoever is able to marry, let him marry, for this will keep him chaste." — **Bukhari Hadith 30:10**

"He created for you mates that you might find rest in them, and He ordained between you love and mercy." — **Surah 30:21**

Choosing a **partner** is often your **parents' responsibility**

Practising Muslims generally want their children to marry other Muslims. Islam affects a Muslim's whole life, and being married to a non-Muslim could create tension, especially with bringing up children.

1) Most Muslims believe it's unwise for young men and women to mix freely, and 'dating' is discouraged or even forbidden.

2) In most Muslim communities, parents search for suitable partners for their children — i.e. Muslims often have 'arranged marriages'.

3) However, as marriage is a contract, both partners must consent to it.

4) Parents also have a responsibility to help if the marriage begins to go wrong.

The **marriage ceremony** — customs **vary**

The marriage ceremony is different in different Islamic cultures, but there's always a religious ceremony (witnessed by Allah) and a public one (witnessed by the community). They usually go like this...

1) A nikah (contract) is drawn up in advance by the families of the bride and groom, and a mahr (dowry) paid by the groom to the bride.

2) An imam (leader of prayers) is often present (though this isn't compulsory).

3) Vows are exchanged, and a marriage declaration is made by each partner. A Hadith (saying) or a khutbah (speech) may also be said.

4) There will be a big feast afterwards, though the men and women may enjoy this separately.

Divorce is the **last resort**

1) Divorce is permitted, but only as a very last resort. If things aren't going well, an arbiter from each family should be appointed to try to sort things out. But if this fails, there can be divorce, and remarriage.

2) When the man says 'I divorce you' three times, the marriage is said to be over. However, there's often a period of three months after the first of these declarations. This allows time for reflection, and also to ensure that the woman is not pregnant.

3) A woman can divorce a man in this way (divorce 'by talaq') if it was written into her marriage contract. Otherwise she has to apply to a Shari'ah court for a divorce 'by 'kuhl'.

"Of all things permitted by law, divorce is the most hateful in the sight of Allah." — **Muhammad**

This kind of divorce isn't legal in the UK — Shari'ah law (see page 114) isn't part of the British legal system.

Marriage is an important part of Islamic life...

There's quite a lot of Arabic words in these Islam sections — and they're in the syllabuses too, so you need to know 'em. The same goes for the sections on Judaism — they contain quite a bit of Hebrew.

Religious Attitudes to Sex

Christianity, Islam and Judaism have all formulated laws concerned with sex. But this doesn't mean that religious people think there is anything wrong or dirty about having sex — quite the opposite.

Christianity, Islam and Judaism have a lot in common

Christianity, Islam and Judaism have a good deal in common when it comes to sex.

1) Traditionally all 3 religions have believed that the only right context for sexual activity is within marriage.

2) But nowadays you find liberal Christians, Jews and Muslims who'll tell you that this belief is outdated.

3) 'Orthodox' members of all faiths say that certain moral principles never change, however.

4) All three religions teach that couples should wait until they are married before having sex. In fact, it's very important to most Muslims that people, especially girls, remain virgins until marriage.

5) Promiscuity (having many sexual partners) is seen as wrong in all three religions — in Christianity it's seen as dishonouring yourself.

They might argue that when their scriptures were written, contraception was unreliable and the danger of unwanted pregnancy very great. This isn't the case nowadays, though, since modern methods can be almost 100% effective.

...but they're not identical

1) Judaism and Christianity are monogamous religions — adultery is forbidden by the 7th Commandment.

2) Islam permits, but does not encourage, polygamy. A man may have up to four wives, but only if he can support them and treat them equally.

Muhammad actually had nine wives during his lifetime — although not all at the same time.

Homosexuality — scriptures say it's wrong

Homosexuality means being attracted to members of the same sex.

1) It used to be illegal in the UK for men to be involved in homosexual activity. In 1967 it became legal for consenting couples, over 21, in private. The age of consent is now the same as for heterosexual couples — 17 in Northern Ireland, and 16 in England, Scotland and Wales.

2) The scriptures of all 3 religions seem to say that homosexual sex is wrong — although the relevant passages are interpreted differently by some people.

"Because of this, God gave them over to shameful lusts. Even their women exchanged natural relations for unnatural ones. In the same way the men also abandoned natural relations with women, and were inflamed with lust for one another: males committed indecent acts with other men, and received in themselves the due penalty for their perversion." — Romans 1:26-27

3) Some people (including some priests) argue that the scriptures were written against a very different cultural background from ours, so we cannot apply their standards today.

4) Christianity no longer condemns homosexuality, but it isn't seen as the ideal.

5) Since 'same-sex marriages' are not recognised in the UK, homosexual sex goes against Church teaching. Therefore many religious gays opt for celibacy — meaning they don't have sexual relationships.

There are some strong religious views on sex...

Homosexuality is a subject that lots of people have strong feelings about — for or against. But even if you strongly disagree with what a religion teaches, you still need to know what they teach, so you can argue against it.

Children and the Church

Practising members of all religions recognise the importance of passing on their faith to the next generation.

Respect your **parents**... and your **kids**

The scriptures of Christianity, Islam and Judaism all say how important respect and honour are.

"Honour your father and mother, so that you may live long in the land which the Lord your God is giving you." — **Exodus 20:12** (the 5th Commandment)

Christian Old Testament (i.e. the Jewish Scriptures)

This verse shows that it is just as important for parents to respect their children as it is the other way round.

"Children, obey your parents in everything, for this pleases the Lord. Fathers, do not embitter your children, or they will become discouraged." — **Colossians 3:20-21**

Christian New Testament

"Be careful of your duty to Allah, and be fair and just to your children." — **Bukhari Hadith**

This Hadith was recorded by Bukhari. (A Hadith is an Islamic 'saying'.)

Parents and **children** should look after **each other**

Parents must care for their children while their children are young. Children must care for their parents when their parents are old. That's pretty much how Christianity, Islam and Judaism all see it. Seems fair.

"Show kindness to your parents. If one or both of them attain old age, do not be rude to them or send them away, but speak to them a gracious word." — **Surah 17:23**

"If anyone does not provide for his relatives, especially his immediate family, he has denied the faith and is worse than an unbeliever." — **1 Timothy 5:8**

Religions' attitudes towards **newly born** children

CHRISTIANITY
1) According to the New Testament, you cannot be 'born a Christian'.
2) It's said that God has no grandchildren. In other words, you can't rely on your parents' faith — you have to find your own. And your parents can't force you to accept Christianity — it's your decision.

JUDAISM
1) Jews believe that if your mother is Jewish, you're Jewish — whether you like it or not.
2) However, practising Jews recognise the importance of encouraging their children to 'keep the faith'.

ISLAM
1) Muslims believe that everyone is born in submission to Allah.
2) They may walk away from Allah as a result of their upbringing, but this is not the way things were meant to be.
3) If someone embraces Islam later in life, he or she is said to be 'returning'.

Different religions, similar views — the family is important...
There are many things Christianity, Judaism and Islam agree on when it comes to the relationship between children, their parents and religion — learn them well by writing a mini-essay on 'Religious attitudes to children'.

Warm-Up and Worked Exam Question

Warm-up Questions

1) What does "monogamy" mean?
2) What does Christianity say is the purpose of marriage?
3) What is the "ketubah"?
4) How do Christian and Jewish views about being born into your religion differ?
5) What does "annulment" of a marriage mean?
6) What did Muhammad say was the "most hateful in the sight of Allah" of all things permitted by law?

Worked Exam Question

You know the drill by now. Read through the worked example, make sure you can see where the answers came from, then have a go at the exam questions on page 34.

1   a)   Explain why family life is so important to Muslims.

It is one of the most important duties of a Muslim to transmit Islam to the next generation. All babies are seen as being born Muslim, but it is the duty of the parents to keep them in the faith by teaching and example.

Extended families provide mutual support and companionship.

It is the duty of husbands to provide for their wives and female relatives, and they also have a duty to care for members of the extended family — for example, to take in orphaned children of relatives.

Young people can learn from the wisdom of the older members of the family.

Families also provide financial support — parents care for their children when they are young and are cared for by them in old age.

There are other possible answers to this question.

Make sure you say as much as you can, as clearly as you can.

(6 marks)

b)   What is the Muslim attitude to polygamy?

Islam permits, but does not encourage, polygamy.

A man may have up to four wives at a time, but only if he can treat them and support them equally.

In practice it would be near impossible to treat four women equally — you would have to love each of them exactly the same amount.

(4 marks)

34

Exam Questions

2   a)   Describe the circumstances under which homosexual activity is legal in Britain.

(2 marks)

b)   "People attracted to the same sex should remain celibate, however difficult it is."

Do you agree? In your answer show that you have considered more than one point of view and refer to religious teachings.

(6 marks)

3   a)   What does it mean when the Bible says that in marriage a couple become "one flesh?"

(2 marks)

b)   Family structure and attitudes towards marriage have changed in Britain over recent decades. Describe some of these changes.

(4 marks)

c)   Describe the views of the Roman Catholic Church regarding divorce and annulment.

(3 marks)

d)   Did Jesus regard adultery as a sin? Explain your answer.

(3 marks)

4   a)   What is the most important commandment of the Torah regarding how a person should treat his or her parents?

(2 marks)

b)   Define the following words:

i)   kiddushin,

ii)   ketubha,

iii) huppah.

(3 marks)

c)   Why are many British Jews concerned about the high proportion of Jews who marry non-Jews?

(2 marks)

d)   What determines whether a newborn baby is a Jew or not?

(1 mark)

Prejudice and Equality

The world we live in is full of people from different <u>religious</u>, <u>racial</u> and <u>cultural</u> backgrounds. And the way each religion deals with this is important, as it can help or hinder the building of <u>communities</u>.

Prejudice has many causes

1) People are prejudiced in all sorts of ways. The main forms of prejudice you need to know about are those based on <u>race</u>, <u>gender</u>, <u>religion</u>, <u>class</u>, <u>age</u>, <u>sexual orientation</u> and <u>disability</u>.

2) Prejudice has many <u>causes</u>, and is often the product of <u>early influences</u>. It frequently comes about as a result of being influenced by <u>widely held</u> (yet <u>inaccurate</u>) beliefs of a particular community or family.

It's worth being very clear about what a few words mean...

Justice	the principle of <u>fairness</u> — both <u>legally</u> and more <u>generally</u>.
Equality	being <u>equal</u>, and being <u>treated equally</u>.
Community	the <u>people</u> living in a certain place, or a group of people with the <u>same</u> religious or cultural <u>characteristics</u>.
Prejudice	<u>prejudging</u> something or someone with no good reason, or without full knowledge of a situation.
Discrimination	<u>unjust treatment</u>, often resulting from prejudice.

3) Although prejudice is usually born of <u>ignorance</u>, those who are prejudiced against a particular individual or group will often <u>resist</u> education and continue to <u>discriminate</u>.

4) <u>Discrimination</u> comes in many forms... <u>Individuals</u> may discriminate by being <u>violent</u> and <u>abusive</u>. Whole <u>societies</u> may discriminate by passing <u>laws</u> which prevent certain people from doing certain things.

The Bible has plenty of 'anti-prejudice' stories

For Christians, the <u>Bible</u> has plenty to say on the subject...

1) The idea of 'do unto others as you would have them do unto you' is a fundamental part of Christian teaching (sometimes called the '<u>Golden Rule</u>'). See page 62 for more info.

2) Generally Christians believe that everyone was created <u>equal</u> by God, and so they try to <u>avoid discrimination</u> and <u>promote equality</u>. They look to the example of Jesus, who told <u>stories</u> about equality, and acted true to his own teaching by <u>mixing</u> with a variety of people himself.

3) Perhaps one of the most famous stories in the New Testament is the Parable of the <u>Good Samaritan</u> (**Luke 10:25-37**) where one man comes to the aid of another simply because he is <u>suffering</u>.

4) But there are plenty of other biblical stories preaching <u>equal treatment</u> for all — these two are from the New Testament.

The Parable of the Good Samaritan

A man is beaten up and left half-dead by robbers. A priest and a Levite walking down the road see him, but carry on walking. But a Samaritan (considered an enemy by the Jews) bandages the man, puts him on his donkey, takes him to an inn and sees that he is looked after.

"My brothers... don't show favouritism. Suppose a man comes in wearing a gold ring and fine clothes, and a poor man in shabby clothes also comes in. If you show special attention to the man wearing fine clothes, but say to the poor man, 'Sit on the floor by my feet,' have you not become judges with evil thoughts?" **James 2:1-4**

"...there is no Greek or Jew... barbarian, Scythian, slave or free, but Christ is all, and is in all." **Colossians 3:11**

5) And <u>Deuteronomy</u> (one of the Books of Law in the <u>Old Testament</u>) includes these...

By the way, 'alien' means 'foreigner' here.

"Do not take advantage of a hired man who is poor and needy." **Deuteronomy 24:14**

"Do not deprive the alien or the fatherless of justice." **Deuteronomy 24:17**

The Good Samaritan — what a nice chap...

This is a serious issue that often makes it into the <u>news</u>. And it's one that you might have <u>personal</u> experience of perhaps — and if you do, you can use that experience to help answer your Exam question. But be careful not to just <u>rant</u> on about yourself — you'll need to refer to the religious teachings as well.

Race and Religion

The United Kingdom is a <u>multi-ethnic</u>, <u>multicultural</u> society, and this leads to questions of how <u>racial issues</u> should be dealt with.

Racism is one form of prejudice

It's a sad fact that some people are prejudiced against anyone from a different <u>cultural</u> or <u>religious</u> background, or simply because of the <u>colour</u> of their skin.

1) There have been many instances of <u>racial discrimination</u> in the UK in recent years — usually as a result of <u>ignorance</u>, <u>misunderstanding</u> or <u>segregation</u>. At times these have culminated in <u>rioting</u> or <u>murder</u>.

2) Racism is often based on <u>stereotypes</u> — fixed and standardised images of people, which can be used to promote <u>negative</u> thoughts and actions.

3) The <u>media</u> has an important role to play. Television and newspapers can <u>educate</u> — or help fuel <u>negative</u> stereotypes (see pages 54 and 55).

4) At the present time in the UK, <u>Asians</u> suffer from racism and racist attacks more than any other ethnic group. This has led to further segregation and increased hostility.

5) The <u>Race Relations Act</u> makes it <u>illegal</u> to discriminate against anyone because of their race, colour, nationality, and so on. It also makes it illegal to publish anything that's likely to <u>cause</u> racial hatred.

Christian Churches are against racism — usually...

1) **Leviticus 19:33-34** contains some basic teaching on the way people from different <u>cultural backgrounds</u> should be treated.

> 'When an alien lives with you in your land, do not ill-treat him... Love him as yourself.' *Leviticus 19:33-34*
>
> This story's actually about foreigners living in Israel, but Christians argue that it also applies to the modern world.

2) There's a story about <u>Simon Peter</u> in Acts that's also relevant:

> **Acts 10:1-35** tells a story about <u>Simon Peter</u>. He is told by God not to consider <u>impure</u> anything that <u>God</u> has made. So when a Roman soldier Cornelius sends for Peter, Peter goes willingly, even though it is <u>against the law</u> for Jews to associate with non-Jews. Peter says, "...*God does not show favouritism, but accepts men from every nation...*"

3) The parable of the <u>Good Samaritan</u> (see page 35) is an example of Christian teaching on the treatment of people from other <u>cultures</u>. The Samaritans were a <u>mixed race</u> who suffered a great deal of discrimination at the time Jesus told the story.

4) More recently, Dr George Carey (the former Archbishop of Canterbury) spoke about the fundamental Christian belief that <u>racism</u> is <u>wrong</u>, and that everyone is created in God's image.

> "*Racism has no part in the Christian Gospel... it contradicts our Lord's command... It solves no problems and creates nothing but hatred and fear.*" Dr George Carey

5) Although Christians generally work <u>against</u> racism and inequality, there have been occasions when this hasn't been the case. The most infamous example was the system of <u>apartheid</u> laws in South Africa.

> The Dutch Reform Church of South Africa (DRC) believed that God had <u>divided</u> mankind into different races and made <u>white people</u> superior. This idea became <u>law</u>. <u>Trevor Huddleston</u> (an English bishop working in South Africa) was appalled by this and struggled against it using <u>nonviolent</u> methods, e.g. political pressure and boycotts. He became President of the <u>Anti-Apartheid Movement</u>, and argued that apartheid was against God's will. Apartheid eventually came to an end in 1992.

Racism — still a big issue today, unfortunately...

In the UK prejudice against Muslims has increased in recent years. This has led to further mistrust and calls for <u>segregation</u> from some, and an increased desire for <u>tolerance</u> and <u>integration</u> from others...

Injustice and Protest

There are different kinds of discrimination. And many people and organisations have fought in their own ways against what they see as unfair treatment.

Sex discrimination — also illegal

Most societies have always been male dominated, and have only started to change relatively recently.

1) The Bible gives different messages on the subject of sex discrimination. In the New Testament, women are found among Jesus' followers and he treated them equally — remarkable for the time.

2) But this is taken from St Paul's letter to his young assistant Timothy:

3) In 1975 the Sex Discrimination Act was passed by Parliament. This made it illegal to discriminate against people on account of their sex — especially in the employment or education fields.

"I do not permit a woman to teach or to have authority over a man; she must be silent... For Adam was formed first, then Eve... it was the woman who was deceived and became a sinner... but women will be saved through childbearing." **1 Timothy 2:12-15**

But in **Galatians 3:28** St Paul writes, "There is no difference between... men and women; you are all one in union with Christ Jesus."

Many people have fought against prejudice

1) Christianity teaches that we are all born equal in the eyes of God.

2) Most Christians would, therefore, argue that we should avoid prejudice on the basis of race, gender, religion, age, disability, colour or class. The Bible has plenty of specific teaching on these matters.

'From one human being he created all races on earth and made them live through the whole earth." **Acts 17:26**

"...loose the chains of oppression and untie the cords of the yoke, to set the oppressed free... then your light will break forth like the dawn..." **Isaiah 58:6-10**

3) There are many examples of individual Christians struggling against injustice — e.g. Dietrich Bonhoeffer, Archbishop Desmond Tutu, Bishop Trevor Huddleston, Oscar Romero, Martin Luther King...

4) There are also Christian organisations working against injustice, such as the *Catholic Association for Racial Justice*, and the *Church of England Race and Community Relations Committee*. Christians can also be found working for charities such as *Amnesty International*.

Oscar Romero was Archbishop of El Salvador. He struggled against the authorities who were badly mistreating the people of his country and, in 1984, was murdered for speaking out.

See page 62 for more about Martin Luther King.

Dietrich Bonhoeffer was a German Christian who felt the Church had a duty to speak out against the Nazis' treatment of Jews. He later became actively involved in a conspiracy against Nazism. For this, he was hanged in a concentration camp.

Archbishop Desmond Tutu and Bishop Trevor Huddleston (see also page 36) were active in the struggle against apartheid in South Africa.

Amnesty International campaigns around the world to promote human rights — especially those of prisoners of conscience.

Prisoners of conscience are imprisoned for their beliefs

1) Prisoners of conscience are those imprisoned for acting or speaking out against government policy.

2) They are usually found in countries where human rights are not valued and governments are unfair.

Father Thadeus Nyugen Van Ly, a Vietnamese Catholic priest, was sentenced to 15 years in prison in October 2001. It's believed that Father Ly is being held for peacefully expressing his view that people have a right to freedom of worship and expression. His views are not in line with the policy of the Vietnamese government, and his public speaking on these matters probably led to his arrest.

The Bible teaches that we are all equal...

We're starting to get onto some very serious topics now — prejudice, racism. These pages have got plenty for you to think about. You need to learn it all for the exam — it's really important. OK, lecture over...

| JUDAISM |
Jewish Attitudes Towards Equality

Like Christianity and Islam, <u>Judaism</u> teaches that God created people <u>equal</u>.

*The **Hebrew Bible** preaches **tolerance***

<u>Racism</u> is disapproved of in Judaism. The Hebrew Bible (the <u>Old Testament</u>) has a lot to say on the matter.

1) The Book of Genesis suggests that all of humanity comes from the <u>same source</u> and is, therefore, <u>equal</u> before God.

"Adam named his wife Eve, because she would become the mother of all the living." **Genesis 3:20**

2) Other messages of <u>tolerance</u> can be found in **Deuteronomy 23:7**, and **Leviticus 19:33-34** (see page 36).

"Do not abhor an Edomite, for he is your brother. Do not abhor an Egyptian, because you lived as an alien in his country." **Deuteronomy 23:7**

3) **Deuteronomy 23** contains a discussion of who should be called 'the Lord's people'. This could be taken as meaning we should show <u>tolerance</u> for other nationalities. However, the same chapter does contain references to certain people or nations who should be <u>excluded</u>.

4) The Jewish people are sometimes called the '<u>chosen people</u>'. This doesn't mean they think they're <u>better</u> than anyone else — simply that God gave them additional <u>responsibilities</u>.

5) The stories of <u>Ruth</u> and <u>Jonah</u> (both in the Hebrew Scriptures, i.e. the Old Testament) could also be used to promote <u>social</u> and <u>racial</u> harmony.

The Story of Jonah...

Jonah was told to preach to the people of Nineveh, who had <u>upset God</u>. When he preached God's message, the people of Nineveh were humble and repentant, which pleased God, and so God <u>spared</u> the city, <u>upsetting</u> Jonah. But God said he was right to spare the city, and that Jonah was wrong to be upset. The message is, *"If God can love and forgive, we should be able to live with others too."*

Before he got to Nineveh, Jonah was eaten by a big fish and stayed there for 3 days.

*And **Isaiah 42:6** shows that God does not want the Jews to turn their backs on non-Jews.*

The Story of Ruth...

Naomi and her husband leave Judah because of a famine — they end up in <u>Moab</u>. Naomi's sons marry Moab girls — but soon after, Naomi's husband and sons <u>die</u>. <u>Ruth</u> (one of Naomi's daughters-in-law) stays very <u>loyal</u> to her <u>Israelite mother-in-law</u>, and becomes devoted to God. This line eventually produces <u>King David</u> (see page 91). The message is, *"Good things happen to those who are nice to people from other lands."*

*"**Male** and **female**, He **created** them"* — **Genesis 1:27**

1) The above passage is sometimes read as meaning that men and women are seen as <u>equals</u> before God, although <u>different</u>, and with different <u>responsibilities</u>. (God did create two different <u>sexes</u> after all, so he can't have wanted us all to be identical.)

2) Some people involved with the <u>feminist</u> movement (fighting for women's rights) argue that the expectation for women to become wives and mothers is <u>unfair</u>, and has <u>hindered</u> women's progress.

3) Judaism doesn't suggest that women should <u>not</u> be able to follow their chosen career. However, there is still a belief that motherhood is a <u>privilege</u>, and women should devote some of their life to it.

4) But there are definitely differences of opinion on this. <u>Orthodox Jews</u> (see page 95) aim to uphold many of the ancient Jewish <u>traditions</u>, and so would be more likely to suggest that women should remain at home as <u>mothers</u> and <u>wives</u>.

There are also rules governing <u>synagogue</u> <u>worship</u>. Usually ten <u>men</u> (called a minyan) are required for a service, and it is <u>men</u> who read from the Torah. Also, men and women usually have <u>separate</u> areas for prayer. <u>Reform Jews</u> don't accept all these rules, however — women can form a minyan, and even become rabbis.

5) However, <u>Reform Jews</u> are willing to <u>interpret</u> traditional teachings so that they are, perhaps, more relevant to the <u>modern age</u>. For this reason they're less strict when it comes to the roles of men and women.

Tolerate thy neighbour...

Jews have suffered from a great deal of racism and persecution over the years. By far the most extreme form of social injustice was the <u>Holocaust</u> (see page 94), when discrimination became <u>government policy</u>. It serves as a reminder to everyone of how much suffering can arise from racial hatred.

Muslim Attitudes Towards Equality

Islam is truly <u>international</u> — with followers from many countries, and many ethnic and cultural backgrounds.

Islam says people are created equal, but not identical

1) Islam teaches that all people were created by Allah, and were created <u>equal</u> (although not the <u>same</u>). He intended humanity to be created with <u>differences</u>. But this just means we're all individuals. Hurrah.

> "And among His signs is the creation of the heavens and the earth, and the differences in your languages and colours." **Surah 30:22**

2) Muslims all over the world are united through the <u>ummah</u> — the community of Islam. The ummah consists of <u>all</u> Muslims, regardless of colour, nationality, tradition (i.e. Sunni or Shi'ite) and so on. This can help promote social harmony, as no one is <u>excluded</u> or <u>discriminated</u> against.

3) <u>Hajj</u> (pilgrimage to Makkah, see page 120) especially demonstrates <u>equality</u>. Those on pilgrimage all wear simple white garments, showing that <u>everyone</u> is equal before Allah — wealth, status and colour don't matter.

4) The fact that <u>all</u> Muslims should <u>pray</u> five times a day at set times, and face Makkah whilst doing so, also demonstrates <u>unity</u> and <u>equality</u>. However, in a mosque, women and men must pray <u>separately</u>.

> "You must live at peace with one another. Everyone must respect the rights and properties of their neighbours. There must be no rivalry or enmity among you." **Hadith**

5) There's also a message of <u>tolerance</u> and <u>equality</u> in the last sermon given by Muhammad before his death. He was addressing Muslims, but many <u>interpret</u> the message as meaning that we should <u>all</u> live together in peace and harmony.

6) Muhammad also warned against <u>nationalism</u> (i.e. fanatical devotion to a country): "*Nationalism means helping your people in unjust causes.*" — **Hadith**

Muslims are more likely to be subjected to <u>racially motivated</u> attacks, abuse and murder than their white neighbours in the UK. As a result a number of peaceful <u>pressure groups</u> have been established — some working within Muslim communities, others working with the Government or with other faith groups.

The Qur'an teaches that men and women are equal

1) There's often a feeling amongst non-Muslims that women are treated <u>poorly</u> in Islam. However, the Qur'an says that Allah created men and women as <u>equal</u> but <u>different</u>:

> "All people are equal…as the teeth of a comb. No Arab can claim merit over a non-Arab, nor a white over a black person, nor male over female." **Hadith**

2) Having said this, there are also some teachings which might be <u>interpreted</u> as meaning men are <u>superior</u>. Although what it actually means is that men and women just have different <u>roles</u> within the community or family — men are responsible for <u>providing</u> for the family, and women are responsible for the <u>home</u>.

> "Men are the protectors and maintainers of women." **Surah 4:34**
>
> *For this reason, the Qur'an says a woman's inheritance need only be half as big as a man's.*

3) However, there's nothing that prevents women from <u>working</u>. In fact, one of Muhammad's wives was a successful <u>businesswoman</u>.

4) Some believe that Muslim women who wear a <u>veil</u> (or <u>hijab</u>) are being treated as second class — but many Muslim women would argue that it's a sign of <u>modesty</u> and allows them to go about their business without being seen simply as <u>sex objects</u>.

We're not all the same, but everyone should be treated equally...

In Islam, a woman's <u>traditional</u> role has been to create a <u>halal</u> homelife where a family could be raised, while the man went out to work and made sure the children were good Muslims. However, that's not to say that all Muslims, no matter where they live, will live in this traditional way. It's more likely in some cultures that there will be complete equality between Muslim men and women — in education, religion and everything else.

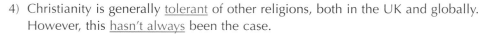

| CHRISTIANITY & GENERAL |
Christianity and Other Religions

Christianity is a very <u>diverse</u> faith, with many different <u>denominations</u> under the Christian umbrella. But that's not to say that it's always been particularly tolerant of <u>other</u> religions.

The UK is a diverse, multi-faith society

1) The United Kingdom is a very <u>diverse</u>, <u>multi-faith</u> society, and religious freedom is a legal <u>right</u>.

2) In most major towns and cities you will find a <u>variety</u> of places of worship — including different <u>churches</u>, <u>synagogues</u> and <u>mosques</u>.

3) Children in most UK schools are taught about <u>all</u> major world faiths in an attempt to increase <u>understanding</u> and <u>tolerance</u>.

Although some Roman Catholic and other church schools limit the amount of time spent looking at other religions.

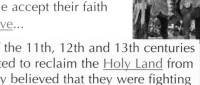

4) Christianity is generally <u>tolerant</u> of other religions, both in the UK and globally. However, this <u>hasn't always</u> been the case.

5) In the past, Christians often believed they had the right to <u>make</u> people accept their faith as the <u>only</u> true way. Other religions were often seen as being <u>primitive</u>...

In the 19th century (when Britain ruled about a third of the world), Christianity was often <u>forced</u> upon other cultures.

In the <u>crusades</u> of the 11th, 12th and 13th centuries Christians attempted to reclaim the <u>Holy Land</u> from the Muslims. They believed that they were fighting a <u>Holy</u> or <u>Just War</u> against <u>infidels</u> (or unbelievers).

Christians believe Christianity is the only true faith

1) Christians generally believe that people have the right to practise <u>any</u> faith, although they might argue that only Christianity has the <u>truth</u> about God. This passage stresses the Christian belief that it is only through following the teachings of <u>Jesus Christ</u> that people can reach God.

"I am the way and the truth and the life. No one comes to the Father except through me." **John 14:6**

2) Some, however, <u>abuse</u> this idea and are <u>less tolerant</u> of other faiths.

3) The *New Catechism of the Roman Catholic Church* (a sort of religious instruction book) makes it clear that "...the Church still has the <u>obligation</u> and also the <u>sacred right</u> to evangelise all men".

4) '<u>Evangelise</u>' means <u>spread</u> the Christian message with the aim of <u>converting</u> people to the faith. Many so-called evangelical preachers or evangelical churches base much of their work on this principle.

The <u>ecumenical movement</u> works within Christianity — it tries to create unity amongst the <u>different Christian</u> traditions (see also page 67).

5) There are also Christian <u>missionaries</u> who believe they have a mission to spread the message of Christianity and <u>convert</u> people.

6) Some of these approaches may be described as <u>exclusive</u> — they don't particularly <u>welcome</u> other faiths, and may even <u>reject</u> them because Christianity is seen as the only way.

Pluralists say there's room for everyone

1) Most Christians are happy to live alongside other faiths in the UK. Many Christian organisations (along with those from many other faiths) belong to 'The Inter Faith Network for the UK'.

2) The aim of this network is to promote <u>mutual understanding</u> and combat <u>prejudice</u>. This is an example of <u>pluralism</u> — the idea that there's room for everyone.

The <u>Inter Faith Network</u> for the UK describes itself as based "...on the principle that dialogue and cooperation can only prosper if they are rooted in respectful relationships which do not blur or undermine the distinctiveness of different religious traditions".

Many faiths, with many different beliefs and customs...

<u>Exclusivism</u> and <u>inclusivism</u> are also things you need to know about. Exclusivism is when a religion teaches that it is the <u>only</u> way to salvation. Inclusivism means the opposite — that salvation need not come through Christianity, say — other religions are 'just as good'. Ooh, it's a tricky subject, is this... make no mistake.

Judaism, Islam and Other Religions

Islam, Christianity and Judaism have a great deal in common, and their approach to other religions is generally one of tolerance and mutual understanding. Over the years, however, there have been times of misunderstanding, ignorance, intolerance and prejudice which have led to discrimination and even war.

Jews believe Judaism is the only true faith (for Jews)

1) Judaism teaches that it is the only true faith for Jews to follow, but is tolerant of other faiths.

2) Most faiths have similar moral and spiritual laws and are, therefore, tolerated by Judaism. Because of this, there's no real desire to convert people.

3) People of any religion are generally deemed to be righteous if they follow the Noahide Code (seven moral laws given to Noah after the flood), or a similar spiritual path which guides them to God. And all righteous people will have a share in a world (or a new age) where humanity will be united under God.

> "And so we wait for you O Lord our God... to establish the world under the kingship of the Almighty... when all human beings will call upon your name..." from a **Jewish prayer**

4) Islam and Judaism have very similar beliefs in one God (they're both pure monotheistic religions — see page 5).

5) However, some Jews have difficulties with the Christian belief that Jesus Christ was the incarnation of God, and with the use of icons in Roman Catholic and Orthodox Christianity.

6) But there's still a great deal of mutual respect, and Jewish participation in interfaith groups (see page 40) is common. One example of an interfaith group is 'The Council for Christians and Jews'.

7) It's sometimes suggested that Islam and Christianity grew from the same seed as Judaism, making the three faiths similar and creating a general air of understanding and tolerance.

Muslims believe Islam is the only true faith

1) It's said that Allah created all humanity from "a single soul" and "made you into nations and tribes, that you may know each other, not that you may despise each other." **Surah 49:13**

> "Those who believe in the Qur'an, and those who are Jews, and Christians — whoever believes in God and the Last Day and does right — surely their reward is with their Lord." **Surah 2:62**

2) Islam believes that it is the only true faith — although there is an acceptance that all righteous people will be favoured by Allah, as he knows all we do.

3) Some Muslims (like some Christians and Jews) might interpret some of the words in the scriptures to argue that Islam should be exclusive, and should not have anything to do with other faiths.

4) Some Muslims may even feel that they have a mission to lead non-Muslims to Allah.

5) However, many Muslims in the UK live side by side with other religious believers, and some take part in interfaith groups.

E.g. The Centre for the Study of Islam and Christian-Muslim Relations.

6) It must be remembered that Muslims believe that men such as Adam, Nuh (Noah), Ibrahim (Abraham), Musa (Moses) and Isa (Jesus) were all Prophets of Allah. So the Torah and the Bible are also seen as holy scriptures which were revealed by Allah (albeit edited from their original form).

Not too different after all...

Christianity, Judaism and Islam have a lot in common — which comes as a shock to some people. But don't go getting the idea that these are the only three religions in the world. If you want to do another RS Exam after this one, there'll be plenty of other stuff to learn about. Hurrah! ...

Warm-Up and Worked Exam Question

Warm-up Questions

1) Describe a rule followed by Orthodox Jews that treats men and women differently.
2) Who are prisoners of conscience?
3) What does the Christian ecumenical movement seek to do?
4) What is prejudice?
5) Who was Dietrich Bonhoeffer?
6) Name the parable Jesus told about a man who came to the aid of a robbery victim, even though the victim was from an enemy nation.

Worked Exam Question

It's time to test what you've learnt over the last few pages. Read the worked exam question carefully, then make your way on to the next page. Don't worry if you're struggling, there's still time to flick back over this section.

1 a) Give an example of a situation in which Christians have used their religion to encourage racism.

The system of apartheid laws in South Africa.

This is unusual — Christian churches are normally against racism.

(1 mark)

b) Briefly describe a story from the Old Testament that deals with the treatment of foreigners.

You could have described the Story of Jonah here instead.

In the Story of Ruth, the Moab daughter-in-law of an Israelite woman stays loyal to her through thick and thin. She becomes devoted to God and one of her descendants is King David.

(3 marks)

c) When Jesus was asked, "Who is my neighbour?" he replied by telling the story of the Good Samaritan. Briefly describe the parable and explain how it answered the question.

The parable tells how a Samaritan, considered an enemy by Jews at that time, helps a robbery victim after a Jewish priest and a Levite had ignored him. The moral is that all people are our neighbours.

(3 marks)

d) Describe another passage from the New Testament that deals with the attitude Christians should have to foreigners.

In the letter of St Paul to the Colossians, Paul says, "There is no Greek or Jew... barbarian, Scythian, slave or free, but Christ is all, and is in all."

(3 marks)

Exam Questions

2   "Allah does not look upon your outward appearance; he looks upon your hearts and deeds."

   a)   What does this Hadith mean for a Muslim?

(2 marks)

   b)   What is the ummah?

(1 mark)

   c)   How does the dress of pilgrims on the Hajj demonstrate Muslim teaching on racism?

(2 marks)

3   a)   What does Islam teach about the relative status and roles of men and women?

(2 marks)

   b)   The Qur'an says that a woman's inheritance need only be half as big as a man's. Does this necessarily mean that the Qur'an teaches that a woman is worth only half as much as a man in the sight of God? Explain your answer.

(2 marks)

   c)   What conclusion do Muslims draw from the fact that Khadijah, the first wife of Muhammad, was a businesswoman?

(2 marks)

   d)   What practical advantage do some Muslim women see in wearing the veil?

(2 marks)

4   a)   What is an evangelist?

(2 marks)

"Deep down all religions are the same." — Betsy

"Where religions say different things one of them must be wrong." — Pete

   b)   Who might argue that his or her faith should be exclusive — Betsy or Pete?

(1 mark)

   c)   Why might Pete argue that his statement does not necessarily mean he is hostile to people of other religions?

(1 mark)

   d)   Write down a famous saying of Jesus that stresses the Christian belief that it is the one true faith.

(3 marks)

Christianity and Poverty

Poverty causes great suffering in the world. So its causes and effects are of great concern for Christians.

Poverty occurs for a number of reasons

1) The Brandt Report in 1980 identified an imbalance between the developed and the developing worlds. The developed world contains around 25% of the world's population but around 80% of the wealth. Little has changed since 1980.

2) Causes of poverty in the Third World include population growth, war, and the sale of raw materials at low prices. In the UK causes range from unemployment and homelessness to gambling.

3) Although possessing wealth is not against Christian teaching, occupations which may bring suffering to others are disapproved of — e.g. working in the arms trade, sex industry, or gambling industry.

Christians have a duty to relieve poverty

"Rich nations have a grave moral responsibility towards those which are unable to ensure the means of their development by themselves", from the Catechism of the Roman Catholic Church.

1) All Christian denominations have become more concerned with a fairer distribution of wealth. A key question is whether wealth ultimately belongs to God, and should therefore be for the good of everyone.

2) Charity is an important part of Christianity, and a concern for Christians is whether or not they should be wealthy. Though Jesus spoke of giving up wealth to help the poor, being wealthy is not against Christian teaching. Indeed, the Church is an extremely rich institution — this is a worry for some believers.

3) The Church often becomes involved in debates about poverty. Recent discussions have focused on issues like the National Lottery and the minimum wage, and whether these contribute to suffering.

4) There's also the question of who should be responsible for the relief of poverty — does the Government have an obligation here, or should it be left to local communities or charities...

"...the love of money is a root of all kinds of evil." **1 Timothy 6:10**

5) A number of Christian organisations exist to tackle poverty — both in the UK and on a global level. These include Christian Aid, CAFOD and Tearfund.

Catholic Agency For Overseas Development

The example of Jesus

Christians believe they have a duty to care for other people and use many sources of authority to stress this. The Bible contains many passages demonstrating Jesus' compassion.

'The man with two tunics should share with him that has none, and the one who has food must do the same." **Luke 3:11**

"Go, sell everything you have and give to the poor, and you will have treasure in heaven." **Mark 10:21**

'I was hungry and you fed me, thirsty and you gave me a drink... whenever you did this for one of the least important brothers of mine you did it for me." **Matthew 25:35-40**

Luke 16:19-31, **Luke 6:20-31**, **Matthew 6:19-21** and **Amos 8:4-6** also contain teachings on poverty.

CASE STUDY — CHRISTIAN AID

Christian Aid was set up after World War II to help refugees. It now has over 40 member churches in the UK and Ireland, and works globally to relieve poverty. It raises money through donations, fund-raising and collections. Most of Christian Aid's work is in development. Although they do contribute to emergency disaster relief, they believe the best way to help people is by *'helping them to help themselves'*. They set up projects in the Third World drawing on the skills of local people. This is seen as more dignified than receiving handouts. Development projects set up by Christian Aid aim to help with problems such as poor sanitation, education and healthcare, as well as disease and population control. The organisation also aims to change government policy which adds to the suffering of the world's poor, e.g. through Third World debt relief, and fair-trade products.

Christianity has many beliefs about poverty...

The basic message here is pretty simple, I think. And if you need to learn about a Christian organisation working to relieve poverty, Christian Aid is just an example — there are many others you can choose from...

Judaism, Islam and Poverty

Islam and Judaism have similar views on poverty. Both believe it's our duty to look after those less fortunate than ourselves, and both expect people to give some of their income to the poor and needy.

Judaism says, "Do not be hardhearted or tightfisted..."

1) The above passage from Deuteronomy sums up Jewish teaching on poverty. Maimonides said that the best way to give was "to help a person help themselves so that they may become self-supporting".

2) There are two main ways of giving to charity — Tzedaka and Gemilut Hasadim:

   TZEDAKA: Tzedaka is financial aid — even the poorest in society are expected to contribute 10% of their wealth. All wealth belongs to God, and not giving to the poor deprives them of what they're owed.
   GEMILUT HASADIM: This refers to kind and compassionate actions towards those in need.

3) Many Jewish homes have collection boxes (called pushkes) in which money for charity can be placed. Children are encouraged to use these boxes — maybe donating some of their pocket money each week.

4) Although Judaism doesn't teach that everyone should try to be wealthy, it does suggest that extreme poverty will make others responsible for you, and that the love of wealth may turn you from God.

5) Unfairness and dishonesty in business is condemned — you're answerable to God for any wrongdoing.

> **Examples**
> i) There are a number of Jewish organisations working to raise money and promote kind actions. These include 'Jewish Care' and 'Norwood Child Care'.
> ii) On a more global level is 'Tzedek' — this charity, using the slogan 'Jewish care for a just world', is concerned with things such as aid, debt relief, refugees and the environment.

The Islamic view is very similar

1) In Islam, the principle is much the same — greed and waste are frowned upon and possessions ultimately belong to Allah. Muslims are encouraged to act responsibly and help those in need.

2) Any work involving gambling, alcohol or anything sexually suggestive is forbidden, and moneylending is seen as immoral if those in debt are being exploited through the charging of interest. Some Islamic banks exist to get around this.

3) Again, there are two main ways to help the disadvantaged — Zakah and Sadaqah:

See also page 117 for more about Islamic living.

   ZAKAH: This is one of the Five Pillars of Islam — 2.5% of your yearly savings should be given to the needy, no matter how rich or poor you are.
   SADAQAH: This is additional aid — maybe financial donations or an act of compassion and love.

> **Examples**
> i) Muslims raise money for their local mosque which is then distributed to the poor.
> ii) In addition, there are global charities such as 'Muslim Aid' and 'Islamic Relief'.
> iii) 'The Red Crescent' is the Islamic equivalent of the Red Cross, and the two often work together to bring aid to countries in times of war and famine.

It all sounds like good advice to me...

Both Islam and Judaism teach that we have a responsibility to the planet, its resources and our fellow humans. We are stewards of the Earth and should not exploit what we have been given at the expense of others. It's a message that crops up in the 'environment' section as well. So I'd learn it pretty well, if I were you.

Religion and the Environment

Environmental problems today mean the Earth is suffering. Sadly, many of these problems are man-made...

Our **small planet** has some **big problems**

The environmental problems facing the world include...

i) Global warming (and the Greenhouse Effect),
ii) Deforestation,
iii) Extinction of animal and plant species,
iv) Pollution (leading to problems like acid rain),
v) Scarcity of natural resources.

1) Developed countries are the worst (but not the only) polluters. Competition means that businesses often feel forced to put profit before the welfare of the planet — if they don't, they may not survive.

2) Some governments look more to short-term benefits than long-term care for the planet.
They may say they're trying to do the best for their people, and that people should be our first priority.

3) Governments in developing nations often claim that they're only doing now what richer countries did in the past, and that it's hypocritical for richer countries to tell them what they should be doing.

Religious ideas about the *environment* — 'Stewardship'

Christianity, Islam and Judaism have pretty similar ideas when it comes to looking after the Earth. All three religions teach that God has put us in charge of the Earth, and that we must do our duty responsibly.

Christianity

1) Christians of all denominations believe that God gave us the Earth, but expects us to care for it — this idea is called 'stewardship'. We have no right to abuse God's creation — we must act responsibly.

2) There's pressure on governments and companies to sell goods and services, even at the expense of the environment. Although it can be difficult to balance taking care of the Earth with providing for humankind, this is what Christians believe we must try to do.

"We have a responsibility to create a balanced policy between consumption and conservation."
Pope John Paul II, 1988

3) Christianity teaches that everything is interdependent (i.e. everything depends on everything else), so driving species of animal or plant to extinction, or harming the planet, eventually ends up harming us.

4) Christian organisations such as CAFOD, Christian Aid and Tearfund are concerned with putting this responsibility into practice. They put pressure on governments and industry to think more about how we are abusing the planet.

"The earth is the Lord's, and everything in it, the world and all who live in it; for he founded it upon the seas and established it upon the waters." Psalms 24:1-2

"You made him [humankind] a little lower than the heavenly beings, and crowned him with glory and honour; You made him ruler over the works of your hands; you put everything under his feet." Psalms 8:5-6

Judaism

1) Jews believe that we are the custodians of the Earth, and a concern for the natural world is often seen as being at the heart of Jewish teaching.

2) God's creations should remain as he intended, and we have no right to abuse them. Everything is interdependent, with trees being particularly important. Since the creation of Israel in 1948, millions of trees have been planted to aid the reclamation of the desert and help rebuild the nation.

"The Lord God took the man and put him in the Garden of Eden, to work it and take care of it." Genesis 2:15

Islam

1) Muslim teaching on environmental issues is very similar to that of Judaism.

2) At the Day of Judgement questions will be asked of us. We will be required to answer for any ill-treatment of the planet and its resources.

3) The Earth is seen as being a product of the love of Allah, so we should treat it with love.

Dr Abdullah Omar Nasseef stated at the 1996 World Wide Fund for Nature conference that, "His [Allah's] trustees are responsible for maintaining the unity of his creation, the integrity of the Earth, its flora and fauna, its wildlife and natural environment."

Religion and Animals

Christianity says animals come below people

According to the Bible, God created the world, mankind was created to populate it, and animals were created for the use of mankind. But animal-rights issues are still of interest to many Christians. For example...

i) Animal experimentation (e.g. vivisection)

ii) Factory farming,

iii) Destruction of natural habitats (e.g. deforestation), leading to extinction,

iv) Hunting,

v) Genetic modification and cloning,

vi) Zoos and circuses,

vii) Vegetarianism.

1) One of the major issues for Christians is whether animals have souls or not. If they don't, then some people will argue that God created us as superior, and that animals are here for our use.

> "They [human beings] will have power over the fish, the birds and all the animals, domestic and wild, large and small."
> **Genesis 1:26**

2) Christianity teaches that we should treat animals with kindness, but that they can be used to benefit mankind (as long as their suffering is considered). It's also thought that excessive money should not be 'wasted' on animals when human beings are suffering. So humans are very definitely 'on top', with animals below.

3) But some Christians point out that as everything is interdependent, our treatment of animals reflects on us. Indeed, the Church of England teaches that the medical and technological use of animals should be monitored 'in the light of ethical principles'.

4) The Roman Catholic Church is more likely to tolerate things like animal experimentation, but only if they bring benefit to mankind (e.g. if the experiments lead to the development of life-saving medicines).

5) Certain denominations are generally more opposed to the ill-treatment of animals — especially for our pleasure. For example, Quakers are particularly likely to frown upon zoos, animal circuses, hunting and the wearing of fur.

> The Bible tells us that Jesus ate fish, and as a Jew he would have eaten meat at certain festivals.

6) Unlike some other religions, there are no specific food laws to be followed in Christianity. So vegetarianism (not eating meat) and veganism (not eating or using any animal products) are a matter for individual Christians to decide about.

Judaism and Islam have similar views

JUDAISM

1) The Noahide Laws (given to Noah after the Flood) clearly forbid cruelty to animals. Animals are here to help us, and not to be abused. And there are many stories in the Torah which demonstrate care for animals.

> *Deuteronomy 5:14 says that animals deserve a day off on the Sabbath, just like people.*

2) In Judaism, if meat is to be eaten, the animal must be slaughtered in a 'humane' fashion. This involves cutting the throat of the animal with a very sharp blade to bring about a quick death (see page 104).

> "I am putting you in charge of the fish, the birds and all the wild animals." **Genesis 1:28**

3) Experiments on animals may be tolerated if they result in a benefit for mankind, but only as a last resort. Cruel sports are seen as an abuse of God's creatures.

> "If someone kills a sparrow for sport, the sparrow will cry out on the Day of Judgement 'Oh Lord, that person killed me for nothing. He did not kill me for any useful purpose.'" **Hadith**

ISLAM

1) Khalifah is the idea that we're responsible for the Earth — Khalifah means Vice-Regent, or Trustee.

2) Cruelty to animals is forbidden, as is their use simply for our pleasure.

3) Muslims believe in demonstrating mercy and compassion for all living creatures, and animals used for meat must be slaughtered humanely.

Most religions believe we have a duty to look after animals...

The issue about how we treat animals isn't a simple one — this is the page where animal experimentation and stuff comes in, which means benefits for people at the expense of animals. Which complicates things...

Warm-Up and Worked Exam Question

Warm-up Questions

1) What does Luke's Gospel say that a man who has two tunics should do?
2) What does "khalifah" mean?
3) What does "interdependence" mean?
4) Name a Christian denomination that generally disapproves of circuses and hunting for sport.
5) What are the Jewish and Muslim words for giving a portion of your wealth to the poor?

Worked Exam Question

Jews, Christians and Muslims all have similar views on the poor, the environment and cruelty to animals. Make sure you know the subtle differences, then have a go at these questions.

1 Compare Christian and Muslim beliefs about the relationship between people and animals.

Both Islam and Christianity say man is above the animals. In the book of Genesis it says that man should rule the animals. Many Christians believe that animals do not have souls. If they do not, then some people argue that they are here for our use.

Both Muslims and Christians have an idea of "stewardship". Animals are part of God's creation and so should be cared for.

Both permit people to eat animals. The Bible tells us that Jesus ate a meal of fish with his disciples after the Resurrection. The instructions in the Qur'an about humane slaughter of animals assume Muslims will eat meat.

Both religions hold that you should slaughter animals humanely, but only Islam has exact rules on how the slaughter is to be done. Islam stresses more strongly than Christianity that animals should not be killed frivolously. A Hadith describes a sparrow crying out at the Day of Judgement that it was killed by someone for no reason.

This is a "compare" question, so you need to say how their views are similar, and how they are different.

(8 marks)

Exam Questions

2   a)   State some of the causes of poverty in Less Economically Developed Countries.

(4 marks)

b)   What do TWO religions you have studied teach about relieving poverty?

(6 marks)

c)   Describe how a Christian charity such as CAFOD or Christian Aid helps people in underdeveloped countries.

(6 marks)

3   a)   State FOUR environmental problems facing the world.

(4 marks)

b)   "We should never put the environment ahead of the needs of human beings."

Do you agree? Give reasons for your answer, showing you have thought about different points of view. Refer to at least one religion in your answer.

(6 marks)

4   Read the following passage from the Gospel of Mark and then answer the question.

Jesus sat down opposite the place where the offerings were put and watched the crowd putting their money into the temple treasury. Many rich people threw in large amounts. But a poor widow came and put in two very small copper coins, worth only a fraction of a penny.

Calling his disciples to him, Jesus said, "I tell you the truth, this poor widow has put more into the treasury than all the others. They all gave out of their wealth; but she, out of her poverty, put in everything — all she had to live on."

(Mark 12:41–44)

a)   What was Jesus trying to teach about generosity?

(2 marks)

b)   Briefly describe TWO other parables or sayings of Jesus that deal with money, poverty and giving.

(4 marks)

c)   "Jesus' teachings about charity are not practical in real life."

Do you agree? Give reasons for your answer, showing you have thought about different points of view.

(6 marks)

Religion and Crime

Christians believe that Jesus was forgiving and compassionate. Islam and Judaism also stress the importance of forgiveness and reconciliation, although the three religions do approach matters in slightly different ways.

Crime or sin — state law versus religious law

1) Most nations believe the rule of law is the best way of protecting people in society. Without law there would perhaps be chaos. With it, people know what they can and cannot do. The police enforce the laws of the land. The judiciary (i.e. the system of courts and judges) tries people suspected of committing a crime, and punishes those that are found guilty.

2) For Christians, there's a difference between a sin and a crime. A sin is when religious law is broken, i.e. when God's teaching is disobeyed. A crime is when the state laws are broken. The laws in the UK are fundamentally Christian, but are not actually religious.

3) Judaism teaches that Jews should obey the laws of the land they live in, as well as following the 613 mitzvot (religious laws or commandments) in the Torah.

4) Muslims have a clear and detailed religious law (Shari'ah — see page 114), and this is often the basis for state law. Saudi Arabia, for example, is run according to this religious law.

5) All three faiths believe that God has commanded us to follow law.

> For Christians:
> "You must obey the authorities — not just because of God's punishment but also as a matter of conscience."
> **Romans 13:5**

> For Jews:
> "You shall appoint judges… and they shall judge the people righteously."
> **Deuteronomy 16:18**

> Muslims believe that Allah sees all. He will know if you have committed a crime and you will be made to answer for it on the Day of Judgement.
> A truly repentant sinner, however, will be forgiven.

Rabbinical courts (called Bet Din) exist in many countries to sort out Jewish disputes (see p 93).

Punishment can have various aims

1) Most people believe that punishment should do some or all of the following:
   1) deter criminals
   2) make the criminal pay
   3) protect society
   4) show the authority of law
   5) help reform the offender
   6) provide retribution (revenge)

2) Punishment can take a variety of forms, including: community service, a fine, probation, a prison sentence, corporal punishment (inflicting pain, e.g. flogging or beating), and capital punishment (death).

   ### CAPITAL PUNISHMENT
   i) Many people say that capital punishment doesn't seem to deter criminals at all — most murders are committed in the heat of the moment (i.e. they're not premeditated), and in the case of terrorists, the death penalty might even encourage people as it makes the executed offender a martyr. (Also, there seem to be more murders in places that use the death penalty than in places where capital punishment isn't used.)
   ii) There have been cases where someone has been proved innocent after having been put to death.

3) Many Christians are opposed to capital punishment, as it does not allow for reform — although some in the United States believe that it's a good thing. They say it protects the innocent and deters others.

   The 'Howard League for Penal Reform' was set up by Christians to campaign for punishments that allow offenders to reform.

4) Judaism has allowed execution in certain circumstances, but only if there are witnesses.

   "If anyone takes the life of a human being, he must be put to death." **Leviticus 24:17**

5) The same is true of Islam — in many Muslim countries people are executed for murder, or for speaking out against Islam. Also, adulterers can be flogged, and thieves can have hands cut off.

Crime and punishment is a really contentious issue...
Not for the first time, I'll say that this is a subject with lots of different shades of grey. Should we just lock people up and throw away the key... or is there something else we should be doing...

Christianity and War

Although Christianity is generally 'anti-war', many denominations accept that a war can be 'just'. Individuals may not agree with this, however. They may be against war under any circumstances.

There are **5 conditions** for a *just war*

Although Christians recognise that war goes against the teachings of Jesus, Christianity accepts that there can be such a thing as a 'just war'. A just war should satisfy these 5 conditions:

PROPER AUTHORITY   A war must be declared by a proper authority, e.g. an elected government, a president or a monarch.

JUST CAUSE   A war must have a just cause, e.g. self-defence, or reclaiming lost territory.

JUST AIM   A war must have a just aim, and should stop when that aim has been achieved.

DISCRIMINATION   A war must be waged without endangering civilians (i.e. with discrimination).

PROPORTIONALITY   A war must be waged without undue force (i.e. with proportionality) — don't use a nuclear missile against someone with a bow and arrow.

A 'Holy War' is one where people believe God is 'on their side' — e.g. in the 11th, 12th and 13th centuries, Christians went on crusades to 'free' the holy places in Palestine.

"Declare a Holy War. Call the troops to arms."
Joel 3:9

Pacifists and *martyrs*

1) A pacifist is someone who has strongly-held beliefs that war and physical violence are wrong under any circumstances.

2) There were pacifists in Britain who refused to fight in the world wars. These 'conscientious objectors' went to prison — they were prisoners of conscience.

3) They suffered humiliation in prison and after they'd been released.

The Quakers is a Christian denomination opposed to war under all circumstances.

"Put your sword back in its place. All who draw the sword will die by the sword."
Matthew 26:52

4) Martyrs are those who have chosen to die for their faith. This willingness to sacrifice your own life for what you believe in is fundamental to Christianity (see page 58) and other religions.

5) Many people risk their lives today by preaching the Gospel of Jesus and speaking out against governments (see page 37).

Unconventional war — *nuclear* war and *terrorism*

Terrorism and nuclear war could both be described as unconventional warfare.

1) Terrorism is a form of violent protest that goes on all over the world.

2) Terrorists target any person, building or institution that could help their cause.

3) All Christian denominations are against nuclear weapons and weapons of mass destruction, because these weapons don't discriminate between civilians and people fighting the war.

4) The Church of England wants countries to reduce the numbers of nuclear weapons they have. However, it recognises that unilateral disarmament (where just one country gives up its weapons) is a difficult thing for a government to do.

5) That's why it calls for countries to work together and agree on multilateral disarmament, where many countries give up their arms at the same time.

Just cause, just aim, just war...

People go to war for all kinds of reasons, and there's nearly always a war or some kind of terrorist activity going on somewhere in the world. For the Exam, it's worth learning about a current conflict, especially why it started, and what efforts are being made to end it. Then you can include something topical in your answers.

52

Judaism, Islam and War

Despite the fact that there have been a number of wars between Muslims and Jews, there are many <u>similarities</u> in the way the two religions approach the subject of <u>war</u>.

The **Jewish** view — **obligatory** and **optional** wars

1) The universal greeting amongst Jews is '<u>shalom</u>' (peace) — this is the <u>ideal</u>. War is hated, but there's a belief that war is sometimes <u>necessary</u> to bring about peace.

2) War is divided into two categories — <u>milchemet mitzvah</u> (obligatory war) and <u>milchemet reshut</u> (optional war).

3) An obligatory war might be:
i) a war fought in <u>self-defence</u>.
ii) a <u>pre-emptive strike</u> in order to avoid being attacked — the Six-Day War in 1967, for example.
iii) a war to help neighbouring countries — so that your <u>own</u> country is not invaded.
iv) a war commanded by <u>God</u>.

4) An <u>optional</u> war should only take place when all attempts to secure peace have <u>failed</u>.

5) No war should be fought to colonise or take <u>revenge</u>. This is <u>forbidden</u>.

> **THE SIX-DAY WAR**
> In June 1967, Israel launched a series of attacks against its much larger Arab neighbours, destroying the Egyptian Air Force on the ground. After six days' fighting, Israel had won a war against Egypt, Jordan and Syria.

The **Islamic** view — "Hate your enemy mildly"

Muslims believe that war is sometimes <u>necessary</u>, although the concept of <u>jihad</u> is often misunderstood. These passages sum up Muslim teaching:

> *"The person who struggles so that Allah's word is supreme is the one serving Allah's cause."* **Hadith**
> *"Hate your enemy mildly; he may be your friend one day."* **Hadith**

Jihad — there are two kinds

1) There are two kinds of jihad (or 'striving')...

i) a <u>Greater Jihad</u>, which is when a Muslim makes a special effort to be a '<u>pure</u>' Muslim, or fights against his or her own selfish <u>desires</u>.

ii) a <u>Lesser Jihad</u> — <u>war</u> is an example of a lesser jihad, but it must be fought only as a last resort. These wars are often thought of as '<u>Holy Wars</u>'.

See page 117 for more about jihad.

2) Military jihad has very strict <u>rules</u>, and is similar to the Christian idea of a 'just war':
i) It is justified if it will bring about <u>freedom</u> from tyranny, restore <u>peace</u>, combat <u>oppression</u>, or right <u>injustice</u>.
ii) It must <u>not</u> be used to colonise, suppress or impose Islam on non-believers.
iii) The sick, the elderly, women and children should <u>not</u> be harmed, the natural world must not be damaged, and <u>indiscriminate</u> killing should be avoided.
iv) Jihad must be in the name of <u>Allah</u>, and according to his will. It must be declared by a <u>religious leader</u>, not any old politician.
v) Dying in the service of Allah turns a Muslim into a <u>martyr</u>. True martyrs go <u>straight</u> to paradise as an <u>instant</u> reward — martyrs don't have to wait for the Day of Judgement.

3) There is no real concept of <u>pacifism</u> in Islam, although <u>peace</u> is always the goal of war.

Peace, love and harmony — seems that's what we all want...

Judaism and Islam seem to have quite a lot in common when you find out a bit more about them. That's true when it comes to war and peace as well. Neither religion believes in unwavering pacifism — the attitude of both religions is that war is sometimes necessary, though always (and inevitably) unpleasant.

Religion and Drugs

Everyone has a view on drugs and drug abuse. But not all drugs are the same — and there are 3 kinds you especially need to know about:

HARD   Drugs like <u>heroin</u> and <u>cocaine</u> — these are Class A drugs, the most <u>serious</u> category.

SOFT   Although soft drugs are still <u>illegal</u> in Britain (Class B or C), they're not regarded as being so bad, and penalties for possessing these aren't as harsh as for hard drugs. Cannabis is widely seen as a soft drug. Drugs like ecstasy and amphetamines (speed) are often put in this category too.

SOCIAL   Social drugs include <u>alcohol</u> and <u>tobacco</u>. Cannabis is viewed by some people as a social drug.

Christianity, Judaism and Islam all say **drugs are bad**

"Your body is a temple of the Holy Spirit..." — Although this is a line from the New Testament (**1 Corinthians 6:19**), the message is similar for Islam, Christianity and Judaism. Drugs are seen as <u>bad</u>, as they damage the <u>mind</u>, abuse the <u>body</u> God has given to us, and can lead to <u>poverty</u> or even <u>death</u>.

1) Illegal drugs are completely <u>disapproved</u> of by Christianity, Judaism and Islam — they're seen as a way of escaping the <u>realities</u> of life, and existing instead in an artificial <u>fantasy</u> world.

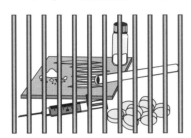

2) All three religions teach that the mind and the body are <u>gifts</u> from God, and that we do not have the right to <u>abuse</u> them. On a more practical level, drug taking is also seen as leading to <u>irresponsible</u> behaviour (e.g. neglecting your family or responsibilities), and possibly <u>criminal</u> activity.

3) Drugs taken to enhance performance in <u>sport</u> are also disapproved of, as they do not allow a person to properly display the skills they have been given. Again, they create a <u>false</u> world.

CANNABIS — THE SUBJECT OF MUCH RECENT DEBATE

Cannabis has been hotly debated recently. Some people believe it may have medical benefits, although others say it's a 'gateway drug', meaning users are more likely to end up using harder drugs. Although cannabis is now a Class C drug, it's still illegal — but many people (including some doctors, policemen and politicians) would like to see it legalised. Some say that drugs like ecstasy should also be legalised.

Islam is against cannabis for the same reasons it's against alcohol. And Sheik Ibn Tayumiyyah (a famous scholar and Islamic teacher) had this to say on the subject: "Sinful people smoke hashish (i.e. cannabis)... it disturbs the mind and temperament... excites sexual desire."

The religions have **different** views on **alcohol**

1) Christianity <u>allows</u> the consumption of alcohol — it's used in Holy Communion after all. However, <u>drunkenness</u> is frowned upon. Some denominations (e.g. The Salvation Army) are more disapproving than others.

2) Likewise in Judaism, alcohol is <u>permitted</u>, although drinking to <u>excess</u> is disapproved of. The Midrash (a collection of moral stories) contains the line, *"wine enters, sense goes out."*

3) Alcohol is <u>forbidden</u> in Islam, as it causes people to lose control — it's seen as a weapon of Shaytan (the Devil). A Muslim should have a <u>clear mind</u> when praying, and so there can be no place for alcohol.

See also page 117.

4) <u>Tobacco</u> isn't mentioned in the Torah or the Qur'an — not surprising, as it hadn't been discovered when they were written. However, it's <u>harmful</u> to the body, and so should really be avoided.

Christians, Jews and Muslims all have similar views on drugs...

This is a social issue that's often in the news. And as it's a very 'people-oriented' issue, you'd expect all religions to have something to say on the matter. But it's a Perspectives topic, so in the Exam, you can mention your own opinions as well — often there are no right or wrong answers necessarily, just different opinions.

| GENERAL | # Religion and the Media |

The term 'media' refers to any form of mass communication.
So it'd be stuff like television, radio, newspapers, magazines, film, the Internet...

The media is becoming more important

1) The amount of money spent on the media has become massive in recent years — especially with the recent launch of satellite and digital television, and the Internet.

2) At the same time, church attendances have been falling dramatically.

3) So as the role of the media in our lives increases, the role of organised religion declines in importance.

There are religious programmes on the telly

1) The majority of television programming is secular (non-religious), although there are a few dedicated religious programmes to be found, as well as religious content in drama and current affairs programmes.

2) Traditionally the BBC has always transmitted religious programmes on a Sunday — during the so-called 'God slot'. The programmes themselves are nearly always Christian.

3) The best-known religious show is probably 'Songs of Praise' — on the BBC at around 6 p.m. on Sunday. It's broadcast from different locations, and each week focuses on a particular religious community and their church. BBC Radio 4 also broadcasts religious programmes on a Sunday.

4) On a Sunday, you can usually find a service of morning worship on one of the terrestrial television channels. This is to allow those who can't get to church (or those who would prefer to worship in private) to take part in an act of worship.

5) Evangelical Christian preachers can also be seen on television in the USA, and increasingly on cable and satellite TV in the UK. They speak to people in their homes, deliver God's message and raise money.

6) There are currently no specifically Jewish programmes on television, and this is a cause of concern and frustration for the Jewish community. Many feel that Jewish issues are often not dealt with fairly, and Jews are portrayed in a stereotypical way.

7) At its best, the media can be used to educate people about a particular faith or issue. However, misrepresentation and bias are a serious concern for followers of all faiths. Muslims and Jews especially often feel that they are sidelined or misrepresented in TV news and other forms of media.

> Some other religious (or part-religious) programmes:
> 1) 'The Heaven and Earth Show' — covers a variety of religious and secular issues from the point of view of various faiths.
> 2) 'Everyman' — a religious documentary programme.

TV or church? TV or church? Hmmm...

There's not an awful lot of religion on the TV or in the newspapers. And because of the nature of the media, when religion is covered, it's more likely to be a story about an extreme weirdy cult than about people practising their faiths quietly, as they have done for years. It's the nature of the job, I guess.

Religion and the Media

It's not just religious TV programmes that grapple with the important issues of the day, however. There's also Dale Winton, Graham Norton, the Teletubbies... and others I don't have room for in a short page intro.

Soaps and newspapers tackle difficult issues

1) **Soap operas** also deal with moral and spiritual issues. In recent years euthanasia, HIV, homosexuality, prostitution, celibacy, lesbianism, incest, death, marriage, infidelity and racism have all been covered in soaps (although rarely all in the same episode).

2) Even though soaps are often seen as a form of escapism, they enable us to see how a variety of characters deal with issues and emotions that we all may face at some point in our lives.

3) However, characters are sometimes criticised for being one-dimensional stereotypes. The same might also be said of characters in comedy programmes — they can easily cause offence to people.

1) **Newspapers** carry a range of stories, e.g. coverage of wars, terrorism, racist crime and refugees, as well as a variety of moral issues. This is where many people find out the 'truth'.

2) But some people worry about how the ideas of the people who own or write for newspapers affect their content. This might include political bias or a degree of xenophobia (i.e. hatred of foreigners). You might find completely different versions of the same story in 'The Daily Telegraph', 'The Sun', 'The Guardian' and 'The Daily Mail'.

The media can also be a bad influence

1) Many people worry about the way the media influences people, especially children. Their main concerns are about how scenes containing sex, violence, bad language and drug taking might affect the young.

2) In the UK there's a 'watershed' — for the BBC this is 9 p.m. After this time, programmes are aimed at adults, and it's the responsibility of parents to decide whether children watch or not. However, before this time "...all programmes...should be suitable for a general audience, including children."

3) There are also strict guidelines on sex, bad language and the treatment of religious issues.

4) However, some people would argue that sex, violence and other unsuitable material has been creeping into mainstream programming, and that this reflects a general lack of morals in society.

5) Sometimes the content of television programmes, films, newspapers and books is considered blasphemous, meaning that it's caused offence to followers of a specific faith. Salman Rushdie's novel 'The Satanic Verses' caused great offence to Muslims around the world.

REFLECTION OR CAUSE...

Some people say that violence on TV reflects what already happens in society. But others say that it has a direct influence on society, and makes violence more likely. The same argument is used in relation to drugs, sexual behaviour, and so on.

Some issues are specific to certain types of media

1) Films are officially classified to warn people about their content, and they may be censored too (i.e. the makers might be told to cut certain bits out). Some films urge 'parental guidance' (PG), while others are only deemed suitable for people over a certain age (e.g. 15 or 18).

2) More recently there have been grave concerns about the Internet, and the ease with which it can be used to access various materials — pornography, for example.

3) Advertisements have also been criticised for using sexual images to sell products to children.

That's all folks! It's the end of Section One.

People sometimes say that programmes on TV chip away at the moral fabric of society. What shocks us today may seem normal tomorrow. But those in the TV industry usually dispute that they have any kind of detrimental effect on society. Yep, once again, there's no right or wrong answer... just points of view.

Warm-Up and Worked Exam Question

Warm-up Questions

1) To Christians, what is the difference between a crime and a sin?
2) Explain the meaning of these words: (a) pacifist, (b) martyr.
3) "Religious people don't drink alcohol." True or false? Explain your answer.
4) What does the term 'mass media' mean?
5) What is film classification, and why are films classified?

Worked Exam Questions

This worked example's just like the sort you might get in the exam. Have a good, careful read of it.

1   Most people believe that society should punish criminals.

   a)   Give three aims which this punishment might try to achieve.

   To deter others from committing crimes, to protect society

   and to help reform the offender.

   There are other possible answers too.   *(3 marks)*

   b)   Explain why most Christians oppose capital punishment.

   It does not allow criminals to reform.

   (1 mark)

   c)   Give one example of a situation in which Judaism or Islam might allow capital punishment to take place.

   If a murder has been committed.

   (1 mark)

   d)   Do you think capital punishment should ever be allowed? Explain your answer.

   No. It does not seem to deter criminals. It may also encourage

   terrorists, because if they are executed, they will become martyrs.

   You could have answered "Yes" here. You just need *(2 marks)*
   to put two reasons that back up your point of view.

2   a)   Are all drugs illegal? Explain your answer.

   No. Tobacco and alcohol are drugs, but are not illegal in Britain.

   (1 mark)

   b)   Explain why committed members of most religions disapprove of illegal drugs.

   They damage the mind and body that God has given to us. They are

   an escape from real life and can lead to irresponsible behaviour, such

   as neglecting your family, or to criminal activity. If they are taken to

   enhance performance in sport, this is another kind of falseness.

   (5 marks)

Exam Questions

3   According to Christian teaching, there are five conditions required for a 'just war'.

a)   What are these five conditions?

(5 marks)

b)   "It is never right for a country to go to war."

Do you agree? Give reasons for your answer, showing that you have thought about more than one point of view. Refer to at least one religion in your answer.

(5 marks)

4   a)   Give two examples of unconventional warfare.

(2 marks)

b)   What is the difference between unilateral disarmament and multilateral disarmament?

(2 marks)

c)   Why are most governments unwilling to try unilateral disarmament?

(1 mark)

d)   Describe the attitude of the Church of England to nuclear weapons and disarmament.

(3 marks)

5   The media is becoming increasingly important in daily life.

a)   Describe how TV and radio can be used for religious purposes.

(3 marks)

b)   Why might some religious groups be unhappy with the media?

(3 marks)

c)   "Soap operas have a bad influence on those who watch them."

Do you agree? Give reasons for your answer, showing that you have thought about more than one point of view. Refer to at least one religion in your answer.

(5 marks)

Basic Christian Beliefs

Worship offered to Jesus is what distinguishes Christianity from all other monotheistic (one-god) religions. While not all Christians believe exactly the same things, most accept the doctrines of the Apostles' Creed.

The Apostles' Creed — a summary of the Christian Faith

The Apostles' Creed summarises the basic Christian teachings about Jesus: *'Creed' just means a set of beliefs.*

(1) Jesus is the Christ   'Christ' isn't a surname, it's a title — it means 'Messiah', i.e. 'Anointed One of God'.

(2) The Incarnation   This was the act by which God became a human being.
Christians don't believe Jesus was 'half God and half man' — he was fully both.

(3) The Virgin Birth   The Gospels say that Jesus was born of a virgin — Mary became pregnant through the influence of the Holy Spirit. This is why Christians say "God's Son", or "God the Son".

(4) The Crucifixion   It was Jesus' death on the cross which "bought" his people forgiveness of sin.

(5) The Resurrection   Jesus rose from the dead on Easter Day, and is still alive today.

(6) The Ascension   After the resurrection Jesus 'ascended into Heaven' (not necessarily 'in the sky').

1) The Apostles' Creed also includes important teaching about the Holy Spirit.

2) Although Christians believe in only one God, this God exists in 3 forms — God the Father, God the Son and God the Holy Spirit. Together, these three make up the Trinity.

3) The Holy Spirit is God's influence in the world, and is often pictured as fire, or as a dove, or thought of as wind.

After the Ascension, God sent his Spirit down upon Jesus' followers in 'tongues of fire' at Pentecost (see page 77).

At Jesus' baptism the Spirit descended on him in the form of a dove.

There's some more basic Christian beliefs on pages 8 and 10.

Jesus sets an example for Christians today

Jesus' self-sacrifice

1) Christians believe that in his willingness to suffer and die on their behalf, Jesus set an example which they themselves should be prepared to follow.

2) In **Mark 8:34** Jesus says, *"If anyone would come after me... he must deny self and take up his cross and follow me."*

Jesus' death

1) Christians believe that Jesus' death was not a sign of his failure, but the climax of his ministry.

2) In dying on the cross, Jesus paid for all the sin of mankind. Because he himself was sinless, and because he was God Incarnate as well as Man, his death was able to redeem mankind.

3) The Bible teaches that God is merciful, but he is also just, so our sins have to be paid for. Jesus sacrificed himself in order to pay that price.

Jesus' resurrection

1) In rising from death, Jesus demonstrated to Christians the truth of his claims, and proved that the debt of man's sin had been paid. He also demonstrated that there is life after death.

2) Christians believe that everyone who has died will be 'resurrected' at the Last Judgement (this is a personal day of judgement, not the same one for everybody). Those that God finds acceptable as a result of Jesus' sacrifice will enter Heaven — the rest will not.

Three is one doesn't work in maths — but this is RS...
The Trinity isn't three Gods — just different forms of the same God. A bit like water, steam and ice...

The Bible

The Bible is a collection of books in different styles and languages written over a period of about 1000 years. It's also the Christian Scriptures — meaning that for Christians, it's sacred.

The Bible — the Old and New Testaments

The Bible's divided into 2 main parts — the Old and New Testaments:

THE OLD TESTAMENT

The Old Testament is the Jewish Scriptures (i.e. it's considered sacred by Jews). Written in Hebrew and Aramaic, its 39 books include the Creation story, the books of the Law (Torah), the 10 Commandments, various histories of Ancient Israel, prophecy, poetry and psalms.

THE NEW TESTAMENT

The New Testament is the specifically Christian part of the Bible. Written in Greek in the 1st Century CE, its 27 books include the 4 Gospels, the Acts of the Apostles (describing the early years of Christianity), 13 letters by St Paul (giving advice about the Christian life), 8 letters by other early Christian leaders, and the Revelation of St John — an apocalyptic vision.

The 4 Gospels are Matthew, Mark, Luke (called the Synoptic Gospels, as they are all very similar stories of Jesus), and John (which portrays Jesus in a very different way). The word 'Gospel' means 'good news', and the Gospels tell the good news about Jesus Christ.

The Bible is used as a Christian faith guidebook

Christians accept the Bible as authoritative in forming their beliefs and guiding their actions.

1) Christians believe the Bible offers directions for living a moral life. It presents Jesus Christ as our example for godly living, and teaches that we best love God by showing love to others.

2) Both the Old and New Testaments (but especially the New) include rituals for worship, large parts of which are still included in modern worship services (e.g. Holy Communion and baptism).

3) The faith of the Roman Catholic Church is based largely on the Scriptures, but Catholic tradition and the Magisterium (i.e. the teaching of the pope, his cardinals and bishops) are also very important. The Protestant Churches claim their authority mainly from the Scriptures.

4) Different groups of Christians interpret the Bible in different ways (depending on their conscience):

1 **Literalism** Many Christians believe that pretty well everything in the Bible is literally true, e.g. Jesus really did 'walk on water'.

Some people argue that there are contradictions in the Bible, and so it's impossible for everything to be literally true.

2 **Fundamentalism** This is a form of literalism. Fundamentalists believe that it's wrong to question anything in the Bible, since it was dictated by God.

3 **Conservative View** This view is probably the most common among Christians. They believe that the Bible was inspired by God but not dictated — the writers' own interests also come through. Readers must use their intelligence and the guidance of the Holy Spirit in order to understand the writers' intentions.

4 **Liberal View** Liberals believe that pretty well everything in the Bible can be interpreted 'symbolically', e.g. Jesus didn't really 'walk on water' — the story has some other 'spiritual' meaning.

The Bible has been influential for centuries

1) There are many different versions of the Bible in use today.

2) The Gospels (which contain the teachings of Jesus) are central to Christian faith.

3) Christians often meet to study the Bible and to pray, and it's also read for guidance, or as an act of devotion towards God.

The Bible — sells more than any revision guide...

Arguments over the many interpretations of the Bible are common — make sure you learn the issues...

Christian Values

Christians, like all people with a religious faith, try to act in a way consistent with their beliefs.

The Ten Commandments are religious rules

Jesus was a Jew, so his values were based in Jewish belief. There are 613 commandments in the Torah (see page 93), but the most famous are the Decalogue, or Ten Commandments, found in **Exodus 20**:

1) You shall have no other Gods before me.
2) You shall not bow down before idols.
3) You shall not misuse the name of the Lord.
4) Observe the Sabbath and keep it holy.
5) Honour your father and mother.

6) You shall not murder.
7) You shall not commit adultery.
8) You shall not steal.
9) You shall not give false testimony (lie).
10) You shall not covet (want someone else's stuff).

Basically the 10 Commandments are about showing respect — to God, and to other people.

Jesus said, "Don't just respect — love"

1) Jesus' Jewish opponents often accused him of breaking religious laws — e.g. he healed people on the Sabbath when Jews were not supposed to do any work.

But Jesus said he wasn't trying to undermine the law — "Do not think I have come to do away with the Law of Moses... I have come to fulfil it." Matthew 5:17.

2) Jesus thought the Jewish authorities had missed the point of God's Law, and that the 'spirit' of the law was more important than the 'letter' — if you were a good person, you'd do good things.

3) In fact, he taught that your motivation was even more important than your actions — being angry with someone could be just as bad as killing them (**Matthew 5:21-22**).

4) For Jesus, even respect wasn't enough — he wanted his followers to love. When asked which was the most important commandment, he gave a pretty neat answer which summed up his beliefs...

"The most important one is this... love the Lord your God with all your heart, soul, mind and strength; the second is this: love your neighbour as you love yourself." — Mark 12:28-31

Four types of love — Eros, Philia, Storge and Agape

At the Last Judgement (**Matthew 25:31-46**), Jesus says that we shall all be judged according to whether or not we helped those in need. This is a form of love, but it has little to do with 'liking' and everything to do with serving. Ancient Greek actually had four words for 'love':

(1) **EROS** — this is erotic or sexual love, based on physical attraction.

(2) **PHILIA** — this is friendship. It involves 'give and take', and is usually between equals.

(3) **STORGE** — or affection, as felt between members of a family, or as affection for pets, places, and so on.

(4) **AGAPE** — this is Christian love, a reflection of the love God has for us. It gives without needing to take.

*In the Parable of The Good Samaritan (**Luke 10:25-37**), the Samaritan demonstrates love (agape) by giving practical help to a 'neighbour' in trouble. See page 35 for more info.*

In some versions of the Bible, 'agape' is translated as 'charity'.

Agape is a guiding Christian principle...

1 John 4:7-21 encourages Christians to love because love comes from God, and that someone who doesn't love doesn't know God. God showed his love for us by sending his son so that our sins could be forgiven.

1 Corinthians 13 is a famous passage summarising the Apostle Paul's concept of love. He says that it matters more than faith or hope, or anything.

"Love is patient and kind. It envies no one, is never boastful... rude... selfish, or quick to take offence. Love keeps no score of wrongs... There is nothing love cannot face... love never ends."

All you need is love...

Love and respect are the basic principles of Christianity — a good starting point for discussion questions.

Love and Forgiveness

Love and forgiveness go together

1) Christianity teaches that forgiveness comes from love, and that love needs forgiveness.

2) Jesus taught that God is always ready to forgive us, but we must accept that forgiveness, and forgive others in turn.

3) Forgiveness is also closely related to repentance. Christians believe that God's forgiveness can only be achieved when we repent of our sins (i.e. say we are sorry).

4) Christians believe the same sort of reconciliation is needed between people.

Zacchaeus the tax collector (Luke 19:1-10)
A story showing Jesus putting forgiveness into practice... Jesus goes as a guest to the home of the hated tax collector Zacchaeus, whose life is completely changed after he decides to repent.

Forgiveness and punishment

Dick's 'turn the other cheek' philosophy seemed somehow inappropriate, given the circumstances.

1) Jesus taught that people should not seek revenge when wronged — they should 'turn the other cheek'. But this doesn't mean being a submissive victim — just that we should base our response on the principles of love and forgiveness.

2) For example, most Christians don't believe that if someone commits a crime, we should do nothing. They believe punishment can be more constructive. Punishment can be used to reform an offender and to deter others from offending, as well as for retribution.

3) Likewise with bullying — it may be right to face up to the situation and sort it out, rather than allow someone to become a victim. But once the situation has been sorted, Christians believe we must forgive, and not remain bitter.

It sounds easy — but it can get very complicated...

Jesus' teachings aren't simplistic — and they're certainly not a recipe for a life full of easy decisions. Moral decisions about things like abortion, contraception, genetic engineering, and global warming are a bit hard to base on love alone, so in practice Christians seek to base their moral decisions on:

1) Love 2) Scripture — for guidance, 3) Advice — from people they respect,

4) Conscience — their own sense of right and wrong, 5) Tradition — authority of Church tradition.

Christian values can be applied to real-life situations...

1) It can be hard to decide which matters more — compassion or justice. For example, in the Criminal Justice System, is it more 'loving' to let criminals off, or to punish them — not an easy question to answer.

2) Christians helped create the Welfare State in Britain after World War 2. In a welfare state the government protects citizens' well-being, providing free health care, education, and so on. But in seeking to help the underprivileged, does giving too much help create dependency (i.e. do they become too reliant on that help)...

...but love doesn't give the answers for everything...
By preaching 'love your enemies', Christianity isn't trying to tell everyone to be a submissive victim. But it does mean exercising a bit of imagination when it comes to responding to difficult situations.

Sermon on the Mount

The Sermon on the Mount — the **Christian ideal**

The <u>Sermon on the Mount</u> is possibly the most important moral teaching found in the Gospels.
It appears as a collection in **Matthew 5:1 - 7:29**, but much of the same material is also in <u>Luke</u>.

The Beatitudes (Matthew 5:3-12) and the Teaching on 'Salt and Light' (Matthew 5:13-16)

The sermon begins with a passage on true happiness
(what it means to be 'blessed') — this is not to be found
in wealth or pride, but in a simple, humble life lived in
obedience to God.

"Blessed are the meek, for they will inherit the earth."

Jesus' followers are meant to be 'salt and light',
i.e. a source of godly influence in the world.

"You are the salt of the earth."

Jesus' Reinterpretation of the Law of Moses (Matthew 5:17-48)   *See page 60.*

Jesus speaks about anger, adultery, divorce, vows, revenge and love for our enemies.

"If someone strikes you on the right cheek, turn to him the other also."

'Displaying Religion' (Matthew 6:1-18)

Good deeds must not be done for show, but for God.
Prayer must be sincere. (The Lord's Prayer is in this bit as well.)

"Our Father in heaven, hallowed be your name..."

Christians and Money (Matthew 6:19-34)

"You cannot serve God and Money." Also Earthly
riches are useless, but spiritual riches last for ever.

Christians and Judgement (Matthew 7:1-5)

Christians should not pass judgement on others
— that's God's job. It's also hypocrisy.

"Why do you look at the speck of sawdust in your brother's eye and pay no attention to the plank in your own eye?"

The Golden Rule (Matthew 7:7-12)

"Do to others what you would have them do to
you, for this sums up the Law and the Prophets."

Christian **values** in **action**

Christians have found various ways of expressing these values <u>in action</u>. Christian <u>vocations</u> include:

Service to others
(e.g. health work, education)

Showing compassion to those who suffer
(e.g. visiting hospices for the dying)

Seeking justice for the oppressed
(e.g. helping political prisoners)

People seek to be **'Salt and Light'** in **different ways**

Many people have tried to be 'salt and light' in their own ways — here are <u>two famous</u> examples:

Dr Martin Luther King

A Baptist minister who dedicated his life to trying to change the way <u>black people</u> were treated in the USA
— they earned only half as much as whites, and many were not allowed to vote, or go to 'white only' public
places. Despite <u>death threats</u> he organised many types of <u>peaceful</u> protest — marches, rallies, boycotts etc.
In 1965 blacks were given equal voting rights with whites, but in 1968 King was <u>assassinated</u> aged only 39.

Mother Teresa

She was an Albanian Roman Catholic nun who <u>devoted herself</u> to the destitute and dying in India.
She founded the Order of the Missionaries of Charity, whose nuns now work amongst the poor all
over the world. She said that it isn't <u>what</u> you do for God that counts, but <u>how much love</u> you pour
into it. She won the Nobel Peace Prize in 1979, and died in 1997 at the age of 87.

Spreading the Gospel

Christians believe it's wrong to display their religion just for <u>show</u> (see page 62). However, most Christians do think it's important for them to <u>stand up</u> for their beliefs, and <u>not</u> be a '<u>secret Christian</u>'.

The **Great Commission** — *'Spread the Gospel'*

1) Jesus told his followers to '<u>spread the gospel</u>' (**Matthew 28:19-20**),
   so that other people would have the chance to become Christians too.

2) He also taught that they were to be '<u>salt and light</u>' in society (see page 62).

So Christians seek to <u>challenge</u> society around them in 2 ways...

   1) They seek to challenge people's <u>beliefs</u>.
   2) They seek to challenge people's <u>behaviour</u>.

'Mature' Christians seek to present this challenge by means of their <u>own</u> words and conduct. They see that it's very important for their actions to <u>mirror</u> their words — otherwise they would just be <u>hypocrites</u>. (Of course this doesn't mean that, in practice, no Christian is a hypocrite.)

Challenging beliefs — *easy does it...*

1) Many Christians like the chance to <u>talk</u> about their faith with their family, friends and neighbours (and many feel it is their duty — see page 64). Some will even look for opportunities to do this in a <u>wider</u> context — e.g. they may write books or appear on TV.

2) Putting forward <u>reasoned arguments</u> to support your religious beliefs is called <u>apologetics</u>.

3) <u>Evangelical</u> Christians in particular consider it a priority to '<u>win people</u> for Christ'. This is because they believe that a person can't get to Heaven unless they 'come to know Christ'.

4) However, people don't always appreciate their concern... No one likes to have religion 'rammed down their throat'. It's important to maintain a <u>balance</u> between saying too much and saying too little.

Challenging behaviour — **absolute** *and* **relative morality**

Christians don't always agree about <u>how</u> (if at all) they should try to influence the conduct of <u>society</u>.

1) Some Christians consider it wrong to '<u>impose</u> their morals on other people' — while others think it's wrong to sit by and '<u>watch</u> society go down the drain'.

2) This is why some Christians campaign <u>vigorously</u> against abortion, euthanasia, and so on — while others would prefer to let people make up their <u>own</u> minds. They believe it's more effective to show <u>compassion</u> than to act like a moral police force.

3) Also, some Christians strongly support the idea of <u>absolute morality</u>, which means that they think many things are <u>always right</u> or <u>always wrong</u>.

4) Others favour <u>relative morality</u>, which holds that most things are sometimes right and sometimes wrong, depending on the circumstances. This view is sometimes called <u>situation ethics</u>.

Jesus' own attitude is summed up in **John 8:1-11**, where a woman who has committed adultery is to be <u>stoned</u> by a crowd.

"If any of you is without sin... let him be the first to throw a stone at her."

I never preach — except to tell you to learn this stuff...

Christian ethics have greatly influenced societies over the years. Most people today might say that this has been a good thing, but remember that the answers to many of society's moral issues are quite often pretty controversial...

SECTION TWO — CHRISTIANITY (CORE BELIEFS)

Living the Christian Life

All practising Christians seek to obey the instructions of the <u>Great Commission</u> (see page 63), but they do this in different ways, depending on their <u>denomination</u>, <u>culture</u>, <u>background</u>, <u>personal taste</u> or <u>talents</u>.

'Witnessing for Christ' — the duty of every Christian

1) <u>Evangelicals</u> (who can belong to any denomination or to a specifically evangelical church) particularly stress the importance of <u>conversion</u>. Others put more emphasis on <u>praying</u> for the souls of unbelievers.

2) But all true Christians acknowledge the need to '<u>witness for Christ</u>' in their speech and lives, so that those people they come into contact with may be given the opportunity to respond to Jesus.

Through Speech

1) Christians often welcome opportunities to talk to non-Christians about their beliefs (e.g. Alpha courses).

2) This sort of <u>evangelism</u> is difficult, as non-Christians aren't always keen to listen.

Through Lifestyle

1) Christians should try to live their lives based on <u>love</u> for God and for their neighbours (see page 60).

2) Jesus said, *"If you have love for one another, everyone will know you are my disciples."* — **John 13:35**

3) Christians also seek to live by the Bible's <u>moral code</u>, with integrity, witnessing to Christ through their marriages, family life, work, how they spend their free time, and so on.

Through Vocation

1) Some Christians feel that God is calling them to <u>full-time</u> Christian work.

2) This may be as a <u>deacon</u>, <u>priest</u> or <u>bishop</u>, through <u>charity</u> or <u>missionary</u> work, or in a Christian <u>community</u>, e.g. as a monk or nun in a <u>religious order</u>.

Monks and nuns are members of religious orders

1) Those who adopt the <u>monastic</u> life of <u>renunciation</u> take vows of:
   i) **POVERTY**: a monk or nun must not be tied down by possessions, but 'hold everything in common'.
   ii) **CHASTITY**: a monk or nun may have no sexual relationships. They must seek intimacy with God.
   iii) **OBEDIENCE**: a monk or nun must be completely dedicated to God and to his/her community.

2) Some religious orders stress <u>service</u> to the poor/sick/destitute (called <u>apostolic congregations</u>). Others go in for <u>prayer</u> and <u>study</u> — usually involving 'enclosure', where members rarely if ever leave their monasteries (<u>contemplative congregations</u>).

'The Carmelites' and 'Poor Clares' (for women), and the 'Carthusians' or 'Cistercians' (for men) are examples of <u>contemplative congregations</u>. Mother Teresa's 'Missionaries of Charity' (see page 62), and the 'Franciscans' are <u>apostolic congregations</u>.

3) Most Christians would agree that <u>both</u> are important aspects of Christian life, but that every Christian must find the right <u>balance</u> for him or herself.

L'Arche — A religious community at work

1) <u>L'Arche</u> was founded in France by Roman Catholic <u>Jean Vanier</u> (who has been called a 'modern saint of the poor and servant of the handicapped').

2) He gave up his career as a teacher of philosophy in order to welcome disabled people into his home, so they wouldn't have to live in <u>impersonal institutions</u>.

3) His idea has <u>inspired</u> Christians of many denominations to do the same, and L'Arche houses now exist in several countries including the UK.

Religious orders — learn all this Christianity stuff well...

Depending on what syllabus you're studying, you might need to know about the <u>purpose</u> and <u>practice</u> of a <u>religious community</u>. L'Arche is just one example you could use, but don't feel as though it's the only one...

Warm-Up and Worked Exam Question

Warm-up Questions

1) In which century was the New Testament written?
2) Name the three Persons in the Christian Trinity.
3) Write brief explanations of the following terms: (i) repentance, (ii) the Incarnation, (iii) agape.
4) Briefly describe what Jesus meant when he said that people should "turn the other cheek."

Worked Exam Question

With "opinion" questions, you need to give both sides of the argument — a rant won't get you the marks.

1 Some people are called to take up a vocation as a member of a religious order.

   a) Religious orders fall into two main groups. What is the difference between an apostolic congregation and a contemplative congregation?

   Members of an apostolic congregation serve the public (often the poor or sick). Members of a contemplative congregation rarely, if ever, leave their monasteries or convents and spend most of their time in prayer and study.

   (2 marks)

   b) "Religious orders are irrelevant to modern society because they are out of step with the values of everyday life."
   Do you agree? Give reasons for your answer, showing that you have thought about more than one point of view. Refer to Christianity in your answer.

   Give one side of the argument...
   The vows of poverty, chastity and obedience taken by monks and nuns certainly are out of step with the desire for money, sex and power common in everyday life. This can make it extremely difficult for ordinary people to relate to members of religious orders. Although many people can appreciate the practical help monks and nuns give the poor and the sick, fewer can see the point in living a secluded life of prayer.

   ...then the other — use religious arguments if you can...
   However it is not fair to say that people outside monasteries are entirely dominated by worldly desires — many ordinary people, not all of them religious, also seek to live an unselfish life. People can be inspired by an example of a religious life simply because it is so out of step from the ordinary rat race, making it more relevant to them, not less. Also, many Christians believe that the prayers of contemplative congregations genuinely help others.
   So, although contemplative congregations are less immediately relevant than apostolic ones, there still seems a place in the modern world for both.

   ...then come to a personal conclusion. If you don't, you haven't answered the question. *(8 marks)*

Exam Questions

2 a) In what language was the New Testament written?

(1 mark)

    b) Briefly explain what Christians mean by saying that Jesus' death "took away the sin of the world."

(2 marks)

    c) "I do not believe that the resurrection of Jesus described in the Gospels was a physical event."

       Is this statement an example of a Literalist, Conservative or Liberal interpretation of the Bible? Give reasons for your answer.

(3 marks)

3 a) State two of the Ten Commandments.

(2 marks)

    b) In the Sermon on the Mount, Jesus said that behaving in a certain way summed up the Law and the Prophets. What was it he said to do?

(1 mark)

    c) "Christians should campaign to make adultery illegal."

       Do you agree? Give reasons for your opinion, showing that you have considered more than one point of view.

(6 marks)

4 a) What does "absolute morality" mean?

(2 marks)

    b) Describe some different ways in which Christians seek to spread the Gospel in their daily lives.

(3 marks)

    c) Not all Christians agree on how strict punishments for crimes should be. Explain why, using moral and religious arguments.

(8 marks)

The Church

The 'Church' traces its roots back to its founder, Jesus Christ. It's basically a community of believers. Those who profess faith in Jesus as God's promised Messiah become part of that community.

The Church — more than a building

The mission of the Church is to teach that Jesus Christ is our Saviour, and to make people disciples for him. It does this by teaching the things Christ commanded, and also by teaching that his death on the cross is a means by which sins are forgiven, and that his resurrection confirms his identity as God's Messiah.

The Church as the Body of Christ

1) St Paul taught that the community of believers was the "Body of Christ" on Earth, with Christ as its head.
2) Christians who have died remain part of the faith community
   — this group is referred to as the Communion of Saints.
3) Christians believe the Church was called into existence by the Holy Spirit, and is therefore 'holy'.
4) Despite its fragmentation into various traditions and denominations, the Church claims a spiritual unity.
5) Ecumenism is work carried out by different churches aimed towards actual unity.
   This might include joint acts of worship or joint service in the community.

The Church has a powerful influence

The Pope has a massive influence over Roman Catholics — e.g. in respect of abortion and contraception (see p20).

1) The teachings of the Church on moral issues (such as abortion, sexuality, and social responsibility) continue to exert strong influence.
2) Church leaders are held in respect, and their pronouncements are adhered to by faithful followers.
3) The Church also offers guidance to those who believe they may be called by God into a specific vocation, e.g. the ordained ministry, and the lay ministry (who aren't ordained, but who act for the Church in helping the needy).
4) The church also influences social and political development through its involvement in peace and justice movements.

The Church has various functions in the community

The role and function of the local church is to put the Christian faith into action. It does this in the following ways:

i) by providing a regular pattern of worship,
ii) by providing 'rites of passage', e.g. baptism, confirmation, weddings, funerals...
iii) by providing Christian teaching,
iv) by ministering to the sick and needy,
v) by supporting causes for justice and peace.

The Church — it's more than just a place of worship...

Remember — don't go assuming that when the Exam asks a question about the Church, it's talking about that building near where you live that rings its bells once a week. It's a bit more than that. Anyway, as long as you know all of this stuff as well, then you should be okay on the 'Church' question in the Exam

68

Traditions and Denominations

There are some significant variations among Christians' beliefs, which have sometimes led to heated conflict. But what they share is some kind of 'relationship with Christ'.

Three main traditions — Roman Catholic, Orthodox & Protestant

There have been a couple of major splits in the history of the Christian Church.

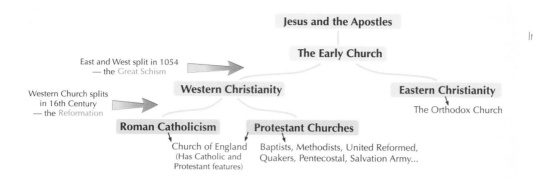

Jesus and the Apostles

The Early Church

East and West split in 1054 — the Great Schism

Western Christianity

Eastern Christianity
The Orthodox Church

Western Church splits in 16th Century — the Reformation

Roman Catholicism
Church of England (Has Catholic and Protestant features)

Protestant Churches
Baptists, Methodists, United Reformed, Quakers, Pentecostal, Salvation Army...

In the Great Schism, the Pope and the Orthodox Patriarch excommunicated each other from their churches.

The Reformation began when Martin Luther challenged the authority of the Pope.

Roman Catholics

1) Roman Catholics are Christians who accept the authority of the Bishop of Rome (the Pope).
2) They believe in the 7 Sacraments as 'vehicles of God's grace' (see page 78).
3) They respect the authority of the Bible, the traditions of the Church, and the Magisterium (see next page).

The Church of England has both Roman Catholic and Protestant features.

Protestants

1) Protestants base their beliefs and practices on the Reformation.
2) The Reformers stressed the importance of the Bible rather than Church Tradition or the teachings of the Pope.
3) Members of the Protestant clergy are usually referred to as ministers.

Orthodox Christians

1) Orthodox Christians are found mainly in Eastern Europe, Russia and what was the Greek-speaking part of the Roman Empire.
2) They believe that their clergy are in direct succession from the Apostles.
3) They also have 7 sacraments, and honour (but don't worship) icons — pictures of saints.

There are loads of Protestant denominations

The different groupings within Protestantism are known as denominations.
Numbers 2-7 below are known as the 'Nonconformists' or 'Free Churches'.

1) **Anglicanism** is the worldwide 'communion' of churches in fellowship with the parent Church of England. This is the 'established' (i.e. national) church in England. It's kind of between Catholicism and Protestantism — but there's a lot of variety within it. The 'more catholic' churches are known as Anglo-Catholic or 'high church'. Those that are more like Methodists are called 'low church'.
2) **Methodists** favour simple services where hymns and the sermon are particularly important.
3) **Baptists** believe in baptising only those who place their faith in Christ — rather than all babies.
4) **Pentecostals** favour the 'gifts of the Holy Spirit' — their worship includes plenty of enthusiastic singing.
5) **Quakers** are best known for their pacifism and for their largely silent services.
6) The **Salvation Army** is organised along military lines, and works particularly among the underprivileged.
7) The **House Churches** are informal groups that originally met in houses, but outgrew them.

Christians are grouped by tradition and denomination...

There are at least 20,800 denominations worldwide, so don't think that the above list is all there is to know. But at the same time, don't feel as though you need to know everything about all 20,800.

Traditions and Denominations

The Roman Catholic Church is the largest Christian group in the world.

The Roman Catholic church has its own customs

The Magisterium — this is the teaching authority of the Pope and bishops of the Roman Catholic Church. To Roman Catholics, the authority of the Church rivals that of the Bible itself.

1) The Magisterium rests on the concept of Apostolic Succession — meaning the Pope is believed to be a direct successor of St Peter, the first pope.

2) The Pope is believed to be infallible on questions of faith and morals (i.e. he can't make a mistake).

3) Dogmas are firm beliefs of the Catholic church. Most of them are set out in the Catechism — a series of questions and answers used to help its members understand what they should believe.

The Importance of Mary

1) Mary is seen as the model for Christian living, because she cooperated fully with God's will.

2) Catholic doctrine teaches that she was born without original sin, meaning she had none of the flaws that all other humans have — this is known as the Immaculate Conception.

3) She remained a virgin all her life, and after she died she was taken up to Heaven in the Assumption (see page 77).

4) Catholics don't worship Mary, but they do pray to her and ask her to pray for them (for example in the 'Ave Maria/Hail Mary'). She is also known as 'Mother of God'.

Transubstantiation and the Mass

1) Virtually all Christians except the Salvation Army and the Quakers recognise the importance of Holy Communion (also called the Eucharist — or often 'Mass' by Roman Catholics), but most see it as just a symbol.

2) However, to Roman Catholics, by the power of the Holy Spirit, the bread and wine become the body and blood of Christ (this is known as transubstantiation), and it is through these that Jesus takes up residence in his people. This is why it's vital for Roman Catholics to attend Mass regularly.

See page 76 for more about Eucharist and the Mass.

Influential movements in the 20th Century

Two movements profoundly affected 20th century Christianity across traditions and denominations:

1) The Charismatic Movement began in the Pentecostal churches, but later spread worldwide. It stresses the importance of 'spiritual gifts', such as speaking in tongues and prophecy. Charismatic Worship is characterised by expression of emotion (e.g. clapping or dancing), and is meant to be entirely spontaneous. There are charismatic groups among Roman Catholics and Anglicans, but most charismatics are evangelicals, who emphasise the importance of spreading the Gospel.

2) Liberation Theology began in Latin America with the aim of fighting oppression. It works by influencing national institutions (like those for health and education), but protest is also considered legitimate. Some priests even supported the use of violence as a last resort, since the regimes they fought against were causing entire populations to suffer.

Christians have different customs and beliefs...

It's important to realise that not all Christians are the same. Roman Catholics make up the largest group of Christians, and so it's pretty important that you at least know something about them (and even more if you're doing one of the units dedicated to Roman Catholicism). Well, lots of stuff is important, I guess.

Members of the Church

The **Roman Catholic** church has a **hierarchy**...

The Roman Catholic Church is arranged in a <u>hierarchy</u>, with the Pope at the top.

THE POPE — The <u>Bishop of Rome</u> and head of the worldwide Roman Catholic Church. Jesus is believed to have chosen St Peter as the first pope, and the current pope is his spiritual descendent. On matters of faith and morals, the pope is regarded as <u>infallible</u> and <u>binding</u> upon all Roman Catholics (see also page 69).

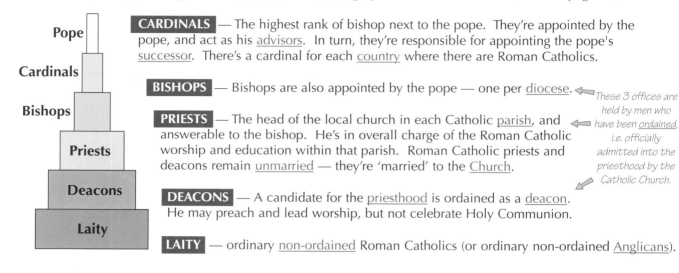

CARDINALS — The highest rank of bishop next to the pope. They're appointed by the pope, and act as his <u>advisors</u>. In turn, they're responsible for appointing the pope's <u>successor</u>. There's a cardinal for each <u>country</u> where there are Roman Catholics.

BISHOPS — Bishops are also appointed by the pope — one per <u>diocese</u>.

PRIESTS — The head of the local church in each Catholic <u>parish</u>, and answerable to the bishop. He's in overall charge of the Roman Catholic worship and education within that parish. Roman Catholic priests and deacons remain <u>unmarried</u> — they're 'married' to the <u>Church</u>.

These 3 offices are held by men who have been <u>ordained</u>, i.e. officially admitted into the priesthood by the Catholic Church.

DEACONS — A candidate for the <u>priesthood</u> is ordained as a <u>deacon</u>. He may preach and lead worship, but not celebrate Holy Communion.

LAITY — ordinary <u>non-ordained</u> Roman Catholics (or ordinary non-ordained <u>Anglicans</u>).

Pyramid labels (top to bottom): Pope, Cardinals, Bishops, Priests, Deacons, Laity

Holy Orders and Ordination

The act of <u>ordination</u> distinguishes members of the <u>clergy</u> from those who are <u>laity</u>. Ordination is conferred by the 'laying on of hands' by a <u>bishop</u>. Only priests and above can administer the <u>sacraments</u> of the Church. In the Roman Catholic Church, being ordained as a <u>priest</u> is called receiving the 'Sacrament of Holy Orders'.

Cathedral Staff

A <u>cathedral</u> is the central church of a <u>diocese</u>, and contains the <u>throne</u> of the bishop or archbishop. Cathedral life and worship is governed by a <u>dean</u> and a committee called a <u>Chapter</u>, who are assisted by the <u>canons</u> — priests appointed by the bishop.

...and so do the **Protestant** and **Orthodox** churches

1) The <u>Anglican Church</u> is also a hierarchy of bishops, priests and deacons, with the Archbishop of Canterbury (the head of the Church of England) at the top.

2) For much of its history <u>women</u> weren't allowed to be ordained, since Christ only ever commissioned <u>men</u> to administer the sacraments. This has now changed and there are women priests, but it remains a <u>controversial</u> issue. Anglican priests are allowed to marry.

3) In the Presbyterian Church, <u>presbyters</u> (or elders) are church leaders with the specific responsibility of preaching and teaching from the Bible. They're appointed by the local congregation and answerable to the church members when they meet.

4) In the Orthodox Church, <u>patriarchs</u> are at the head of each national church, with the Patriarch of Constantinople (or Istanbul) being the 'first among equals'. Men can become priests at 30, and are allowed to marry (but if they do, they can't become a bishop).

<u>Lay ministers</u> are <u>non-ordained</u> church members who are allowed to perform certain duties e.g. visiting the sick, leading worship.

The leadership of the Church is structured like a pyramid...

I bet you thought vicars would get a mention. Well, here you are. 'Vicar' is a general title that's come to be used to refer to any parish priest. 'Minister' is also a general title — used to describe anyone who's been ordained. And the clergy consists of anyone who's been ordained. Lots of words for the same kind of thing.

A Christian Church

A Christian place of worship is a <u>church</u> or <u>chapel</u>. Churches often have a similar layout to each other. (Chapels are usually smaller than churches, and not quite so fancy.)

The **location** of a **church** is often **symbolic**

1) Christian churches are often found on tops of <u>hills</u>. This is because they would have been the most <u>important</u> building in the area, and so needed to be easy to <u>see</u> and <u>defend</u>.

2) Churches were traditionally built from <u>local</u> stone and materials which would have been easily available. The quality of the decoration and fittings reflected the church's <u>status</u> and <u>wealth</u>.

3) They were sometimes built on ancient <u>pagan</u> sites — e.g. <u>sacred</u> groves of trees. Pagans were people who worshipped a number of <u>different</u> gods, a practice much more common before Christianity became popular.

4) The <u>size</u> of the church reflected the size and wealth of the <u>parish</u>, or the wealth and status of the local <u>people</u>.

5) Seen from above, churches were often built in the shape of a <u>cross</u> aligned from east to west, so that the church faces the rising sun. This is because east is the direction of the <u>Holy Land</u> where <u>Jesus</u> lived. It also symbolises <u>God's goodness</u> lighting up the darkness.

A **parish church** has some **typical features**

1 TOWER This draws people's eyes up to Heaven to remind people of God. It was also used in the past for <u>defence</u>, and houses the <u>church bells</u>.

2 TRANSEPTS The two wings of a **cross-shaped** church, at right angles to the nave (see page 72).

5 WEATHER-VANE This provided a medieval public service (weather was important to farmers), and is often in the shape of a <u>cock</u> to remind people of the story of <u>St Peter</u>.

(This is usually on top of the tower.)

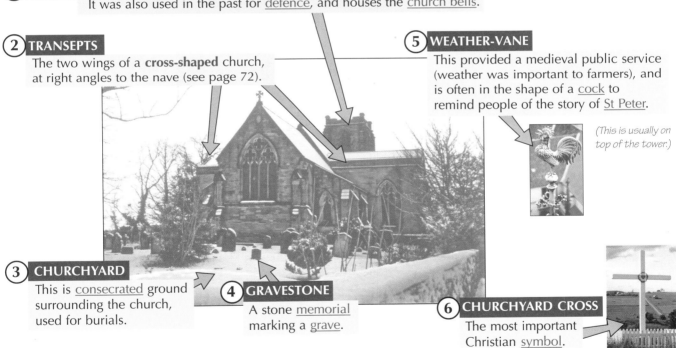

3 CHURCHYARD This is <u>consecrated</u> ground surrounding the church, used for burials.

4 GRAVESTONE A stone <u>memorial</u> marking a <u>grave</u>.

6 CHURCHYARD CROSS The most important Christian <u>symbol</u>.

Many churches also have these extra features:

7 PORCH The <u>day-to-day</u> entrance.

8 WEST DOOR The main <u>ceremonial</u> entrance.

9 LYCH-GATE <u>Coffins</u> were placed in the gate to await the arrival of the minister to conduct the <u>funeral</u> service.

10 NICHE This is just a recess to hold a <u>statue</u>.

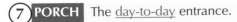

The architecture of a church is often symbolic...
You find most parish churches built more than a century ago look pretty similar. Chapels tend to vary more, as do more modern chapels and churches. The Roman Catholic cathedral in Liverpool is very untraditional.

A Christian Church

Inside a typical parish church

Roman Catholic and Church of England churches are often very similar in layout:

1 ALTAR
The most important place in the church — a table which holds the items for the Communion service. The altar is in the east end.

2 EAST WINDOW
Often of stained glass, it's right behind the altar and draws attention to it.

3 PULPIT
A raised box from which the minister gives the sermon or talks to the congregation.

4 REREDOS
A painted or sculpted screen behind the altar. Often has pictures of Jesus, Mary or saints. Helps to focus attention on the altar.

5 SANCTUARY
A raised platform where the most important parts of a service take place.

6 COVERED FONT
Used to hold holy water for Baptism.

7 LECTERN
A stand for the church bible. Often made from brass in the shape of an eagle.

8 NAVE
The main part of the church where the congregation sits (or originally stood).

9 AISLE
Aisles are often used in processions.

1) Roman Catholic, Orthodox and most Anglican churches use liturgy (see page 76) — where the focal point of the building is usually the altar — but there will also be a pulpit, lectern and pews (benches).

2) In Methodist, Baptist and United Reformed churches, there will be no altar, but a very large pulpit reflecting the centrality of the word of God. There will be pews or chairs.

A church isn't used just for religious services

Okay, a church is a religious building — but it often has a more general use in the local community as well. Make sure you learn the kind of things a church is commonly used for:

RELIGIOUS SERVICES — Especially on Sundays, but also during the week.
(Evensong is the name given to daily evening prayers.)

SPECIAL SERVICES — E.g. baptisms (christenings), confirmations, weddings, funerals, memorial services.

RELIGIOUS FESTIVALS — E.g. Christmas, Easter, Whitsuntide (Pentecost), Harvest Festival.

COMMUNITY USE — E.g. fêtes, talks and lectures, coffee mornings, playgroups and youth clubs, etc.

PARISH COUNCIL — Sometimes used for meetings and fund-raising events.

Learn the different features and uses of a church...
You need to learn this stuff and understand why it's important — try writing it all down now, from memory.

Religious Symbolism

Symbols are used within the Christian tradition to represent what's believed.
An obvious example is the symbol of the cross — used to represent the sacrificial death of Jesus Christ.

Religious architecture is often symbolic

1. Cathedrals can be enormous, demonstrating their importance. Like parish churches, they were historically built at the centre of the community to represent God's kingship on Earth. Inside, the focus of attention is always towards the altar, where the main act of worship (the celebration of Holy Communion) takes place.

2. Orthodox churches are often in the shape of a cross, with a large dome on top symbolising Christ's presence, eternity and the nearness of heaven. Inside they are richly decorated with friezes and carvings.

3. Free Churches (e.g. Baptists) meet in simple halls where the pulpit is the focus of attention. This shows the importance to them of preaching from the Bible. Also in a Baptist church, the prominence of the Baptistry (a pool for baptism by total immersion, see page 79) shows the central importance of baptism.

Icons, statues and stained-glass windows are symbolic

1. Icons are paintings (mostly of saints) often found in Orthodox churches, and are often greeted with a kiss on entering the building. They're used to represent the presence of saints, and as a means to pray — 'prayers captured on wood'.

Statues also represent the presence of the saints.

In certain festivals a madonna (a statue of Mary) or another saint is paraded through the streets as an appeal to bless the community.

2. Large cathedrals and churches are often decorated with colourful murals or frescoes, and many feature beautiful stained-glass windows depicting biblical stories. For centuries the finest work of leading artists was made for churches — all to offer to God the highest expression of worship, and to create a sense of awe.

Church music is also symbolic

Church music is symbolic as it is used to praise God and to express belief. Mozart, Bach, Beethoven and many other great composers wrote music for worship — e.g. Handel's Messiah, Mozart's Requiem Mass...

1. Hymns have been part of Christian worship for many centuries — they're often derived from passages of scripture.

2. In Protestant churches, choirs have an important role leading the singing. There are many types, from Anglican schoolboys to Pentecostal gospel.

3. Many different musical instruments are used in worship — from pipe organs to brass bands and guitars. The music used in worship can be solemn and dignified or loud and lively depending on the type of church.

4. Dancing is common in Charismatic churches — it's a sign of the Holy Spirit's presence.

Symbolism plays a vital part in religious expression...

Don't forget that Christian beliefs are commonly expressed through worship in ritual form (e.g. baptism), and that this is also a kind of symbolism. There's also a link between religious symbolism and spirituality (see page 1).

74

Warm-Up and Worked Exam Question

Warm-up Questions

1) What is the job of a presbyter in the Presbyterian church?
2) Which of the following Christian traditions believe that there are seven sacraments: Orthodox, Protestant, Roman Catholic?
3) Name four of the main physical features inside a typical Catholic or Anglican parish church.
4) What is the main difference between "low church" and "high church" Anglicanism?
5) In which part of the world did "liberation theology" begin?

Worked Exam Question

Work through this example carefully, then have a go at the questions on page 75.

1   The Christian Church is split into many denominations.

   a)   State the views that Roman Catholics, Protestants and members of the Orthodox Church have on priests getting married.

   Roman Catholics believe priests must remain unmarried.

   Protestant priests are allowed to marry.

   Ordinary Orthodox priests may marry, but bishops may not.

   Roman Catholic priests are considered
   to be married to the church.
                                                              (3 marks)

   b)   In the history of Christianity, what were the Great Schism and the Reformation?

   The Great Schism was the split between the Eastern and Western

   Churches (1054). The Reformation was when Protestants,

   starting with Martin Luther, split off from Roman Catholicism.
                                                              (2 marks)

   c)   Read the following paragraph and answer the questions below.

   Church A is organised along military lines. Members often work helping the poor, alcoholics, drug addicts and the homeless.

   Church B focuses on receiving gifts of the Holy Spirit, such as "speaking in tongues".

   Church C is pacifist. All members are equal. Worship meetings are silent until someone feels led to speak by God.

   Name Churches A, B and C.

   A = Salvation Army, B = Pentecostal Church, C = Quakers

   Even though Christianity is one religion, there's heaps of diversity within it.
   Make sure you know the main differences between the denominations.
                                                              (3 marks)

SECTION TWO — CHRISTIANITY (THE CHURCH)

Exam Questions

2   a)   What is meant by ordination?

(1 mark)

     b)   As well as Sunday services, for what other occasions are services held at a parish church?

(3 marks)

     c)   Describe some of the roles of the priest or minister of a local church.

(4 marks)

     d)   Christians do not just use the word Church to mean the building where they worship. What else do Christians mean by the Church, and what did St Paul teach about it?

(3 marks)

3   a)   State one way in which music is used in Christian worship.

(1 mark)

     b)   Look at the plan of the church below:

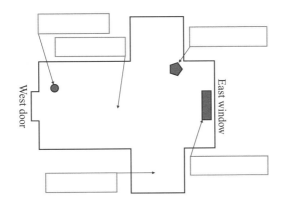

West door   East window

Fill in the blanks to label the **nave**, **transept**, **altar**, **pulpit** and **font**.

(3 marks)

     c)   Explain two ways in which a Baptist church building differs from an Anglican church building.

(4 marks)

     d)   Explain how ONE of the differences between an Anglican and a Baptist church building that you stated in your answer to (c) is the result of a difference in belief between the two denominations.

(3 marks)

4   a)   What is a Cardinal in the Roman Catholic hierarchy?

(2 marks)

     b)   State what is meant by the following Roman Catholic terms:

       (i) Papal infallibility, (ii) the Immaculate Conception, (iii) the Magisterium.

(3 marks)

     c)   "The bread and wine at Communion are purely symbolic."

       Do you agree? Give reasons for your opinion, showing that you have considered more than one point of view. Refer to the beliefs of different Christian denominations.

(4 marks)

76

Sunday Worship

Christianity grew out of Judaism, so Jesus would have kept Saturday as the Sabbath.
However, Christians soon made Sunday their special day.

Sunday is 'The Lord's Day'

Sunday is holy to Christians because it is the day Jesus rose from the dead.

This is the reason you should give in an exam.

Sunday could also have been made special for one of the following reasons:

1) It was a Sunday when the Holy Spirit visited the disciples at Pentecost.
2) Christians wanted to distinguish themselves from the Jews, though at first both Saturday and Sunday may have been regarded as holy by Christians.

1) The Roman Emperor Constantine adopted Christianity as the legal religion of the Roman Empire, and it was he who made Sunday an official day of rest — he even forbade town-dwellers to work on Sundays.
2) Few Christians today feel there should be a law requiring people to observe the Sabbath, but most see the value of devoting one day each week to God and to their families.
3) However, the 'Keep Sunday Special' campaign seeks to ban sport and non-essential work on a Sunday.

Sunday worship in Church can take many forms

1) The exact form of Sunday worship will vary between denominations.
2) Most churches have their main service on a Sunday morning. It may be structured or spontaneous, but virtually all denominations use hymns or songs, Bible readings, and a sermon.
3) In Roman Catholic, Orthodox, and most Anglican churches it will be structured and liturgical (i.e. it will follow a pattern laid down in writing — with set prayers, and readings).
4) Methodists and other nonconformists have structured but non-liturgical services, e.g. following the 'hymn sandwich' pattern, where the service consists of hymns alternating with readings and a sermon.
5) Roman Catholic and Orthodox Sunday services always include Holy Communion (called Mass in the Roman Catholic tradition), and Anglican churches usually do.
6) Pentecostals, House Churches and other independent Christian fellowships may have spontaneous, often charismatic worship (see page 69).

There are several reasons for all this variety. Christians share the same basic beliefs about the importance of Holy Communion, the Bible, the sermon, the Holy Spirit etc., but they differ as to which matters most.

Holy Communion remembers the Last Supper

1) At the Last Supper, Jesus said that the bread and wine on the table represented his body and blood. The disciples were to eat and drink in remembrance of him whenever they ate together.
2) Roman Catholics believe in transubstantiation (i.e. the bread and wine used at Mass become the flesh and blood of Christ), and every Mass is a re-enactment of Christ's sacrifice (see also page 69).
3) Any leftover consecrated bread and wine must be consumed by a priest, or placed in a ciborium (a lidded chalice) inside a 'safe' called a tabernacle.
4) Many nonconformists simply regard Communion as a memorial service, and the Salvation Army and Quakers do not have Communion at all.

A Roman Catholic Mass or Anglican Eucharist will include:

A creed is a brief summary of religious beliefs.

i) Penitential Rite — confession of sin and absolution from it.
ii) The Liturgy of the Word — readings, sermon (called Homily by Catholics), creed, prayers.
iii) The Eucharistic Prayers — the priest consecrates the bread and wine using the words of the Last Supper.
iv) The Rite of Communion — the Lord's Prayer is recited and the bread and wine distributed.

Christian Festivals

According to the Bible, no time of year is any more sacred than any other. However, certain times of year are used by Christians to commemorate, give thanks and celebrate specific aspects of their faith.

Christian *festivals* occur **throughout the year**

ADVENT — November / December

Advent marks the beginning of the Christian year, and begins 4 Sundays before Christmas. It's a period of preparation for Christmas and for Christ's Second Coming. Advent candles are lit in homes and churches, and Advent calendars may be used by children to count off the days until Christmas. Orthodox Christians observe 40 days' penance (showing true sorrow for sins).

CHRISTMAS — December 25th

Christmas celebrates the Incarnation — when God's Son came to Earth as a human being. We don't know the exact date of his birth, but we celebrate on December 25th. Customs vary around the world, but often date from pre-Christian times (e.g. Christmas trees). In many RC and Anglican churches there is a 'Midnight Mass' to welcome Christmas Day, and a crib (nativity scene).

EPIPHANY — January 6th

Epiphany commemorates Jesus being shown to the wise men, and his baptism and first miracle (turning water into wine at Cana). It marks the end of the '12 days of Christmas'. Decorations are taken down, and the transfiguration may be remembered.

Transfiguration was when Jesus' clothes became a dazzling white, and he appeared to 3 disciples to be talking with Elijah and Moses.

LENT — February / March

Lent celebrates the 40 days and nights of Jesus' fasting in the wilderness after his baptism. The day before Lent is called Shrove Tuesday, a day for being 'shriven' (absolved from sin). Rich foods should be eaten up. Mardi Gras carnivals may be held ('carnival' means 'farewell to meat'). On Ash Wednesday (the first day of Lent) ash is put on believers' foreheads to show they are sorry for their sins. Few Christians today fast during Lent, but many still give up certain luxuries. Lent ends on the day before Easter.

HOLY WEEK — March / April

This is the final week of Lent, lasting from Palm Sunday (the Sunday before Easter, recalling Jesus' triumphal entry into Jerusalem — some churches distribute palm crosses) until the day before Easter. It commemorates Jesus' final week on Earth. Maundy Thursday recalls the Last Supper, and Good Friday Jesus' crucifixion. There are special services, especially on Good Friday between noon and 3pm — the hours when Jesus was dying on the cross.

EASTER SUNDAY — March / April

This commemorates Jesus' resurrection. Special services are held. Roman Catholics and some Anglicans hold an Easter Vigil beginning at midnight on the Saturday. Orthodox Christians gather outside their church until midnight, when the doors are flung wide and they file into a church flooded with light.

ASCENSION & PENTECOST — May / June

Ascension (40 days after Easter Saturday) marks the day when Jesus returned to his father in Heaven. Pentecost (or Whitsun) remembers the subsequent 'Coming of the Holy Spirit' upon the disciples (when they 'spoke in tongues'), empowering them to go out and spread the message of God's Kingdom — this is 50 days after Easter Saturday.

ASSUMPTION OF THE BLESSED VIRGIN MARY — August 15th

Roman Catholic and Orthodox Christians don't believe that Jesus' mother Mary died a normal death — instead she's believed to have been taken directly up to Heaven. This doctrine is not in the Bible, so Protestants don't accept it. In the Mediterranean world there is feasting and dancing, along with lavish processions and fireworks.

Some Catholic and Orthodox Christians observe saints' days too — in theory, every day of the year celebrates something.

Holy Days (or holidays) — celebrations of religion...

Because there are Christians all over the world, there's huge variety in the way festivals are celebrated. Many customs are cultural rather than Christian (e.g. Easter bunnies). Make sure you learn what the festivals celebrate and why, rather than how things are done.

Private Prayer and the Sacraments

Christian prayer is a <u>conversation</u> with God, and should take place both in <u>church</u> and in <u>private</u>.

Private **prayer** draws a **believer** closer to **God**

The whole point of prayer is for the believer to draw close to God to <u>communicate</u> with Him and <u>hear</u> what He's saying. Different Christians use different methods to accomplish this:

The 'Quiet Time' — time spent <u>alone</u> with God, perhaps reading the Bible and praying.

Meditation — a form of prayer where the believer clears his or her mind of <u>distracting</u> thoughts and concentrates on God's nature or work. It may involve <u>repeating</u> a prayer over and over again.

Contemplation — true Christian contemplation is not merely deep thinking — it's <u>intimate</u> wordless prayer in which the believer senses God's presence <u>strongly</u>.

The Rosary — used by Catholics, this is a string of <u>beads</u> arranged in groups. As the beads are moved through the fingers, prayers are said, e.g. the Lord's Prayer, Ave Maria (Hail Mary) and Gloria.

Icons — Orthodox Christians use <u>icons</u> (sacred pictures of saints) to help them focus on God. Although they may light a candle in front of the icon or kiss it, they don't pray to it.

Many <u>parents</u> pray with their <u>children</u>, believing this encourages them to grow up as praying Christians. And many Christians believe praying while ill helps them <u>accept</u> their suffering as part of God's plan.

The **Seven Sacraments** — vehicles of **God's Grace**

Roman Catholic and Orthodox Christians believe in <u>Seven Sacraments</u>, through which they claim that God can communicate His <u>grace</u> (i.e. His 'saving energy') directly. The sacraments are:

1 Baptism Baptism or christening marks a person being officially <u>accepted</u> as a Christian.

2 Confirmation In this ceremony a Christian <u>renews</u> the vows made on his or her behalf at baptism.

3 Reconciliation This involves <u>confession</u> of a sin, followed by <u>contrition</u>, <u>penance</u> and <u>absolution</u>.

4 Eucharist In taking Holy Communion the believer <u>receives</u> Christ into him or herself afresh.

5 Ordination This is the rite in which people are made <u>deacons</u>, <u>priests</u> or <u>bishops</u>.

6 Marriage When a couple are joined in <u>Holy Matrimony</u> they receive a special blessing.

See pages 27 and 28 for more about <u>marriage</u>.

This is when a priest applies consecrated oil. → **7 Anointing of the Sick** This may be for <u>healing</u>, or to prepare a <u>dying</u> person for his or her journey into the next life, when it's also called <u>extreme unction</u> or <u>viaticum</u>.

Most Protestants accept only <u>baptism</u> and <u>Eucharist</u> as sacraments.

God is thought to communicate His grace directly through sacraments, whether or not the recipient <u>understands</u> what it all means.

<u>Nonconformists</u> generally regard baptism as a <u>symbol</u> — not a <u>sacrament</u>.

Fasting and pilgrimage — not vital in Christianity

1) There are no longer any compulsory <u>fasts</u> for Christians, or <u>special</u> foods they must eat or avoid. However Roman Catholics shouldn't eat meat on Ash Wednesday and Good Friday, and they should fast for an hour before Holy Communion.

2) <u>Festival foods</u> (e.g. Christmas pudding, hot-cross buns) tend to be more <u>cultural</u> than <u>religious</u> in origin.

3) There are no compulsory <u>pilgrimages</u> either, although many like to visit the <u>Holy Land</u> (Israel). Catholics may also visit Rome, or places where the Virgin Mary has been seen — like Lourdes, or Knock.

4) They may make these pilgrimages to seek <u>healing</u>, or to deepen their <u>faith</u>.

Baptism

Ritual bathing to symbolise <u>purification</u> or <u>conversion</u> was already practised by Jews.
The word 'baptism' comes from the Greek 'baptizo' meaning 'dip in water'. Not a lot of people know that.

Baptism **symbolises** the **washing away** of sin

1) In the Gospels, <u>John the Baptist</u> (Jesus' cousin) instructed people to 'repent and be baptised'.
<u>Jesus</u> himself was baptised by John (**Mark 1:9-11**), but John objected to this, saying Jesus should baptise <u>him</u>.

2) After the Resurrection, Jesus told his followers to *"Go and make disciples of all nations, <u>baptising</u> them in the name of the Father, Son and Holy Spirit."* — **Matthew 28:19**. This is known as the 'Great Commission'.

3) Baptism symbolises a <u>new life</u> and the washing away of <u>sin</u>.
A baptised person is sometimes said to be '<u>born again</u>'.

4) Christians are baptised in nearly all denominations except the <u>Salvation Army</u> and <u>Quakers</u>.

Roman Catholic, Orthodox and many Anglican Christians regard baptism as a <u>sacrament</u> (see page 78).

Baptism — meant for **infants** or **believers**...

Adults can be baptised in <u>any</u> denomination,
if they haven't already been baptised as <u>babies</u>.

1) Those who regard baptism as a <u>sacrament</u> see no problem with baptising <u>infants</u>.
They believe that this cleanses the baby from <u>original sin</u>, giving it a fresh start in
life and making it a member of God's family.

2) Traditionally infant baptism was especially important if the baby was <u>sick</u> and likely
to die — unbaptised babies were thought to be unable to enter <u>Heaven</u>.

In the Early Church, it tended to be <u>adults</u> who were baptised, though whole <u>families</u> (including children) could be baptised too.

3) Baptist, Pentecostal and House Church Christians, plus those from
independent fellowships, tend to receive <u>dedication</u> as <u>babies</u>, and
baptism only as <u>believers</u>. They believe you shouldn't be baptised
until you are old enough to say you accept Christianity yourself.

Baptism **services** can be pretty **varied**

Infant Baptism

1) <u>Parents</u> and <u>godparents</u> make promises on the child's behalf, which the child will later <u>renew</u>
(if he or she chooses) at <u>confirmation</u>.

2) A sign of the <u>cross</u> is made on the baby, and <u>holy water</u> is poured three times over the forehead (in the
name of the Father, Son and Holy Spirit), though Orthodox Christians baptise babies by <u>total immersion</u>.

3) The baptism is conducted over a <u>font</u>, and the baby is usually dressed in a <u>white robe</u> called a <u>chrisom</u>
(white is the colour of <u>purity</u>).

4) A lighted <u>candle</u> may be given to parents and godparents to remind them of their duty to bring the
<u>light of Christ</u> into the baby's life.

5) At the age of 7, Roman Catholic children have a special service of <u>First Communion</u>.

Believer's Baptism

1) This can take place in a church, a lake, a swimming pool, or even a skip. <u>Several</u> people are
usually baptised at one special service.

2) Each candidate is asked <u>questions</u> about his or her faith, and may <u>explain</u> how and why he or she
decided to become a Christian. He or she is then baptised by the minister by <u>total immersion</u>.

Baptism means a fresh start...

Loads to learn: a) <u>what baptism is</u>, b) <u>why it's important</u>, and c) some of the <u>common baptism rituals</u>. Get stuck in.

Funerals, Burial and Cremation

Christians don't believe that only Jesus could be resurrected — they claim that they will be resurrected too (see page 15 for more on Christian beliefs about death).

"Whoever **believes** in me will **never die**"

This is how the Christian Church sees death and resurrection:

1) Human beings sin, meaning that they don't live up to God's perfect standard. Because of this, they're not fit to be accepted into Heaven.

2) But Jesus broke the power of sin and death — his power and goodness were so great that after he was crucified, death could not keep hold of him. Jesus conquered it, both for himself and for his followers.

> "I am the Resurrection and the Life. He who believes in Me will live, even though he dies; and whoever lives and believes in me will never die." **John 11:25-26**

See also page 58 for more about Jesus' resurrection.

Funeral services are **sad**, but with a note of **hope**

Funeral services vary according to denomination, but all Christian funerals contain a note of hope. For many this doesn't mean wishful thinking — it means confident expectation based on God's promises.

1) The coffin is carried into the church, and the above verses from John 11 are often read. There are hymns, other Bible readings and prayers. The priest (or someone else) often gives a short sermon about Christian belief in life after death, and may also talk about the life of the person who has died.

2) Of course there will be sadness too, particularly if the person died young or very suddenly. There are prayers for the bereaved, and members of the congregation will express their sympathy for the family and close friends of the deceased. Black clothes are often worn, though some Christians consider this inappropriate and may even request guests not to dress in this way.

3) It doesn't matter whether the body's buried or cremated — Christians believe that at the Resurrection they will have new 'spiritual bodies', not their old ones. There's usually another short service at the graveside or crematorium, then afterwards often a meal for family and friends.

Roman Catholic Requiem Mass

A Roman Catholic funeral includes Holy Communion (the 'Requiem Mass'). The purpose of a Requiem Mass is to pray for the soul of the dead person. The priest wears white vestments, and the coffin is covered with a white cloth (a pall). The coffin is sprinkled with holy water and the priest says, *"In the waters of baptism (name) died with Christ, and rose with him to new life. May s/he now share with him in eternal glory."* The coffin is later sprinkled again, and also perfumed with incense.

Funeral **customs** help **support** the **bereaved**

1) Christian funeral services have a great deal to say about the hope of eternal life. The bereaved person is encouraged to believe that one day she or he will be reunited with the deceased.

2) In the days following the funeral, family and friends often try to contact those who were closest to the deceased, and encourage them to talk through their grief.

3) Usually the priest or vicar will also try to visit, and may offer counselling, or suggest someone who can. There are several stages to the process of grief, and it can help to talk to someone who understands this.

Symbolism plays a vital part in religious expression...

Christians try not to see death as depressing — after all, they believe the person who died is going to Heaven (probably). Now see how much you can remember by writing a mini-essay on 'Christian funeral customs'...

Warm-Up and Worked Exam Questions

Warm-up Questions

1) Describe how meditation might be used as part of private prayer.

2) Give another name for Holy Communion.

3) What do the following Christian festivals celebrate:
   a) Epiphany,   b) Ascension,   c) Pentecost?

4) Which festival marks the beginning of the Christian year?

5) Describe a typical Christian funeral service.

Worked Exam Questions

It's exam question time, and look — we've done the first ones for you. That doesn't mean you get out of doing it though. Work through the question yourself, and compare your answer to ours — that's the best way to learn.

1   a)   What does baptism symbolise?

Baptism symbolises the washing away of sins and the start of a new life.

(2 marks)

b)   Why do some Christians only baptise adult believers and not infants?

Baptists, Pentecostals and other House Church Christians believe that you should not baptise people until they are old enough to accept Christianity for themselves. Instead, they have a "dedication" service for babies.

Some Christians see baptism as a sacrament which cleanses babies from original sin.

(2 marks)

2   a)   Why is Sunday "The Lord's Day"?

Sunday was the day of Jesus' resurrection.

(2 marks)

b)   Why do some Christians not celebrate the festival of the "Assumption of the Blessed Virgin Mary"?

The doctrine that Mary did not die a natural death and was instead taken directly into Heaven is not based on the Bible, therefore Protestants do not celebrate this festival.

Protestants base all their beliefs and practices on the Bible.   *(2 marks)*

SECTION TWO — CHRISTIANITY (WORSHIP)

Exam Questions

2   a)   Which day of Holy Week recalls the Last Supper?

(2 marks)

     b)   How do many Christians re-enact the Last Supper?

(4 marks)

     c)   "Easter is more important than Christmas."

        Do you agree? Give reasons for your opinion, showing that you have considered more than one point of view.

(6 marks)

3   a)   Describe a typical Roman Catholic Mass or Anglican Eucharist.

(4 marks)

     b)   Discuss the differences between structured and spontaneous forms of Sunday Worship, using examples from different Christian denominations.

(6 marks)

     c)   Describe two methods of private prayer.

(4 marks)

4   a)   What is a sacrament?

(2 marks)

     b)   Roman Catholics and Orthodox Christians believe in seven sacraments. List these and state which of these sacraments are accepted by most Protestants.

(6 marks)

Jesus and Mark's Gospel

The Gospels — good news, but not biographies

See page 59 for more about the Gospels.

1) Three of the Gospels (Matthew, Mark and Luke) are very similar, and are called the Synoptic Gospels.

2) The Early Church believed that all 4 Gospels in the New Testament (the Synoptic Gospels, plus John) were written by apostles, or by men who had known the apostles well — this is how they got their authority.

3) They quickly established their place as Scripture (holy writings inspired by God).

There's a lot of uncertainty surrounding the Gospels

1) The Gospels were written to preserve the story of Jesus after the apostles died, but they also pointed to the future coming of the Kingdom of God, and answered questions that the early Christians were asking.

2) An early Christian wrote that Mark was the 'interpreter of Peter', but that he hadn't known Jesus personally. Mark may have used early collections of Jesus' words and actions, or he may have got information from Peter.

3) It's accepted that Mark's Gospel was probably written in Rome *(See pages 87 and 88 for more about Peter.)* between 65 and 75 CE — partly to encourage Christians who were facing persecution from the Emperor Nero.

4) It's probably impossible to work out the story of Jesus' life exactly. But since Jesus was Jewish, he will have been circumcised, and educated in the Torah and other Jewish literature and traditions. He will have visited synagogues, observed the Sabbath, and gone to Jerusalem for the 'Pilgrim Festivals'.

The Gospels tell the story of Jesus

All references are to Mark's Gospel.

In the Gospels, Jesus is called by a number of titles, each of which gives a clue as to who he is/was.

Son of God No person uses this title until after Jesus' death. It was blasphemous to Jews.

1) At his baptism (**1:9-11**) a voice comes from Heaven saying, 'You are my own dear Son.'

2) At the Trial before the High Priest (**14:53-65**) the High Priest asks, 'Are you the Messiah, the Son of the Blessed God?' and Jesus answers, 'I am.'

Son of Man This title is the one which Jesus uses when referring to himself. It symbolises the fact that Jesus felt ordinary human emotions. It's also used by Jesus to claim the authority mentioned by Daniel.

The prophet Daniel (Daniel 7:13-14) talks about a 'Son of Man' who would have great authority from God.

1) In response to the Request of James and John to sit at Jesus' side in his glory (**10:35-45**), Jesus says, 'The Son of Man did not come to be served, but to serve, and to give his life as a ransom for many.' James and John have not understood the nature of Jesus as a Messiah.

2) In his Prediction of the Passion (**8:31-33**), he says, 'The Son of Man must suffer much and be rejected... he will be put to death, but three days later he will rise to life.' Jesus seems to see himself as the kind of 'suffering servant' prophesied in **Isaiah 53:2-12**.

Christ, Messiah, Son of David Christ and Messiah mean 'anointed one'. Although Jesus saw himself as the Messiah, he wasn't what most Jews were expecting. Many expected a warrior king, or a prophet like Moses.

1) At Caesarea Philippi (**8:27-30**) his immediate followers recognise Jesus as the Christ.

2) Blind Bartimaeus (**10:46-52**) is the first person to acclaim Jesus as Son of David in public without being told to shut up.

Saviour

'Jesus', 'Yeshua' and 'Joshua' all mean 'Saviour'.

1) The Calming of the Storm (**4:35-41**) and the Feeding of the 5000 (**6:30-44**) show Jesus controlling nature and providing miraculous food to save his people from harm.

2) In healing the Syro-Phoenician woman's daughter (**7:24-30**), Jesus demonstrates that his salvation can extend to Gentiles (i.e. non-Jews) as well as Jews.

| GOSPEL | **The Kingdom of God** |

The 'Kingdom of God' ('Kingdom of Heaven' in Matthew) was a key element in Jesus' teaching. Christians believe that when Jesus began his ministry, God's Kingdom arrived on Earth.

The **Kingdom of God** — there are **two sides**

Jesus uses the phrase in his first and last major speeches:

1 At the outset of his ministry, Jesus went into Galilee proclaiming the good news of God.

"The time has come. The Kingdom of God is at hand. Repent and believe the good news." — **Mark 1:14-15**

2 At the Last Supper:

"I will never again drink this wine until the day I drink the new wine in the Kingdom of God." — **Mark 14:25**

There are 2 sides to the Kingdom of God — i) it has already begun...

Many Jews had expected the Kingdom to arrive spectacularly and undeniably, along with the Messiah. This is why the Pharisees asked Jesus when the Kingdom of God would come (**Luke 17:20**). Jesus' answer was, "The Kingdom of God is within you." (**Luke 17:21**). He may have meant that God's Kingdom was already in people's hearts, but that most of them were preventing its growth.

...and ii) it is still to come. He also taught that when the final judgement comes, all those who accept God as King will be in the Kingdom. Those who have not accepted him will be outside the Kingdom. But at Jesus' Second Coming the Kingdom would be spectacularly revealed "...like lightning, which flashes and lights up the sky..." (**Luke 17:22-37**).

The Kingdom — **conditions for entry**

"It is easier for a camel to go through the eye of a needle, than for a rich man to enter the Kingdom of God."

Jesus and the Children (Mark 10:13-16)
To enter the Kingdom, Jesus said that you must accept it like a little child (i.e. with open trust and gratitude, rather than an adult's cynicism).

The Rich Young Man (Mark 10:17-27)
Jesus told a young man to give away all his property and follow him — he said it was desperately hard for a rich person to enter the Kingdom, although everything is possible for God.

Jesus tells loads of **parables** about the **Kingdom**

These are a few of the parables of the Kingdom of God in Mark's Gospel:

The sower (4:3-20)
Hearers of the Gospel are like types of soil — seed only grows in good soil. Similarly, the word of God will only flourish in a person if they live a 'Kingdom of God' lifestyle.

The growing seed (4:26-29)
The Kingdom grows gradually but there's no stopping it.

The mustard seed (4:30-32)
It's very small to start with, but ends up enormous.

The tenants in the vineyard (12:1-12)
A man leaves his vineyard in the hands of tenants, and sends various messengers to collect the rent — but all are beaten or killed by the tenants. They even kill the man's son so the vineyard will become theirs. Instead the owner throws out the tenants and gives the vineyard to others. This parable is told to the high priests and Pharisees — they are compared to the tenants who would kill the man's son for their own ends. The vineyard owner represents God.

The patches and the wineskins (2:21-22)
Jesus says that no one patches old clothes with a new patch, or pours new wine into old skins. This is about Jesus' way being completely new — it's not merely an update of old stuff.

Parable of the lamp (4:21-25)
You bring a lamp in to make things visible. Jesus is the lamp — he is to help people see the new way.

Parables are a bit like religious fables...
Jesus used parables to get his message across because they were simple stories which paralleled real-life situations — a bit like the 'Hare and the Tortoise' (though I don't think he ever told that one)...

Jesus and Miracles

Jesus performs many miracles in the Gospels. He performs them basically for two reasons — to show that he has God's power, and to demonstrate the importance of faith. (All references are to Mark's Gospel.)

Jesus controls *nature* — inspiring *awe* and *wonder*

Jesus calms the storm (4:35-41)
A storm breaks out and threatens to sink the boat Jesus and the disciples are in. Jesus calmly instructs the wind to die down, which it does. The disciples are filled with awe at what they see.

Jesus walks on water (6:45-52)
Jesus catches up with his disciples' boat by walking across the water. Although they have seen him feed the 5000, they are still shocked at his powers.

Jesus feeds the 5000 (6:30-44)
A crowd has gathered around Jesus and the disciples, but there are only 5 loaves and 2 fish to eat. Jesus gives thanks to God, breaks the bread and the disciples pass the food round. All 5000 people have enough to eat, and there's enough food left over to fill 12 baskets.

Jesus *cures* mental *illness* — but *faith* is *important*

A man with an evil spirit (1:21-28)
While teaching in the synagogue, a man shouts, "What do you want with us, Jesus of Nazareth? Have you come to destroy us?" Jesus sees the man is possessed by an evil spirit and says sternly, "Come out of him!" The spirit shakes the man violently, but comes out of the man with a shriek.

A man with evil spirits (5:1-20)
A man called Legion is possessed by so many evil spirits that he is able to break the chains on his hands and feet. Jesus sends the spirits into 2000 pigs instead, who rush down to the lake and drown themselves. Jesus tells the man to spread the word about what he has done.

The Syro-Phoenician woman (7:24-30)
A non-Jewish woman begs Jesus to drive the evil spirit from her daughter. Jesus tells the woman that the 'children' (i.e. Jews) must be 'fed' first — meaning his healing powers are intended for Jews. She argues that surely the 'dogs' (i.e. non-Jews) can have the scraps the children don't want. For this answer, Jesus heals her daughter. She has faith that Jesus' power is for everyone, even though she doesn't get an instant response.

The boy with an evil spirit (9:14-29) (see page 86)

Jesus *heals* physical illness — and *challenges beliefs*

Jesus heals a man with a dreaded skin disease (1:40-45)
Jesus tells him to keep the story to himself, but the man immediately tells many people, making Jesus more well known.

Jairus' daughter (5:21-24, 35-43) (see page 86)

Jesus heals the haemorrhagic (5:25-34) (see page 86)

Jesus heals a paralysed man (2:1-12)
A paralysed man is brought to Jesus. Jesus forgives the man for his sins. The crowd think that only God can forgive sins, and accuse Jesus of blasphemy. Jesus asks whether it is easier to forgive sins or cure a paralysed man. The man then gets up and walks, proving the Son of Man has authority to forgive sins on Earth.

Jesus heals a deaf mute (7:31-7)
He commands the amazed onlookers not to talk about it. But the more he tells them to keep quiet about it, the more they talk about it.

The man with the paralysed hand (3:1-6)
Jesus cures a man with a withered hand in a synagogue on the Sabbath — this goes against the Pharisees' teaching. Jesus looks at them and asks, *"Which is lawful on the Sabbath: to do good or to do evil, to save life or to kill?"* The Pharisees' stubbornness angers and distresses Jesus.

The blind man at Bethsaida (8:22-25)
Jesus cures a blind man by spitting on and touching his eyes. He then tells the man not to go into the village.

Miracles — they're a matter of faith...
Remember that Jesus performed miracles to show that if you have faith, then anything is possible — these miracles also demonstrate that he has God's authority. Lots to learn on this page, so don't let me keep you...

Miracles, Faith and Conflict

The Gospels teach that <u>faith</u>, <u>prayer</u> and <u>commitment</u> are all needed if you want to enter the Kingdom of God. Jesus demonstrated them consistently in his own life, and encouraged his followers to do the same.

Miracles and *faith* are *linked*

Jesus exercised his own faith every time he performed a <u>miracle</u>. And he showed that people could be cured miraculously of both physical and mental illness — as long as they had <u>faith</u>. (See also page 85.)

JAIRUS' DAUGHTER (Mark 5:21-24, 35-43)
Jairus, a synagogue official, begs Jesus to heal his daughter. When Jesus arrives, the girl is apparently dead already, but Jesus revives her. As in most of the healing miracles, faith is <u>crucial</u>. Here the sick girl's father has demonstrated faith <u>on her behalf</u> (by asking Jesus for help).

This also shows that not all important Jews were against Jesus.

THE BOY WITH AN EVIL SPIRIT (Mark 9:14-29)
The disciples attempt to cure a boy with an evil spirit (some say the boy was epileptic, but who's to say...). When they fail, Jesus says to the father that the boy can only be healed if he shows faith. The father says he has faith, but not enough. Jesus then casts the evil spirit out, and says that 'only <u>prayer</u> can drive this kind out'.

It's also made clear in this story that he expects his followers to perform healings and exorcisms, just as he does himself.

The point of all these stories is to show the importance of <u>faith</u>.

THE WOMAN WITH A HAEMORRHAGE (Mark 5:25-34)
While Jesus is on his way to Jairus' house, a woman with severe bleeding touches his cloak in the crowd. She is healed, even though Jesus says he does not know who has touched him. He tells her that her <u>faith</u> has made her well.

1) In these stories, faith is not merely a <u>passive</u> 'belief in God' — it is <u>active</u>, and involves taking a 'step of faith' in the direction you believe God is leading, and expecting God to intervene as a result.

2) So in the 'Boy with an Evil Spirit' story above, the boy's father claims to have 'faith but not enough' (i.e. faith mixed with <u>doubt</u>). But because he <u>exercises</u> the little faith he has, his son is healed.

*In **Mark 6:1-6** (Rejection at Nazareth), Jesus can hardly perform any miracles because the people didn't have faith — so the faith of the people he dealt with seems just as vital as his own relationship with God.*

Conflict — *Jesus challenges 'pointless' traditions*

The Pharisees were a group of influential Jews that applied the various religious rules very strictly. Jesus wasn't afraid to <u>challenge</u> them, even though he knew it would be <u>dangerous</u>.

Paying taxes (12:13-17)
Jesus avoids the trap of some Pharisees and Herod's men when they ask him who to pay taxes to — Caesar or God. *"Give to Caesar what is Caesar's, and to God what is God's."*

All references are to Mark's Gospel.

Ritual washing (7:14-23)
The Pharisees have elaborate laws about washing before eating. Jesus argues that what a man does makes him unclean, not what he takes in, and says the Pharisees are more concerned with their own traditions than God's word.

Picking corn on the Sabbath (2:23-7)
The Pharisees accuse the disciples of working on the Sabbath when they pick ears of corn. Jesus reminds them that David (see page 91) ate on the Sabbath, and that *"the Sabbath was made for man, not man for the Sabbath"*.

See also '**The man with the paralysed hand**' (**3:1-6**) on page 85.

There are many examples in the Bible of the importance of faith...

The passages from Mark's Gospel on this page are only <u>examples</u> of stories where faith, prayer and commitment are important. There are others, but these ones are in the '<u>got to know</u>' category. And make sure you know how Jesus <u>challenged authority</u> when he felt it was necessary. It's important stuff.

Discipleship

These are the lessons of discipleship, as told in Mark's Gospel.

The **call** of the **disciples** — Jesus **gathers** his **followers**

Call of the disciples (1:16-20)
"Come, follow me, and I will make you fishers of men."

Jesus gathers his 12 Disciples.

Mission of the 12 (6:7-13)
Jesus sends his disciples out with authority over evil spirits. They are to take a staff — but should not take bread, money, a bag or an extra coat. Where they are made welcome, they are to stay in that place until they leave town. Where they are unwelcome, they are to shake the dust from their feet as a marker to others.

The word 'disciple' means 'follower', and is often used to refer to one of Jesus' 12 followers from the Gospels. But it can also be used more generally to mean any Christian.

The calling of Levi (2:13-17)
Jesus has dinner at Levi's house with people the Pharisees call 'sinners'. Jesus says that healthy people don't need doctors — meaning his role is to save 'sinners'. (Note: Levi wasn't one of Jesus' 12 disciples from the Gospels.)

Peter expresses his faith at Caesarea Philippi (8:27-30)
Jesus asks Peter (one of his disciples) how he describes Jesus when people ask. *"You are the Christ,"* replies Peter. Jesus tells his disciples not to tell anyone about him.

Discipleship — there are **duties** and **rewards**

The **duties** and **qualities** of a disciple

A follower of Jesus must:

...love children (9:37)
"Whoever welcomes one of these little children in my name welcomes me; and whoever welcomes me does not welcome me but the one who sent me."

...be faithful in marriage (10:11-12)
Jesus taught that anyone who divorces and remarries is committing adultery.

...be for Jesus
"Anyone who is not against Jesus is for Jesus." (9:40)

...be servant of all (10:43)
"...whoever wants to be first must be slave of all."

...take up their cross (8:34)
"If anyone would come after me... he must deny self and take up his cross and follow me."

...be willing to make sacrifices (The widow at the treasury) (12:41-44)
While many rich people make large offerings at the treasury, a widow gives only two small coins. Jesus says her offering is greater, as it is all she had to live on.

...preach the Gospel (The Commission) (16:14-18)
After his resurrection, Jesus gave his disciples their mission... He urges them to preach the Gospel, saying whoever believes will be saved, but whoever does not will be condemned. And in Jesus' name they will *"drive out demons; they will speak in new tongues; they will pick up snakes with their hands; and when they drink deadly poison, it will not hurt them at all; they will place their hands on sick people, and they will get well"*.

The **rewards** for a disciple

But it's not all hard work. There's some good news too...

True Family (3:31-35)
"Whoever does God's will is my brother and sister and mother."

Rewards of discipleship (10:28-31)
Whatever you give up now, you'll get a hundred times as much, both now and in the future, i.e. you may face persecution now, but there is eternal life in the end.

St Mark's Gospel — Disciple training manual...

At Caesarea Philippi Jesus tells the disciples not to tell anyone about him — maybe Jesus doesn't want to become too famous too soon. This secrecy is also in some (but not all) of the stuff on page 85, and is known as the Messianic secret. And have a look on page 86 for stories of conflict.

GOSPEL	# Jesus' Trial and Death

The Last Supper — Jesus knows he will be betrayed

1) During the Passover meal, Jesus says that one of the disciples will betray him — each disciple denies it will be him.

Jesus says about the disciple who will betray him, "It would be better for him if he'd never been born."

2) Jesus breaks a piece of bread and says, *"Take it; this is my body."* He passes round a cup of wine and says, *"This is my blood of the covenant, which is poured out for many."*

3) Jesus also foresees that Peter will deny him three times — something that Peter refuses to believe.

He is arrested, tried and crucified

1) Jesus and the disciples go to Gethsemane. Jesus is fearful of death, but vows to do as God wishes.

2) Jesus' betrayer arrives — it is Judas. He has come with an armed crowd, and has arranged a secret signal with them — the person he kisses is the one they should arrest. He kisses Jesus, who goes with the crowd.

3) Jesus is put on trial before the Sanhedrin (the Jewish religious court). Various priests and elders testify falsely against Jesus, but their stories don't agree with each other.

4) Eventually, the high priest asks Jesus, *"Are you the Christ?"* Jesus answers, *"I am, and you will see the Son of Man sitting at the right hand of the Mighty One on the clouds of heaven."* This is enough for them to condemn Jesus for blasphemy.

5) In the courtyard below, Peter is accused of being a follower of Jesus. He denies it twice... but then remembers Jesus' prediction. He breaks down and weeps.

6) Jesus is turned over to Pilate — as the governor, he has the power to sentence Jesus to death. But Jesus answers none of the questions Pilate asks, to Pilate's amazement.

7) Pilate is to release a prisoner to mark Passover, and he lets the crowd choose who they want — they can have Jesus or Barabbas, a murderer. But the high priests have primed the crowd to shout for Barabbas... Jesus is flogged, and handed over to be crucified.

8) The Roman guards mock Jesus — they make him a crown of thorns and pretend to honour the 'King of the Jews', while all the time hitting and spitting at him.

9) Jesus is led to Golgotha, where he is to be crucified. Simon of Cyrene is made to carry his cross.

10) Jesus refuses the drugged wine he is offered, and is then crucified next to two robbers. A sign is fixed to Jesus' cross that reads "The King of the Jews". Passers-by and the Roman soldiers throw insults at Jesus, saying that he can work miracles, but he can't save himself.

11) Before dying, Jesus cries out, *"My God, My God, why have you forsaken me?"* As he dies, the curtain of the Temple is torn in two, and a Roman soldier remarks, *"Surely, this man was the Son of God!"*

And then he's resurrected

1) Mary Magdalene, Mary the mother of James and Salome go to Jesus' tomb, only to find that Jesus has gone. A young man there says they are to spread the word among the disciples. The three women flee in terror.

2) Jesus appears first to Mary Magdalene. She passes the news on to the disciples, who refuse to believe.

3) He then appears to the disciples and rebukes them for not believing in his resurrection. He orders them to preach the Gospel, and perform miracles in his name.

4) Jesus then ascends into Heaven and sits at the right hand of God.

The examiners won't be impressed if you don't know this...

Like I said, it's a fairly famous story, but you need to be able to describe in detail all the events of Jesus' death and resurrection — and I mean all of them. The best way to make sure you know this stuff is to write it all down...

Warm-Up and Worked Exam Questions

Warm-up Questions

1) According to Christians, what is meant by the word "scripture"?
2) Describe two parables in which Jesus explains the Kingdom of God.
3) Who were the Pharisees? Give two examples of things that Jesus did that the Pharisees disapproved of.
4) What happened at Caesarea Philippi?
5) Briefly describe the story of Jesus' arrest, trial and death.

Worked Exam Questions

There's lots of stuff to learn for this section. Make sure you've memorised all the Bible bits, then try these questions.

1   In Mark's Gospel, Jesus is called Christ, Messiah and Son of David.

   a)   List three other titles which were given to Jesus. For each title explain what clue you think it gives us about who Jesus was.

Three other titles are: Son of God, Son of Man, and Saviour.

"Son of God" implies that Jesus had a unique relationship with God.

"Son of Man" implies that Jesus was a man with ordinary human emotions.

"Saviour" suggests that Jesus would save his people, either from harm or sin.

(6 marks)

   b)   From Mark's Gospel, briefly describe an occasion when ONE of these titles was used by another person to describe Jesus.

Blind Bartimaeus is the first to call Jesus the Son of David in public without

being silenced (Mark 10:46-52). You need to get the right title in the right context for both marks.

Any of the examples from page 83 would have done here.

(2 marks)

2   a)   For what TWO basic reasons did Jesus perform miracles?

To show God's power, and to demonstrate the importance of faith.

(2 marks)

   b)   Briefly describe TWO miracles performed by Jesus.

Jesus fed 5000 people with 5 loaves and 2 fish (Mark 6:30-44).

Then he walked across water to catch up with his disciples' boat (Mark 6:45-52).

(2 marks)

   c)   Suggest why the Pharisees often reacted to Jesus' miracles with hostility.

Jesus performed miracles on the Sabbath, against the Pharisees' teaching.

They feared Jesus would lead people away from the Jewish faith.

This is only a two-mark question, so you don't need to write an essay

(2 marks)

90

Exam Questions

3   Jesus used stories (parables) in his teaching to help get his points across.
     In Mark's Gospel 12:1–12, Jesus tells the parable of the tenants in the vineyard.

a)   Briefly describe the parable of the tenants in the vineyard.

(4 marks)

b)   Who did Jesus tell this parable to?

(1 mark)

c)   What do you think the tenants in the vineyard parable means?

(2 marks)

d)   Why do you think Jesus used parables in his teaching?

(2 marks)

4   a)   Jesus expected many things of his followers. Describe THREE duties of a disciple,
          making reference to Mark's Gospel.

(6 marks)

b)   There were rewards as well as duties for Jesus' followers.
     What reward did Jesus promise to his disciples?

(1 mark)

5   a)   Briefly explain the role played by each of the following in the story of Jesus' trial
          and death:

     i)   Judas

     ii) the Sanhedrin

     iii) Pontius Pilate

     iv) Simon of Cyrene

(4 marks)

b)   "Pilate is responsible for Jesus' crucifixion."

     Do you agree? Give reasons for your answer, showing that you have thought about
     more than one point of view. Refer to Mark's Gospel in your answer.

(8 marks)

The Beginnings of Judaism

If you're asked to explain the <u>origins of Judaism</u>, remember that there was <u>more than one founder</u>. In fact, there are <u>3 key figures</u> you should know about:

Abraham (between 2000 and 1800 BCE)

1) Jews call him <u>Avraham Avinu</u> ('our father Abraham'). He was the first of the <u>patriarchs</u> — the founders of Judaism.

2) Unlike his neighbours in <u>Ur</u>, he believed in <u>one god</u>. God told him to leave Ur and go to <u>Canaan</u>, also known as <u>The Promised Land</u>, <u>The Holy Land</u>, and later <u>Israel</u>. God promised this land to Abraham's descendants.

3) God made a <u>covenant</u> with Abraham (see below) — this covenant forms the basis of Jewish beliefs.

> *The time since the birth of Jesus is known as the <u>'Common Era'</u> (CE), and BCE just means <u>'Before the Common Era'</u>. Very often, <u>1800 BCE</u> is written <u>1800 BC</u> (Before Christ). And <u>2002 CE</u> (Common Era) is often written <u>AD 2002</u>.*

Moses (around 1300 BCE)

1) <u>Abraham's descendants</u> had to leave Canaan and escape to <u>Egypt</u> because of a <u>famine</u>.

2) In Egypt they <u>multiplied</u> and the Egyptians made them <u>slaves for 400 years</u>.

3) Moses then led them to freedom — an event called the <u>Exodus</u>. Their journey back to Canaan took <u>40 years</u>.

4) On the way back, Moses received the <u>10 Commandments</u> and the rest of the <u>Torah</u> (meaning 'Instructions', or 'Law') at <u>Mount Sinai</u>.

5) Moses is regarded as the greatest of the prophets, and is known as <u>Moshe Rabbenu</u> ('our teacher Moses').

6) Moses' successor <u>Joshua</u> led the <u>reconquest of Canaan</u>.

David (not long after 1000 BCE)

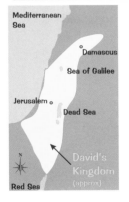

1) For a long time the Israelites lived in <u>Twelve Tribes</u> under warlords called <u>Judges</u>.

2) Unfortunately, the tribes made a <u>dangerous enemy</u>, the <u>Philistines</u>, that the judges couldn't really do anything about.

3) So the tribes asked God for a <u>king</u>, and got <u>Saul</u>.

4) Saul's successor, <u>David</u>, captured <u>Jerusalem</u> from its pagan inhabitants and made it his <u>capital</u>. He reigned for <u>40 years</u> and created a <u>small empire</u>.

5) David's son <u>Solomon</u> built the first permanent Jewish <u>temple</u> in <u>Jerusalem</u>.

> *The remains of this Temple are still <u>very important</u> in Judaism.*

6) After Solomon the kingdom <u>split</u> in two. The 10 <u>northern</u> tribes were soon swallowed up by <u>Assyria</u>. The 2 <u>southern</u> tribes together became known as <u>Judah</u>, and Jews are descended from them.

The Covenant — key to the past and hope for the future

1) Jews think that their relationship with God is like a two-way promise (a <u>covenant</u>).

2) God made a covenant with <u>Abraham</u>, where God promised Abraham many descendants that he would never <u>abandon</u>. In return they had to be <u>circumcised</u>.

3) The covenant was renewed at <u>Mount Sinai</u> with the giving of the <u>Torah</u>.

4) Jews regard their <u>history</u> as the story of the covenant. Some things described in the covenant haven't happened yet — these are believed to describe the <u>future</u>.

5) Jews look forward to the Age of the <u>Messiah</u> ('anointed one'), when all of Israel will belong to them and a new age of universal <u>peace</u> will dawn.

Learn this page — and be as wise as Solomon...

There's a lot more to RS than <u>knowing facts</u> — but still, you can't get far unless you actually know them...

Basic Jewish Beliefs

Jews don't <u>all</u> believe exactly the same things. They have many different opinions on many important issues. But most Jews share some basic beliefs about their <u>God</u>, <u>themselves</u> and their <u>land</u>.

"Hear O **Israel**: the Lord our **God**, the **Lord is One**"

Most Jews believe these 11 things about God. They believe <u>God is</u>...

Belief in one god is called <u>monotheism</u>.

...one — Jews believe there's only one God. The heading above comes from **Deuteronomy 6:4** — it's the opening of a very important Jewish prayer called the <u>Shema</u>.

...a person — i.e. he's not just a 'force' like the one in Star Wars, but neither is he an old man with a beard. Human beings were made '<u>in his image</u>' (but this needn't mean he looks like us).

...the Creator — i.e. he made the Universe and everything in it. Jews don't invent clever arguments for God's existence — they say that creation makes it <u>obvious</u> that he's there.

...the Sustainer — i.e. he didn't just create the Universe and then sit back — his <u>energy</u> keeps it going.

...holy — '<u>Holy</u>' means '<u>set apart</u>' or '<u>completely pure</u>'. God (or <u>YHWH</u> in Hebrew) is so holy that some Jews won't even write or say the word 'God' — they write <u>G-d</u> and say <u>Hashem</u> ('the Name') or <u>Adonai</u> ('the Lord', or 'the Master').

...omnipotent — i.e. <u>all-powerful</u> — although he still allows each person <u>free will</u>.

...omniscient — i.e. he <u>knows everything</u>, even your smuttiest secrets and your wildest dreams.

...omnipresent — i.e. present throughout the <u>whole Universe</u>.

...the Lawgiver — Jewish tradition says '<u>God wrote himself into the Torah</u>'.

...the True Judge — Jews believe they shall all face him one day, for death is <u>not</u> 'the end'.

the Redeemer — Jews believe God is <u>merciful</u>. He will <u>save</u> his people from sin and suffering.

See also pages 8 and 11.

Jews believe they are the **chosen people**

1) Because of the <u>covenant</u>, Jews believe they have a special role to play in history.

2) But they believe they were chosen for <u>responsibility</u>, not for <u>privilege</u> — God wanted people who would dedicate themselves to him, and prepare the world for when all human beings would come to know him.

Israel is the **Holy Land**

<u>Zionism</u> (after <u>Zion</u>, one of the hills on which the holy city of Jerusalem was built), is the belief that the Jews should have a <u>homeland</u> of their own — the land God gave them.

1) The Jews lost their homeland in the 6th century BCE, when much of the population of Judah was taken into <u>exile</u> in Babylon (although many returned in the 5th century BCE).

2) Later, the Jews suffered conquest by the <u>Greeks</u>, and then by the <u>Romans</u>. After a rebellion in 70 CE, the Romans destroyed <u>Jerusalem</u>.

3) For many centuries most Jews had to live <u>abroad</u> — this time is known as the <u>diaspora</u>. It was only after 6 million died in the <u>Holocaust</u> during the Second World War that the state of <u>Israel</u> was established.

4) For many Jews the establishment of the <u>State of Israel</u> in 1948 heralded the fulfilment of the Zionist dream. But others disagreed, for <u>two</u> main reasons:

1) It seemed wrong to <u>displace</u> the <u>Palestinians</u> who were living there. There was likely to be <u>violent opposition</u> to Jewish settlement. And indeed there was — and still is.

2) Some Jews believed it was the job of the <u>Messiah</u> to restore the Jews to their homeland. God's people should have waited for <u>him</u> to come, rather than putting their trust in corrupt <u>politicians</u>.

One God, but many different ways to describe Him...

You might get asked about how these <u>beliefs</u> about God could affect a person's <u>life</u> — so you need to learn this...

Sources of Guidance

The 'Jewish Bible' is the Tenakh. This is basically the same as the Christian Old Testament, except that it's in a different order. The letters in the word 'TeNaKh' even help you remember the order of its groups of books.

The Tenakh — its letters tell you its contents

T = Torah (Instructions / Law / Teachings)

The Torah is the first five books of the Bible (Genesis to Deuteronomy). It contains 613 commandments (mitzvot) which Jews are supposed to live by. Jews regard the Torah as the holiest part of the Tenakh, as it was given to Moses directly by God.

N = Nevi'im (Prophets)

This collection of books is divided into two. The Former Prophets trace the history of the Israelites after the death of Moses. The Latter Prophets contain the words of Isaiah, Jeremiah, Ezekiel and 12 Minor Prophets. All these men encouraged the Jews to keep their part of the covenant, and their words are believed to have been inspired by God. However, the books in the Nevi'im do not have as high a status as the Torah.

K = Ketuvim (Writings)

This is a hotch-potch of other stuff, chiefly the three 'P's: Psalms (hymns), Proverbs (wise and witty sayings), and Philosophy. This part of the Tenakh is less authoritative than the others.

Torah means different things to different people

Some Jews use the word 'Torah' to refer to the whole Tenakh. Others use it to mean the enormous body of teachings which grew up over the centuries to explain how the Torah should be applied in a changing world. Although some of these teachings were originally passed on by word of mouth (and were known as the Oral Torah), they eventually got written down in a number of collections — you need to know the names:

(1) The Mishnah ('Learning' or 'Repetition')

This was a collection of Oral Torah written down by Rabbi Judah the Prince (roughly 200 CE). It ran to 63 volumes.

(2) The Gemara ('Completion')

This is an extended commentary on the Mishnah.

(3) The Talmud (the Mishnah and Gemara combined)

Some Jews think that God gave the entire contents of the Talmud to Moses, so it has a very high status and authority.

(4) The Codes

The Talmud was so huge that summaries had to be made. An important example is the Mishneh Torah written by Maimonides in 1167. Another is the Shulchan Aruch from the 16th century.

(5) The Responsa

New questions arise as technology develops, so panels of rabbis meet to give 'responses' to tricky questions, e.g. whether people should drive on the Sabbath.

The Bet Din is a rabbinical court

1) A Bet Din has three judges (dayasim), who rule on issues which remain unclear (in spite of the huge amount of other guidance available).

2) Individual Jews can approach the Bet Din to sort out legal or business disputes. It also supervises kosher food products and divorces.

The word 'Halakhah' describes Jewish Law as a whole. It means 'going' — in other words, how to 'walk with God' the Jewish way. It's the part of Jewish teaching which is concerned with ritual and behaviour.

Hebrew words can be spelt in different ways in our alphabet...

If you see a word on your exam paper which looks unfamiliar, try pronouncing it in your head — it might make sense after all, e.g., you might see the word 'Tanach' — but it turns out this is just a different way to spell Tenakh.

The Holocaust

The word Holocaust means 'a complete burning up' or 'total destruction'. It refers to the massacre of six million Jews by the Nazis between 1933 and 1945. Jews also call it Shoah ('whirlwind').

The Holocaust — the Nazis' extermination of Jews

1) Towards the end of the 18th century, Jews living in Europe began to face greater persecution than ever before from nationalists who thought that Jewish blood was watering down their own racial identity.

2) This hatred of Jews became known as anti-Semitism, and spread through many countries — especially France, Germany, Austria and Russia. The fact that many Jews regarded themselves as loyal citizens of these countries didn't stop this from happening.

3) Later, during the 1920s, Germany faced huge economic problems. The National Socialist (Nazi) Party seemed to offer solutions. It pinned the blame for the country's problems on 'non-Aryan' people (i.e. those who weren't considered 'pure Germans') living in Germany — especially the Jews.

4) In 1933 its leader Adolf Hitler became Chancellor of Germany, and laws began to be passed which gradually deprived the Jews of their citizenship rights.

5) Eventually Hitler introduced the Final Solution — the plan to wipe out the Jews completely. Throughout World War II (1939-1945) concentration camps and extermination camps were built in the countries under Nazi control. Huge numbers of Jews perished here in gas chambers.

The Holocaust caused Jews to ask "Where was God?"

The holocaust posed very serious problems for Jews — they had to find answers to questions like:

> If God exists, and he is good, and all-powerful, how could he have allowed such terrible suffering?
> If we are the 'chosen people' how could God have let six million of us be wiped out?

See pages 10 and 11 for more about religious questions of evil and suffering.

Holocaust Remembrance Day is 27 Nisan.

'Nisan' is the first month in the Jewish calendar.

Jewish responses to the Holocaust have been varied

Jews have come up with many responses to this type of question:

1) Some Jews have concluded that there is no God.

2) Some have concluded that if God does exist, he either doesn't care, or is powerless to intervene.

3) Some Jews say that the Holocaust, and all suffering, is a test of faith — if good people always got the best things in life, everyone would be good for the wrong reasons.

4) Some Jews say that God could intervene to stamp out evil if he chose to. However, he gave all human beings free will and refuses to override this even when it is abused. Also, it would be impossible for God to 'destroy all evil people' because no one is completely evil or completely good.

5) Some Jews regard all those who died in the Holocaust as martyrs for the faith, and see their martyrdom as 'sanctifying the name of God'.

6) Some say the most important thing is to keep practising Judaism, or else Hitler will have won.

7) Some have devoted their energies to building the State of Israel (established in 1948) so that Jews may never again be forced to live with persecution. But are they persecuting the Palestinians (see page 92)?

Six million people died in the Holocaust.
Six million people. Hard to comprehend.

Different Jewish Traditions

There are certain Jewish <u>cultures</u> and <u>traditions</u> that you need to be aware of.

Different *Jewish cultures* are *described* in *different ways*

1) Some Jews (known as '<u>secular Jews</u>') don't <u>practise</u> their religion at all — they may not even believe in God. But they still regard themselves as Jews. To a Jew, if your <u>mother's</u> Jewish, then <u>you're</u> Jewish.

2) <u>Sephardic Jews</u>' ancestors lived for centuries in Spain, Portugal and North Africa (i.e. mainly in '<u>Muslim</u>' countries).

3) <u>Ashkenazi Jews</u> lived in central and eastern Europe (mainly in 'Christian' countries).

4) The <u>Sephardim</u> and <u>Ashkenazim</u> differ in their <u>customs</u>, their way of pronouncing <u>Hebrew</u>, and in some of their <u>prayers</u>.

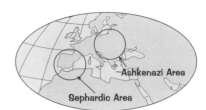

Orthodox Jews live *strictly* by the *Torah*

1) <u>Orthodox</u> means 'right belief'. Orthodox Jews accept that traditional Jewish beliefs and practices are still important <u>today</u>.

2) Roughly 80% of <u>British</u> Jews belong to Orthodox synagogues, though not all are equally <u>observant</u>.

3) Those who *are* observant believe that <u>Progressive Jews</u> (see below) have betrayed Judaism by <u>watering it down</u> and <u>taking liberties</u> with God's word.

4) <u>Ultra-Orthodox</u> Jews take their orthodoxy very seriously — some would say, to extremes. The most famous ultra-Orthodox group are the <u>Hasidic</u> Jews.

Hasidic Jews are ultra-Orthodox

1) <u>Hasid</u> means 'pious one'. The movement was started by Rabbi <u>Israel Baal Shem Tov</u> in 18th century Poland (and most Hasidim still dress in 18th century Polish style).

2) Baal Shem Tov believed in keeping every word of the Torah <u>strictly</u> — but also with <u>joy</u> and <u>enthusiasm</u>.

Progressive Jews interpret the Torah *less rigidly*

1) <u>Progressive Jews</u> apply the Torah to <u>modern life</u> in a very different way.

2) Progressive Jews believe that the Torah is merely people's <u>interpretation</u> of the word of God.

3) They consider the <u>moral</u> commandments <u>binding</u> (although open to <u>interpretation</u>).

4) However, the <u>ritual laws</u> can be <u>adapted</u> or <u>abandoned</u> in response to changes in society. In <u>Britain</u>, there are 2 Progressive movements: <u>Reform</u> and <u>Liberal</u>.

Reform Judaism

1) <u>Reform Judaism</u> began at the end of the 18th century, when Jews in Europe were allowed to take a full part in society.

2) The first reformers tried to update synagogue services by making them more like Christian ones.

3) Reform Jews <u>stopped</u> praying for the restoration of the <u>Holy Land</u> and the rebuilding of the <u>Temple</u> (see page 91). They also gave up believing in the physical coming of a Messiah — instead they hope for a <u>Messianic Age</u> of universal peace.

4) They allow <u>women</u> a much greater role in worship — men and women sit together in services, and there are women rabbis. Also, <u>modern</u> languages are used in worship — not just Hebrew.

Liberal Judaism

1) <u>Liberal Judaism</u> was founded at the start of the 20th century.

2) The originators thought that even Reform Judaism was <u>too strict</u>.

3) They taught that observing any mitzvot is a matter of <u>personal choice</u>.

The <u>Masorti movement</u> (Conservative Judaism) tries to take a <u>middle way</u> between Reform and Orthodox Judaism.

Not all Jews have the same beliefs and customs...

The differences described on this page fall into two basic categories: <u>geographical</u> differences (e.g. where in the world your ancestors came from), and differences in <u>beliefs</u> (e.g. <u>secular</u>, <u>orthodox</u> or <u>progressive</u>).

Judaism and Day-to-Day Life

Observant Jews believe that their day-to-day lives should be lived in a way which is pleasing to God.
For Orthodox Jews this means obeying the 613 mitzvot in the Torah, covering everything from sex to seafood.

Mitzvot means commandments

The most famous mitzvot are the Ten Commandments (see page 60) — but they're not the only ones.
The 613 mitzvot can be divided up in different ways...

248 of the mitzvot are positive, telling Jews what they should do. 365 are negative, telling them what they shouldn't be doing.

Ritual mitzvot are about Jews' relationship with God.
Moral (ethical) mitzvot are about Jews' dealings with other people.

The first four of the Ten Commandments are ritual mitzvot, and the last six are moral mitzvot.

The singular of mitzvot is mitzvah.

1) Orthodox Jews believe that the commandments given by God are his chief method of communicating with his people. Their method of responding is obedience.

2) They also believe that living God's way is in their own best interests.
They reason that if God is our Maker, and the Torah is the 'Maker's Handbook', it makes sense to follow its guidance. **Deuteronomy 10:12-13** says, "Keep, for your own good, the Commandments of the Lord."

3) There's also a belief that observing mitzvot causes people to lead disciplined lives, which in turn builds character.

4) Progressive Jews take a rather different view. They think the Torah is God's teaching as interpreted by human beings. Therefore mitzvot which no longer seem relevant can be adapted or even abandoned.

Morality matters in Judaism

1) Observant Jews think it's vital to live by a moral code, and will generally regard a moral individual as someone who combines religious observance with concern for other people.

2) In deciding how to behave, Jews look first to the Torah, then to the Talmud, then to the wider body of traditional Jewish teaching. But an individual Jew can always ask someone who knows more about these things than they do.

3) Jews realise that no one can live by all 613 mitzvot all of the time.
But they believe that God is merciful and will always forgive someone who is truly sorry for his sins. Rosh Hashanah and Yom Kippur (see page 104) remind Jews of this every year.

The word 'mitzvah' is sometimes translated as a 'good deed'. Doing anything to help a fellow human being is pleasing to God.

The Mikveh is a ritual bath — used for 'family purity'

1) A mikveh is a ritual bath. It should be a special tiled pool about 3-5 metres long and 2-3 metres wide, and contain rainwater.

2) Traditionally, Jews immerse themselves in a mikveh to be purified from 'spiritual uncleanness'.
The mikveh isn't about getting rid of a bit of dirt — Jews have to shower before entering the mikveh.

3) Women should visit the mikveh after menstruation, before marriage and after childbirth.
Men go in preparation for Yom Kippur. All converts to Judaism must go.

4) Progressive Jews tend to reject the use of the mikveh as old-fashioned and sexist.

The mitzvot give religious and moral guidance...
You don't need to know each of the 613 mitzvot in the Torah, but you should learn how these rules affect the day-to-day life of a Jew — and the best way to learn this stuff is by writing down the main issues from memory...

The Synagogue

A Jewish place of worship is called a synagogue, although Jews more often use the word 'shul', or sometimes even 'Bet ha Knesset' (House of Meeting).

It's **not** what's on the **outside** that **matters**...

There are no rules stating what a synagogue should look like on the outside — they can be plain or ornate, traditional or ultra-modern. But you might recognise a synagogue from symbols on its outside walls, such as a menorah (a seven-branched candlestick), or a magen David (a six-pointed star/shield of David).

...it's what's on the **inside** that's **important**

The layout of the synagogue's Prayer Hall is based on that of the ancient Temple. It faces Jerusalem, where the Temple stood, and is usually rectangular. All synagogues share the following four features:

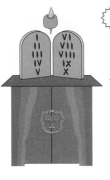

1 Aron Hakodesh (the Ark) — this is the most important item of furniture. It is a large cupboard or alcove, with doors or a screen, set on the wall facing Jerusalem.

2 Ner Tamid (Perpetual Light) — above the ark is a light which never goes out. It represents the menorah which was always kept alight in the Temple.

3 Sefer Torah (Scrolls of the Torah) — parchment scrolls. On each end is a wooden pole for winding it to the required passage. It must be handwritten by a sofer (scribe), and is usually decorated. They're kept inside the ark.

Remember — there will be no 'pictures of God'.

4 Bimah or Almemar — a raised platform with a reading desk, normally in the centre of the hall.

Also, some synagogues have a pulpit, and the Ten Commandments above the ark. Some have an organ (but on the Sabbath, all singing should be unaccompanied), and an Orthodox synagogue will have a gallery where women can sit.

...and **how** it is **used**

A synagogue is a bit like a community centre. In addition to the Prayer Hall, a synagogue will have a hall for wedding receptions and parties, classrooms for study groups, a mikveh perhaps (see page 96), plus rooms for youth clubs, mother and toddler groups, senior citizens' clubs, and so on.

The most **important officials** — the **Rabbi** and the **Chazan**

The Rabbi

1) Every synagogue has a rabbi (meaning 'my master'). To become a rabbi, you have to study for many years and have practical training.

2) The rabbi's role is much like that of a minister in a Christian church — he leads prayers in the synagogue, conducts weddings and funerals, visits the sick, and may be chaplain to a hospital or prison.

3) But rabbis are not priests — Jews don't believe that anyone can mediate between an individual and God.

The Chazan (Cantor)

1) Many synagogues also have a chazan (cantor), specially trained in music and voice projection.

2) His role is to lead the congregation in singing. He chants some of the prayers on Shabbat, and at festivals, weddings and funerals.

3) He may also provide entertainment at receptions and parties.

Synagogues are Jewish centres of worship...

If you're studying Judaism, you need to know about synagogues. There's just no getting away from that.

98

Warm-Up and Worked Exam Question

Warm-up Questions

1) When did the Romans destroy Jerusalem?
2) What is the Jewish name for the first five books of the Bible?
3) In which direction does a synagogue prayer hall face?
4) Where was the Torah given to Moses?
5) What is the difference between ritual and moral mitzvot?
6) When is the Holocaust Remembrance Day?

Worked Exam Question

There's a lot of history in this section, and a lot of times where the Jews have had it pretty hard going. Exam stress suddenly doesn't feel so bad. Read through these worked exam questions carefully before trying the questions on the following page.

1   a)   What are the Mishnah and the Gemara together known as?

The Talmud

(1 mark)

  b)   Name the three parts of the Tenakh and briefly describe them.

The Torah or Law is the first five books of the Bible. The Nevi'im is the history and words of the Prophets. The Ketuvim or Writings consists of sacred psalms, proverbs and philosophy.

Make sure you answer the questions fully. Here it asks you to name AND describe the three parts of the Tenakh. It asks you to briefly describe them, so don't waffle on for ages.   *(6 marks)*

  c)   In which order were the following collections written, starting with the oldest: the Responsa, the Codes, the Mishnah?

Mishnah, Codes, Responsa.

(2 marks)

  d)   What is the purpose of the Responsa?

To give guidance on how religious law should be applied to new situations that arise as technology develops.

The modern day lifestyle causes many issues for all the religions. They each have their own way of tackling the problems.   *(2 marks)*

  e)   Which part of the Tenakh is regarded as most holy by Jews, and why?

The Torah, because it was given directly by God to Moses.

(2 marks)

Exam Questions

2   a)   Who was the first of the Jewish Patriarchs?

(1 mark)

b)   Explain what is meant by the Covenant.

(4 marks)

c)   The Holocaust and the founding of the State of Israel are two important 20th century events that have affected Jewish thinking.

Describe what Jews thought about each of these events.
Make reference to more than one point of view in your answer.

(6 marks)

3   a)   What is the name of the Jewish prayer that begins "Hear O Israel: The Lord our God, the Lord is one."

(1 mark)

b)   This prayer demonstrates that Judaism teaches that there is only one God.
What other beliefs do Jews hold about God?

(6 marks)

c)   Explain the term Zionism.

(2 marks)

4   a)   Describe THREE differences between Orthodox and Progressive Jews.

(9 marks)

b)   Different Jewish cultures grew up in various parts of the world. Name two of these cultures and state which part of the world they came from.

(4 marks)

c)   "The customs and beliefs of Orthodox Jews are outdated. They should think about the future rather than the past."

Do you agree? Refer to Judaism in your answer and show that you have considered more than one point of view.

(6 marks)

Signs and Symbols

Symbols: visible *signs* of invisible *ideas*...

Since God is <u>invisible</u>, <u>symbols</u> are important in just about every religion. Believers use symbols to help them focus on God in private prayer and in communal worship. A <u>picture</u> on a wall, a household <u>object</u> and an item of <u>clothing</u> may all be used as religious symbols.

But Jews have **no pictures of God**

There are <u>two</u> reasons why Jewish art never tries to picture God.

1) No one knows what he looks like.

2) The 2nd of the <u>10 Commandments</u> forbids it as idolatry.

"You shall not make for yourself an idol in the form of anything in heaven above or on the earth beneath." Exodus 20:4

Symbols in the **home** — the **Mezuzah**

"These commandments that I give you today are to be upon your hearts... and you shall write them on the door-frames of your houses."
Deuteronomy 6:6-9

1) The <u>mezuzah</u> is a sign which is put in Jewish houses.

2) It's a tiny <u>parchment scroll</u> containing the words of **Deuteronomy 6:4-9** and **11:13-21** in Hebrew. It must be <u>handwritten</u> by a <u>trained scribe</u>, and is put inside a <u>case</u> to keep it safe.

3) There's one on the front door and every other door of the house except the bathroom and toilet. It constantly reminds the family of the <u>covenant</u>.

Ritual dress is important in *Judaism*

Kippah (Yarmulka, Capel, Skullcap)

Many Jewish men and boys wear a small cap as a sign of <u>respect</u> to God. It reminds them that God's intelligence is vastly <u>higher</u> than ours. There's no actual <u>law</u> commanding men to cover their heads when praying, but it's an almost universal custom.

The Tefillin (Phylacteries)

These are worn during morning prayers, except on the sabbath and on festival days. They are 2 <u>leather boxes</u>, one worn on the upper arm (next to the heart), one on the head. Inside are tiny parchment <u>scrolls</u> containing 4 Bible passages: the first 2 paragraphs of the <u>Shema</u> (see page 8), plus **Exodus 13:1-10** and **13:11-16**. These remind Jews to serve God with <u>head</u> and <u>heart</u>.

The Tallit (Prayer Shawl)

This is also worn by males during <u>morning prayers</u>. It's a square or rectangle of silk or wool. Some Jews wear a 'tallit katan' (small tallit) all the time, under their clothes.

The Tzitzit (Fringes)

Fringes are attached to each corner of the tallit, in obedience to **Numbers 15:37-41** and also **Deuteronomy 22:12**.

Signs and symbols play an important part in worship...

You need to know why these special clothes and symbols are important in Judaism. Learn what each thing <u>represents</u>, and how it's <u>useful</u> — e.g. ritual dress helps people stay focused while praying.

Judaism and Children

<u>Rites of passage</u> are ceremonies marking the <u>transition</u> from one stage of life to the next.
Like most religions, Judaism has ceremonies associated with <u>birth</u>, <u>coming of age</u>, <u>marriage</u> and <u>death</u>.

There are **three** important **birth ceremonies**

Brit Milah

1) This is the '<u>Covenant of Circumcision</u>', and involves the removal of the <u>foreskin</u> from the penis (and so is only for boys). The baby boy is also <u>named</u> at this time, and afterwards there is a celebratory <u>meal</u>.

2) The circumcision is done when a boy is 8 days old, and is for <u>religious</u> rather than <u>medical</u> reasons. The operation is carried out in hospital, at home or in the synagogue by a specially trained '<u>mohel</u>' while being held by the '<u>sandek</u>' (often the grandfather).

Redemption of the first-born

Note: a modern rabbi isn't the same as an ancient priest.

Originally, all <u>first-born boys</u> became priests. Now, when a boy is 30 days old, his father ceremonially releases him from the priesthood by <u>redeeming</u> him (i.e. 'buying him back') with five silver coins.

The naming of a girl

Jewish girls usually receive their names on the Sabbath following their birth, although some Sephardic Jews name <u>girls</u> at a ceremony called <u>zeved habat</u> ('gift of a daughter') when they are 7 days old.

Children are **taught** about Judaism in **different** ways

1) At home, parents might try to create a <u>religious environment</u> using <u>symbols</u> of the faith, and so on.

2) Children might go to the <u>synagogue</u> for Hebrew classes. Some children will also attend <u>Jewish schools</u>, which teach Hebrew, the Torah and the Talmud as well as the normal curriculum.

3) Almost all <u>festivals</u> have features specifically designed to involve children.

At <u>Pesach</u> the youngest child asks questions about the festival. And during the readings in the synagogue at <u>Purim</u>, the children drown out the name of the evil <u>Haman</u> with football rattles.

Bar Mitzvah and **Bat Mitzvah** are **coming of age** ceremonies

Bar Mitzvah is for Boys

1) At 13 a boy becomes <u>Bar Mitzvah</u> (Son of the Commandment) and is responsible for keeping the mitzvot for himself. This is also when a boy begins to wear <u>tefillin</u> for prayer.

2) On the Sabbath after his 13th birthday there is a special service, followed by a small <u>reception</u>, and perhaps a lavish party (although <u>not</u> all Jews approve of such extravagance on a religious occasion).

Bat Mitzvah and Bat Chayil are for Girls

1) A girl becomes <u>Bat Mitzvah</u> (Daughter of the Commandment) at 12, since Judaism recognises that girls mature before boys. The ceremonies vary widely, but among <u>Progressive</u> Jews, Bat Mitzvah ceremonies may be exactly like Bar Mitzvah.

2) Many synagogues have a ceremony for 12-year-old girls called <u>Bat Chayil</u> (Daughter of Excellence). Girls prepare by studying their responsibilities as women, then make a short speech at a special service.

These rites of passage are important...

They're like doors opening to a new part of your life. You could compare them (sort of) to passing your driving test, or getting your first job. They're things you're likely to remember — <u>nothing will be the same again</u>...

Jewish Beliefs About Death

You need to know what Judaism teaches about <u>death</u> and the <u>afterlife</u>, and the <u>rituals</u> surrounding death.

The **Souls of the Dead** end up in **Sheol**

1) Most religious Jews believe in life after death, but as the Torah is very vague on the subject, they don't necessarily agree on what it will be like.

2) The Torah mostly talks about '<u>Sheol</u>', a shadowy underworld where the souls of the dead end up.

3) According to <u>Maimonides</u> (see page 93), belief in the <u>resurrection</u> of the dead is one of the main beliefs in Judaism — when the Messiah comes, the dead will be raised to life, and to <u>judgement</u>.

4) Sheol is sometimes compared to Hell, but Jews don't believe in Sheol as a place of everlasting torment — it's more like a laundry where souls are cleaned up to make them fit for an eternity spent in the presence of God.

Judaism has **customs** to **comfort** the **bereaved**

There are many <u>rituals</u> in Judaism concerned with death. They are designed to <u>help</u> bereaved people <u>accept</u> what has happened, give expression to their <u>grief</u>, receive <u>comfort</u>, and come to terms with their loss.

1) Jewish families <u>gather together</u> to be near a loved one who is dying, while the dying person should spend his / her last moments confessing <u>sins</u> and reciting the <u>Shema</u> (see page 8).

2) After the death, each member of the family makes a small <u>tear</u> in their clothing — a symbol of grief and shock.

3) The dead person must not be left alone, and must be <u>buried</u> (<u>not</u> cremated) as soon as possible, preferably within <u>24 hours</u>.

It's the job of the <u>Chevra Kaddisha</u> (burial society) to prepare the body for burial.

4) The body's washed and put in a <u>mikveh</u> (see page 96). Then it's wrapped in a plain linen <u>shroud</u>, before being placed in a plain, unpolished, wooden <u>coffin</u> — in death rich and poor are <u>equal</u>.

5) At the funeral service in the synagogue, <u>psalms</u> are read and a prayer is said praising God for giving life and for taking it away. The rabbi might make a short speech about the deceased.

6) The first week after the funeral is called <u>shiva</u> (seven). The immediate family stay at home and are <u>visited</u> by relatives and friends who pray with them three times a day and offer comfort. They do not cut their hair, shave, listen to music or have sex. The men recite a prayer called the <u>kaddish</u>. Everyone is encouraged to talk about the person who has died.

7) The first month after the funeral is called <u>Sheloshim</u> (thirty). During this time life returns <u>gradually</u> to normal, and male mourners go to the synagogue to recite the <u>kaddish</u>. Anyone who has lost a parent remains in mourning for a whole <u>year</u>.

8) The anniversary of death is called <u>Yahrzeit</u>. It is on the first yahrzeit that the <u>headstone</u> will usually be erected above the grave. Every year a candle is lit for 24 hours and men say the <u>kaddish</u>.

Death is a part of life...

All religions will have <u>very strong thoughts on death</u>, as it's one of those difficult times that people have always had to face — Judaism is no exception here (take a look at page 16 for more about Jewish attitudes to death).

Jewish Prayer and the Sabbath

The Jewish holy day is the Shabbat (Sabbath), but in Judaism, prayer is important every day of the week.

There are **three** special **times** for **daily prayer**

1) Prescribed daily prayers happen at 3 special times — evening, morning and afternoon.

2) At these times, men will try to attend the synagogue and become part of a minyan — a group of at least ten men, which is the minimum needed for a service. Women (traditionally because of their domestic commitments) are trusted to pray at home.

3) As well as the normal daily prayers, there are also special prayers for when getting up, going to bed, before and after eating... in fact, pretty much every event in life, good or bad, can be a reason to pray.

*Shabbat (Sabbath) is **celebrated** in the **synagogue**...*

The Sabbath is a day of rest to commemorate the 7th Day of Creation when God rested after making the Universe. It begins at sunset on Friday, and ends on Saturday evening when stars begin to appear.

There are 3 separate services in the synagogue on the Sabbath.

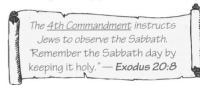
The 4th Commandment instructs Jews to observe the Sabbath. "Remember the Sabbath day by keeping it holy." — **Exodus 20:8**

FRIDAY EVENING Shabbat is welcomed as a queen or a bride with singing led by a chazan (cantor). No instruments are used — in memory of the destruction of the Temple (see page 91) with its instrumental music.

SATURDAY MORNING The main service of the week — the rabbi will read from the Torah and give a sermon. Also, seven men are called up to read or recite a blessing, and an eighth reads a portion from the Nevi'im. In Orthodox synagogues, women sit separately from the men and take little part.

SATURDAY AFTERNOON This service includes a reading from the Torah, and three special prayers.

*...and in the **home***

1) To prepare for Shabbat, the house is cleaned and tidied, and all the food to be eaten on Shabbat is cooked in advance. Family members bathe or shower. At dusk, the mother of the family will light two candles and welcome the sabbath by saying a blessing and gesturing with her arms.

2) At the beginning of the Shabbat meal, a sanctifying ceremony called kiddush takes place. It happens at home and at the synagogue, and includes the reciting of **Genesis 2:1-3** (God resting after creation). Wine is used to symbolise the sweetness and joy of Shabbat.

The Mishnah lists 39 kinds of 'work' not allowed on the Sabbath.

 3) Chalot (singular challah) are eaten — these are plaited loaves which commemorate the double portion of 'manna' which God provided the day before each Shabbat during the exodus. They are blessed, cut and dipped in salt.

4) After the father has blessed his children, the Shabbat meal is eaten.

5) The havdalah ('division') ceremony marks the end of Shabbat, separating it from the six days ahead. Blessings are said over sweet-smelling spices, a cup of wine, and over a special plaited candle.

The Shabbat is a holy day of rest and prayer...

This page describes the behaviour of observant Orthodox Jews. Progressive Jews tend to have a more relaxed attitude to things like exactly when Shabbat should begin and end, and to prayer and worship generally. Also their women are permitted to take an equal part in worship with the men.

Pilgrimage, Food and Fasting

Prayer isn't the only way to worship in Judaism...

Pilgrimage — a religious journey

Pilgrimage is a way to show devotion to God, and is a symbol of spiritual quest.

1) Before the Romans destroyed Jerusalem in 70 CE, Jews from all over Israel were expected to go up to the Temple three times a year for the 3 Pilgrim Festivals — Pesach, Sukkot and Shavuot.

2) Today there are no compulsory pilgrimages for Jews to make, but diaspora Jews (i.e. those living outside Israel) often visit the Holy Land.

Three places are particularly important to pilgrims:

The Western Wall (or Wailing Wall)
This is all that remains of the Temple (see page 91). Here many Jews mourn its destruction, and place prayers in the wall's cracks.

Yad Vashem (the Holocaust Memorial)
The names of the concentration camps are engraved in the floor of a candlelit hall.

Masada
This is a huge fortress in the Judaean desert. Here 1000 Zealots held out against the Romans from 70-73 CE. They eventually committed suicide to avoid being enslaved.

Kashrut — the Jewish food laws

1) Observant Orthodox Jews follow a special diet based on the Kashrut (Jewish food laws).

2) Permitted food is called kosher — everything else is treifah ('torn').

3) These laws were not originally laid down for reasons of health or hygiene — they are an example of statutes from God to test Jews' obedience, and to mark them out as different from other nations.

In Judaism, food is associated with happiness — so fasting shows grief or repentance. Judaism teaches that true repentance can atone (i.e. make amends) for any past transgression — 'the gates of repentance are always open'.

4) To be kosher, a mammal must have cloven (split) hooves and chew the cud. Fish with fins and scales are kosher, but no other seafood is. Some birds are also kosher.

5) Animals and birds must be specially slaughtered with one cut across the throat using a razor-sharp blade. Blood must not be eaten, and meat and dairy products must not be eaten together. Foods that aren't meat or dairy may be eaten with either.

The Days of Awe — Rosh Hashanah and Yom Kippur

These special days aren't really festivals — they're two stages in the process of judgement and atonement.

Rosh Hashanah — Jewish New Year — it falls in the autumn.

1) It's believed that God judges his people for the year's misdeeds on Rosh Hashanah, and decides what their circumstances will be in the year ahead.

2) During the last month of the old year and on Rosh Hashanah itself, a shofar (ram's horn) is blown. The shofar expresses the crying out of the soul as it yearns to be reunited with God.

3) The tashlich ('casting away') ceremony also takes place — a prayer is said to ask God to remove the sins of his people. It should be said by the bank of a river.

Between Rosh Hashanah and Yom Kippur come 10 days of repentance.

Yom Kippur — the Day of Atonement *'Atonement' means making amends for wrongdoing.*

Features include: a visit to the mikveh (ritual bath) the previous evening, fasting for 25 hours, the wearing of the kittel (white smock), chanting of the Kol Nidre ('annulment of vows') and the Neilah (closing service).

Learn the special places, food and times of year in Judaism...

By the time you've finished your revision, you'll have learnt quite a bit of Hebrew. Just make sure you learn Hebrew words carefully — there are sometimes variant spellings, so stick to the spelling you've learnt.

Jewish Festivals

These are the Jewish festivals you need to know about. So learn away...

Learn these **six** major **Jewish festivals**

FESTIVAL	WHEN	TO COMMEMORATE	FEATURES AND FOODS
Purim (Lots)	Early spring	Esther, a Jewish girl who became Queen of Persia in the 5th century BCE, saving the Jews from being annihilated by Haman.	1) The day before Purim is a fast. 2) Reading of Megillah (scroll of Esther). 3) A football rattle is used to drown out the name of Haman. 4) Fancy dress and plays.
Pesach (Passover)	Spring	The exodus from Egypt — when Moses led the Israelite slaves from Egypt to freedom. In Egypt, the angel of death killed the first-born sons of the Egyptians, but passed over the Israelites.	1) Leaven (something that makes bread rise — yeast, for example) is forbidden. 2) Seder (Passover meal) with matzah (biscuit), wine, salt water, bitter herbs, karpas (a vegetable), burnt egg, bone.
Shavuot (Weeks)	Early summer	Giving of the Torah to Moses on Mount Sinai 7 weeks after leaving Egypt.	1) Synagogues are decorated with flowers. 2) Men study the Torah all night. 3) Cheesecake is eaten.
Sukkot (Tabernacles)	Autumn	The Israelites' trek through the desert with Moses, and the shelters (tabernacles) they camped in.	1) Family decorates and lives in a 'sukkah' — a temporary shelter. 2) Use of the '4 species': etrog (citron), lulav (palm branch), aravot (willow) and hadassim (myrtle).
Simchat Torah (Rejoicing of the Torah)	Autumn	End of the annual cycle of Torah readings (and beginning of the next one).	1) Synagogue readings from the end of Deuteronomy and beginning of Genesis. 2) Men take all Torah scrolls from the Ark (see page 97) and dance round the synagogue 7 times, singing and clapping.
Hanukkah (Chanucah) (Dedication)	Winter	Victory of the Jews over the Syrian Greeks under Antiochus Epiphanes (in the 2nd century BCE).	1) Special 8-branched candlestick called a hanukiah (chanuciah) is lit. 2) Doughnuts are eaten. 3) Children play with a spinning top.

Festivals are important expressions fof religious belief...

Celebrations of the key events in a religion's history are important because they help you to remember religious messages. The best way to make sure you learn this stuff is to write it all down — then go and have a doughnut...

Warm-Up and Worked Exam Question

Warm-up Questions

1) What is the word for food NOT permitted under the Kashrut?
2) Whose duty is it to light the Sabbath candles?
3) Where would you see a Mezuzah?
4) What does Sukkot commemorate?
5) What is the Kaddish?
6) At what age does (a) a Bar Mitzvah (b) a Bat Mitzvah take place?

Worked Exam Question

Judaism has heaps of symbols, customs and ceremonies. You don't know which of them are going to crop up in your exam, so you need to know what they're all called and why each of them is special.
Here's an example of the sort of question you might get and how you could go about answering it.

1   a)   i) In the second century BCE, Jewish forces recaptured the Temple at Jerusalem from the army of Antiochus Epiphanes.
Which Jewish festival commemorates this victory?

Hannukah

It's worth learning the six major Jewish festivals, what they commemorate and their features and foods.   *(1 mark)*

ii) Describe three ways in which Jews celebrate this festival.

Jews light an eight-branched candlestick called a hanukiah and eat doughnuts. The children play with a spinning top.

(3 marks)

b)   What event that took place in 70 CE has affected Judaism ever since?

The destruction of the Temple.

(1 mark)

c)   Why is the Western Wall a place of pilgrimage and mourning for Jews?

It is all that is left of the Temple.

Yad Vashem (the Holocaust Memorial) and Masada are the other two important places of pilgrimage and mourning for Jews.   *(1 mark)*

d)   Explain why a Jewish father makes a symbolic payment of five silver coins when his first born son is thirty days old.

Because originally all first-born sons became priests. Nowadays the father makes the payment to ceremonially release his son from the priesthood.

(2 marks)

Exam Questions

2   The pictures below show objects that are important in Jewish customs or worship.
    Name each item and explain how it is used.

a)

b)

c)

(6 marks)

3   a)   Briefly explain Jewish beliefs about sheol.

(4 marks)

   b)   Describe Jewish customs for respectfully dealing with the body of a person
        who has died.

(4 marks)

4   a)   What does the Jewish Shabbat commemorate?

(1 mark)

   b)   Why is the food to be eaten on Shabbat cooked in advance?

(1 mark)

   c)   When does Shabbat begin and end?

(2 marks)

   d)   Explain when and how Jews celebrate Shabbat in the synagogue.

(6 marks)

   e)   Describe how Jews celebrate Shabbat in the home.

(6 marks)

5   "People should be left to choose their own religion once they become adults,
    rather than have one forced upon them during childhood."

    Do you agree? Refer to Judaism in your answer and show that you have considered more
    than one point of view.

(6 marks)

Basic Islamic Beliefs

This stuff is the absolute <u>fundamentals</u> of Islam.
You won't get very far in your study of Islam if you don't know something about <u>Tawhid</u> and the <u>Five Pillars</u>.

Tawhid is the belief in the **Oneness of God**

1) Islam teaches that <u>nothing</u> is remotely like <u>Allah</u>, and nothing can be compared to him.

2) The worst sin for a Muslim would be to believe that God was <u>not</u> supreme —
   this concept is called <u>Shirk</u>. (Shirk is the opposite of tawhid.)

Allah is the Muslim name for <u>God</u>.

And see pages 9 and 11 for more basic Muslim beliefs about God.

> **Muslim beliefs about Allah...**
> Allah is beyond time and space. He is the Almighty One, the Compassionate and the Merciful. All men and women owe their creation, and continued existence, to Allah — the One and Only Creator.

The Five Pillars — a guide to Islam

For Muslims, there is no point in having faith if you don't act on your beliefs.
And this action should be based on the <u>Five Pillars</u> — which are a kind of <u>guide</u> to Muslim life:

 SHAHADAH — the Muslim Declaration of Faith

"There is no god but Allah, and Muhammad is the Prophet of Allah."
Muslims should repeat this <u>several times a day</u>.

See pages 119 and 120 for more info about the Five Pillars of Islam.

 SALAH — Prayer five times a day

This is the <u>second</u> most important duty in Islam, and should be learnt from the age of 12. <u>Exposed</u> parts of the body, including feet and inside the mouth and nostrils, are <u>washed</u> three times before praying. If you happen to be waterless (e.g. in the desert) clean sand will do instead of water. This washing is called <u>wudu</u>.

 ZAKAH — Giving money or possessions to help the poor, sick and needy

It's <u>compulsory</u> in Islam, and the minimum is 2.5% of your disposable income.
Each individual decides whether to give to a relative, to a charity, or to the poor — but come the <u>Day of Judgement</u>, you have to justify your decision.

 SAWM — Obligation to fast in Ramadan

<u>Ramadan</u> is the 9th month of the Muslim calendar, and celebrates Muhammad first receiving the revelation of the <u>Qur'an</u>. No food or drink can pass your lips during daylight hours — not even a cigarette or toothpaste are allowed. This <u>fasting</u> teaches self-discipline, which is believed to draw Muslims closer to Allah.

 HAJJ — Pilgrimage to Makkah at least once in your life (if you're healthy and wealthy enough)

This journey-of-a-lifetime is believed to teach <u>equality</u> — all men wear two unsewn cotton sheets, and women are covered from head to foot. So it doesn't matter how fat your wallet is — you're just like <u>everyone else</u> (like on the Day of Judgement).

Niyyah — it's the thought that counts...

In Islam, it's your <u>intention</u> (<u>Niyyah</u>) that's the key to how you're judged. If you fully intended doing something and you fail, it's counted as though you'd done it anyway. Unfortunately, this principle isn't carried over into your <u>Exam</u>, which seems a bit <u>harsh</u> really, if it's good enough for all other areas of life.

Prophets and Angels

According to the Qur'an, the <u>prophets</u> bring God's message so that people know how to behave. These prophets are <u>not</u> angels, they're <u>humans</u> — though they <u>receive</u> the message from an <u>angel</u>.

Risalah is the idea that Allah uses messengers

1) <u>Risalah</u> is the concept of <u>messengership</u>, which is necessary in Islam because Allah is so great. He doesn't communicate directly with humans — instead he uses angels as messengers. Angels are created by Allah, require no food, drink or sleep, and obey Allah perfectly.

2) His mercy and compassion mean he cannot leave us to mess up our lives without doing something to help. So God gives messages to angels, who then pass on God's words to <u>prophets</u> (or <u>rasuls</u>).

3) In the Qur'an, the first man and the first prophet was <u>Adam</u>.

4) Allah sent many prophets as messengers, maybe because we seem to forget the plot quite quickly. The names of <u>25</u> prophets are mentioned in the Qur'an, although Muslim tradition suggests there have been 124,000.

Five Prophets are 'Mighty Ones'

1) Of all Allah's prophets, five are Mighty Ones. These are <u>Nuh</u> (Noah), <u>Ibrahim</u> (Abraham), <u>Musa</u> (Moses), <u>Isa</u> (Jesus) and <u>Muhammad</u>.

2) <u>Ibrahim</u> rejected the idea of many <u>different</u> gods, and it was Ibrahim who rebuilt the <u>Ka'ba</u> (the first structure built to worship one god) in <u>Makkah</u>. Ibrahim was also told by God to <u>sacrifice his son</u> as a test of his faith. After seeing that Ibrahim was prepared to do this, God told Ibrahim to kill a <u>ram</u> instead.

3) <u>Moses</u> is the only prophet that God spoke to <u>directly</u> rather than through the Angel Gabriel. He was given the tablets of the law (which Muslims believe is the foundation of all religion) on <u>Mount Sinai</u>. The <u>Tawrat</u> (Jews call it the Torah) is the Holy Book inspired by Moses.

According to Islam, the <u>Zabur</u> (a book like the Book of Psalms) was revealed to <u>King David</u> (see page 91 for more about David).

*Allah said, "O Jesus I am gathering you and causing you to ascend to Me, and am cleansing you of those who disbelieve, and am setting those who follow you above those who disbelieve." — **Surah 3:55***

The <u>Injil</u> (Gospel) was given to <u>Isa</u> (<u>Jesus</u>) according to Islam. It gives accounts of miracles, and explains the amazing life of Isa. But don't forget, Isa was just a <u>prophet</u> according to the Qur'an.

4) Allah sent <u>Isa</u> (Jesus) when he thought that humans had strayed from the teachings of Moses yet again. According to Islam, Isa was not <u>crucified</u> (God wouldn't allow it to happen) but after three years teaching he was taken up bodily into heaven to be with Allah.

5) <u>Muhammad</u> was the prophet to whom God revealed the <u>Qur'an</u>, in Arabic, for humanity to follow. Islam teaches that the Qur'an is the greatest <u>miracle</u> of all.

Khalifah — taking responsibility in God's name

1) Muslims believe in the idea of Judgement Day, when God will judge us on the basis of our actions. This suggests we have <u>free will</u>, and can choose how we act.

2) But Muslims also believe God has a divine <u>master plan</u> where everything is determined by him. In Islam this isn't a problem — we're not like God, and so we can't expect to understand all God's ways. *<u>Al-Qadar</u> is the Muslim idea of Allah's complete and final <u>control</u> over all events and destiny.*

3) <u>Khalifah</u> is the idea that while we're on Earth we should take responsibility for the world in God's name, and make it the sort of place he wants it to be. However, if we fail to manage our task Allah will send help, which shows his <u>compassion</u> and <u>mercy</u>.

Muhammad is the Seal of the Prophets...
This comes from the Qur'an — it means Muhammad's like the <u>seal</u> people used to attach to a <u>letter</u> to prove it had come from them, and to make sure nothing could be added. Muhammad was <u>God's seal</u>.

The Qur'an

Muslims believe the Qur'an is the most important book in the world, as it records the exact words of Allah (God). They call these words revelations, because they were revealed by Allah to the Prophet Muhammad.

The Qur'an is treated with respect

For Muslims, the Qur'an is...

1 **A complete record of Allah's words:** The Prophet never forgot any revelations, and his followers recorded them at once, and learned them by heart.

2 **a totally accurate and unchanged record** The early Caliph (Muslim ruler) Uthman made sure there was only one version and that it was completely correct.

3 **a complete guide to Islamic life** The Qur'an says what Muslims must believe, and how they must live, in order to get to Paradise. In the Qur'an, Allah tells Muslims what they need to know, so that they can please him. Since Muslims believe the Qur'an came direct from Allah, they trust it completely. Basically, if the Qur'an says 'Do this,' then a Muslim must do it.

4 **always in Arabic** Allah gave the Qur'an to the Prophet Muhammad in Arabic. If you read it in another language, you might not get the proper meaning. So all Muslims must learn Arabic to be sure they are reading the real Qur'an.

Because the Qur'an is so important, Muslims treat it with great respect. Many Muslims will:

1) keep their Qur'an wrapped up to keep it clean,

2) wash their hands before touching it,

3) keep it on a higher shelf than all other books,

4) place it on a special stand when they read it.

The Qur'an is also read during private and public prayers, so Muslims get to know it really well. In the month of Ramadan, it's read from beginning to end during worship at the mosque.

The Qur'an is divided into 114 surahs

1) The Qur'an is organised into 114 surahs (chapters).

2) The surahs are arranged in order of length — longest first, shortest last (apart from Surah 1, the Fatihah, which is a short and punchy statement of central beliefs).

3) Each surah is made up of ayats (verses).

4) Most surahs begin with the bismillah — an Arabic phrase meaning 'In the name of Allah, the Merciful, the Compassionate'. This means that when Muslims start to read any Surah, they are reminded of the mercy and kindness of Allah.

The Hadith and the Sunnah are also important texts

Muslims also pay a lot of attention to the guidance and example they get from the following:

1 **THE HADITH** — the sayings of Muhammad which were not part of the Qur'an.

2 **THE SUNNAH** — the actions and way of life of Muhammad.

Because Muhammad was chosen by Allah to be his last Prophet, they regard him as a very remarkable man, and pay special attention to his words and actions.

The Qur'an describes what Allah is like...

When Muslims read the Qur'an, they're learning about how Allah relates to humans, and how to live the way Allah wants so they can get to Paradise and avoid the 'unpleasantness' of Hell. Important stuff — so learn it...

The Prophet Muhammad

A pretty central figure in Islam. If you're studying Islam, you'll want to know *all* this...

Muhammad's *early* life was *hard*

1) Muhammad was <u>born</u> around the year 570 AD/CE in <u>Makkah</u> (also known as <u>Mecca</u>).
He had a <u>hard</u> childhood, after his parents died while he was young.

2) He <u>married</u> his widowed employer <u>Khadijah</u> at around the age of 25
— he had previously worked as her business manager.

3) The people of Makkah <u>respected</u> him, and called him <u>Al-Amin</u> — 'Mr Trustworthy'.

Life changed in *610 CE* — the call to be a *prophet*

While he was meditating in a cave on <u>Mount Nur</u>, Allah sent the angel <u>Jibrail</u> (Gabriel) to him...

1) Jibrail passed on Allah's first command to Muhammad, *"Read, in the name of your
Lord, who creates man out of a mere drop of blood."* — **Surah 96**.

*The letters 'pbuh' or 'pboh' are
sometimes written after the
name of Muhammad. They stand
for '<u>Peace be upon</u> (or <u>on</u>) Him'.*

2) Although Muhammad was initially <u>frightened</u>, Khadijah helped him realise that
God was calling him to be a <u>prophet</u>.

3) This was <u>confirmed</u> by the second command, *"Rise and Warn."* — **Surah 74**. As
time went on, Muhammad received loads more <u>revelations</u> from Allah.

This was the message that Muhammad had to take to the people of Makkah:

i) People were to worship <u>one God</u>, <u>Allah</u> — not many gods.	iii) People were to conduct their business <u>honestly</u>, and to look after the <u>poor</u>.
ii) People were to listen to him, because he was <u>Allah's Prophet</u>.	iv) If they did <u>not</u> do all this, they would burn in <u>Hell</u>.

4) Although a few people were <u>converted</u>, this was <u>not</u> a popular message. At first people laughed at him, or said
he was mad. Then they started making life hard for his followers — even <u>killing</u> some. They also stopped
Muhammad preaching within the city limits.

5) Finally, in 622, the Prophet and his followers had to <u>leave</u> Makkah. Muhammad was invited to become the
leader of a place called Yathrib, which was eventually named after him — <u>Madinah</u> (or <u>Medina</u>) short for
<u>Medina Nabi</u>, 'City of the Prophet'. Things got better for the Muslims in Madinah.

6) The journey to Madinah is called the <u>Hijrah</u> or the <u>Emigration</u>.
It was a real turning point. Now, in the safety of Madinah, the
Muslims could make many more <u>converts</u>, build a Muslim
<u>community</u>, and develop their own way of life.

7) Many people see this as the real <u>start</u> of Islam — even the
Muslim <u>calendar</u> starts from the Hijrah in 622.

Madinah and *Makkah* went to *war*

After the Hijrah, Madinah and Makkah were at war. The key events are these...

1) 624 — <u>Battle of Badr</u>. Muhammad won and became very popular in Madinah.

2) 625 — <u>Battle of Uhud</u>. Close, but Muhammad came out ahead on points.

3) 627 — <u>Battle of the Trench</u>. A brilliant victory for Muhammad, leading to...

4) 628 — <u>Treaty of Hudaybiya</u> – preparing the way for a Muslim takeover of Makkah in 630.

5) By Muhammad's death in 632, Makkah was a Muslim city and Islam was advancing through Arabia.

Make sure you learn why the Hijrah was so important...

There are lots of important facts on this page — and the best way to learn them is to read, cover, then write...

Different Islamic Traditions

In <u>Madinah</u>, Muhammad and his followers formed a <u>single</u> community. But this didn't last. After he died, Muslims <u>disagreed</u> about who should be the next leader. This eventually led to a <u>split</u>.

Sunnis and Shi'ites split after the death of Ali

1) The next four leaders after Muhammad were chosen because they were <u>good Muslims</u> and <u>competent leaders</u>. These successors (or 'caliphs') were:

i) Abu Bakr: 632-634 CE   ii) Umar: 634-644 CE   iii) Uthman: 644-656 CE   iv) Ali: 656-661 CE

2) However, some Muslims had wanted Muhammad's close relative <u>Ali</u> to be the first leader after Muhammad's death. Others said Ali should <u>never</u> be leader at all.

3) After Ali's death, two groups were formed — the <u>Sunnis</u> and the <u>Shi'ites</u>. Each group followed a different <u>succession</u> of leaders.

4) The <u>Sunni</u> accepted the next <u>caliph</u> (successor), but the <u>Shi'ites</u> (Shi'at Ali or Party of Ali) followed Ali's <u>descendants</u>.

5) Sunnis call the first four leaders after Muhammad the '<u>Rightly Guided Caliphs</u>'. Shi'ites, on the other hand, believe the first three caliphs shouldn't have been leaders at all.

6) Sunnis and Shi'ites have been <u>separate</u> groups ever since the split, and often in <u>conflict</u>.

The majority of Muslims are Sunnis

In Sunni mosques, <u>imam</u> is simply a title of <u>respect</u> given to the mosque <u>prayer leader</u>. This is very different to Shi'ite beliefs.

About 90% of Muslims are <u>Sunni</u> (or orthodox) Muslims. They believe:

1) The Rightly Guided Caliphs (including Ali) were <u>properly</u> chosen.

2) The followers of Ali were <u>wrong</u> to break away from the majority.

3) No one after Muhammad gets special knowledge <u>from God</u> (including <u>imams</u>).

4) Muslims should be guided by the <u>consensus</u> (majority view) of the community. In particular, it's the <u>community</u> that <u>elects</u> the caliphs. This is how the Rightly Guided Caliphs were chosen.

5) Paying special attention to Ali and his sons takes attention away from <u>Allah</u> and his <u>Prophet</u> (Muhammad), and is <u>wrong</u>.

6) The <u>Qur'an</u> is <u>complete</u> and <u>unaltered</u>, just as Allah revealed it to Muhammad.

Shi'ite Muslims have some different beliefs

<u>Shi'ite</u> Muslims are also referred to as <u>Shi'i</u>, <u>Shi'a</u> or <u>Shi'ah</u> Muslims. They believe:

1) <u>Ali</u> was the first <u>true</u> leader after Muhammad, and all other leaders of Islam should be <u>descendants</u> of Muhammad.

2) Ali had special knowledge given by <u>God</u> to make sure his teaching and actions were <u>right</u>. After him, other leaders called <u>imams</u> had this knowledge too.

3) The last imam (most say the 12th, but some the 7th) went into <u>hiding</u>, and since then other leaders have been chosen by <u>him</u>. The most important of these are called <u>ayatollahs</u> (signs of Allah).

An important group of Shi'ites believe that the 12th and last imam is still in hiding, but will eventually return to revitalise the Muslim community.

4) They take guidance from the Hadith (sayings) of <u>Ali</u>, as well as those of <u>Muhammad</u>.

5) They commemorate the <u>martyrdom</u> of Ali and his sons <u>Hasan</u> and <u>Husayn</u> — they have festivals concerned with Ali and his sons, and make pilgrimage to places connected with them.

The Festival of Ashura

The most important festival is <u>Ashura</u>, celebrated on the <u>10th day</u> of the month of <u>Muharram</u> at <u>Karbala</u>, where Husayn was killed. Shi'ites perform rituals re-enacting the event, and some even wound themselves to share in his suffering.

6) Some Shi'ites believe that the Qur'an was <u>altered</u> by the Sunnis, so that verses which would back up the Shi'ites were got rid of.

Muslim traditions are different, but similar in many ways...

Don't forget that Sunnis and Shi'ites agree on a lot of <u>important</u> stuff — like Allah and Muhammad...

Sufism

For <u>Sufis</u> (as for all Muslims) the <u>Qur'an</u> is the fundamental guide in matters relating to their religious faith. What makes Sufis different from other Muslims is the way they <u>interpret</u> this guide.

Sufism is a **mystical movement**

1) <u>Sufism</u> is often called <u>Islamic mysticism</u> — the aim is to be at one with God and reach truths beyond human understanding. It developed as a <u>reaction</u> to the growing attachment to a life of making money.

2) For <u>Sufis</u>, a symbolic or mystical meaning lies <u>beneath</u> the actual words of the Qur'an. To find this meaning, it's necessary to <u>purify</u> your thoughts and actions, and be constantly aware of the love of God in order to achieve a '<u>joining together</u>' with Allah.

3) Sufis believe that the <u>Prophet Muhammad</u> is the man who most perfectly achieved this close relationship with God — so they try to imitate his way of life. They live a <u>humble</u> life — based on <u>asceticism</u> (self-denial) and <u>meditation</u>, and make use of <u>ritual</u> practices, like sacred dances or chanting.

4) Sufis have tried to show that the heart of Islam is not how a Muslim <u>practises</u> their faith, but the <u>bond</u> between each person and God. In other words Sufis encourage Muslims to look at their relationship with God, instead of just obeying the <u>rules</u>.

> "It is not enough to observe the rituals of Islam... A humble soul may be religious even though ignorant of interpretations of the Qur'an. The core of religion is to repent of one's sins, purge the heart of all but God."
> — 12th century Sufi philosopher <u>Al-Ghazzali</u>.

Jalaluddin Rumi (a 13th century Sufi master) founded a group which uses music and dance to <u>spin</u> at speed. The spinning of these '<u>Whirling Dervishes</u>' is said to lead to a trancelike state, and is regarded as a form of prayer.

Women have played a **big part** in Sufism

1) <u>Women</u> have played a big part in Sufism from its beginnings. <u>Fatima</u> (the daughter of Muhammad and his wife <u>Khadijah</u>) is often regarded as the first Muslim mystic.

2) And as the mystical side of Islam developed, it was a woman, <u>Rabi'a al-Adawiyya</u>, who first described God as the "<u>Beloved</u>". She also gave meaning to the idea that ultimately it is through <u>love</u> that people are brought into unity with God.

Sufism is **different** to other **Islamic traditions**

Sufism's ideas about the relationship between <u>people</u> and <u>God</u> are different from other Islamic traditions.

1) Islam is based on the idea of <u>duty</u> — the word <u>Muslim</u> even means 'one who surrenders his or her life to Allah'. Muslims must follow the <u>Five Pillars</u> and the teaching of the Qur'an.

2) Muslims generally emphasise the radical <u>difference</u> between God and human beings.

3) The idea promoted by some Sufi groups of <u>merging</u> with God would not be acceptable to many Muslims.

Variety is the spice of life...
Religion is like any other 'people' thing — people are different, and will want different things from their religion. Make sure you understand how and why the different Islamic traditions are... erm... different.

Islam and the Shari'ah

'Islam' literally means 'submission' or 'obedience' to Allah. And there are certain day-to-day rules that Allah expects you to follow if you want to <u>show</u> that you're being obedient.

Being **obedient to Allah** is vital for a **Muslim**

The reasons why Muslims should be <u>obedient</u> are as follows...

> 1) Allah <u>expects</u> obedience, and obedience is a Muslim's <u>duty</u>.
> 2) If a Muslim does his or her duty, that person will <u>please</u> Allah.
> 3) If a person pleases Allah enough, they will be sent to <u>Paradise</u> after they die.
> 4) And if Allah is <u>not</u> pleased with someone, they will be <u>punished</u> after they die.

So this is <u>vital</u> stuff. How a Muslim lives in <u>this</u> life will determine where he or she ends up in the <u>next</u> life.

The **Shari'ah** contains the **rules** for **Islamic life**

Fortunately, Allah makes sure Muslims know <u>what</u> to do and <u>how</u> to live.

1) The first and most important source of guidance for a Muslim is the <u>Qur'an</u>. But this doesn't give every <u>detail</u>, and it doesn't talk about <u>21st-century</u> issues — like drugs, for example.

2) So Muslims need extra <u>day-to-day</u> guidance — and this is found in the law-code called the <u>Shari'ah</u>.

'Shari'ah' means 'straight path' in Arabic — and it keeps Muslims 'going straight'. If Muslims obey the Shari'ah, they can be sure they're doing what Allah wants.

The **Shari'ah** is **based** on the **Qur'an**

Scholars and lawyers built up much of the <u>Shari'ah</u> from the following three sources in the early years of Islam. They're the most <u>important</u> sources of Islamic law.

 The Qur'an   The Shari'ah is based on the <u>Qur'an</u>. Any moral guidance in the Qur'an is <u>bound</u> to be in the Shari'ah.

 The Hadith and Sunnah   The Shari'ah also takes guidance from the <u>Hadith</u> (sayings) and <u>Sunnah</u> (lifestyle) of Muhammad.

 Muslim custom and practice   It then looks to the <u>custom</u> and <u>practice</u> of the Muslim community, especially if it can be traced back to the time when <u>Muhammad</u> was alive.

But if the first three don't help with some <u>new</u> problem, the scholars will appeal to <u>two more</u>:

 Consensus or agreement   Based on their knowledge of the <u>Qur'an</u> and of <u>Islamic tradition</u>, the most <u>learned scholars</u> would reach an agreement about how to act. They trust Allah to make sure they get it right.

 Analogy or Similarity   If they <u>can't</u> find guidance on any particular issue, they look for guidance on something <u>similar</u>. The Qur'an says nothing about <u>heroin</u>, for example, but it does forbid <u>alcohol</u>. Both are bad for the user, so the scholars can work out that if alcohol is out, then so are other drugs.

Drawing on all these, the Shari'ah covers the whole of a Muslim's life.

The Shari'ah sets the rules Muslims live by...

So that's pretty much where Islamic law comes from then. And it's pretty important too. Well, it certainly is if you're a Muslim, anyway. And it certainly is if you're studying Islam and you've got an Exam coming up. So although I'm not <u>actually</u> God, I command you to learn all the above. For your own sake, of course.

Warm-Up and Worked Exam Questions

Warm-up Questions

1) What is Al-Qadar?
2) Who are the 5 most important Muslim prophets?
3) Why is the Sunnah important?
4) What is the Hijrah?
5) Where was Muhammad born?
6) What is Shari'ah law?

Worked Exam Questions

Here's a couple of worked exam questions to get your brain juices flowing before you have a go at the practice questions on the next page. Make sure you understand these examples.

1 a) Explain what the word Islam means.

The word Islam means submission or obedience to Allah.

(1 mark)

b) Briefly describe each of the five Pillars of Islam.

Shahadah — The Muslim declaration of faith.

Make sure you know the names of the Pillars and what they are off by heart.

Salah — Obligatory ritual prayer five times a day.

Zakah — Giving charity or alms to help the poor, sick or needy.

Sawm — Obligatory fasting during the month of Ramadan.

Hajj — Making pilgrimage to Makkah at least once in your life.

(5 marks)

2 a) Explain why there are two different Muslim traditions – Sunnis and Shi'ites.

There are two different Muslim traditions because there was a spilt after the death of Ali. Ali was a relative of Muhammad and some Muslims wanted him to lead the faith — but others did not. After Ali died, those who followed his descendants became known as Shi'ites. The rest formed a separate group — the Sunnis.

Make sure you know these Islamic traditions and how and why they differ from each other. *(4 marks)*

b) How is Sufism different from other forms of Islam?

Sufism concentrates on an individual's relationship with Allah. There is less emphasis on following rules and certain practices. Sufism teaches that there is a mystical meaning in the Qu'ran. Sufis try to live a humble life based on meditation and self-denial. Ritual dancing and chanting are used to get closer to Allah.

(5 marks)

Exam Questions

3   What is the difference between Tawhid and Shirk?

(2 marks)

4   Describe the concept of Khalifah and why it is important to how a Muslim lives his or her life.

(3 marks)

5   Compare Sunni and Shi'ite Muslims.

(10 marks)

6   a)   How did Allah communicate with Muhammad? Explain why he did not communicate with him directly.

(3 marks)

   b)   What important messages did Muhammad give the people of Makkah?

(4 marks)

   c)   How did the citizens of Makkah react to Muhammad's message?

(3 marks)

7   a)   The Qur'an is the most important book in Islam.

      i)   What does Islam teach about the Qur'an?

(5 marks)

      ii)   How do Muslims show their respect for the Qur'an?

(4 marks)

   b)   The Qur'an does not cover every area of a Muslim's life, especially 21st-century issues. Describe how a modern-day Muslim may find extra guidance.

(6 marks)

   c)   "Living your life in a good, caring and honest way is more important than following rules written down in a holy book."

      Do you agree? Give reasons for your answer, showing that you have thought about more than one point of view. Refer to Islam in your answer.

(8 marks)

Islamic Living and Jihad

You need to know about some particular bits of the Shari'ah laws which affect a Muslim's daily life.

The Shari'ah says things are either halal or haram

HALAL means 'allowed'   **HARAM means 'forbidden'**

You need to know these two Arabic words. Think of the letter L — haLaL is aLLowed. And HARaM can HARM.

Dress laws — basic principles are modesty and cleanliness

1) Everyone should wear loose, modest clothing, so they don't arouse desire. (Sexy figure-hugging clothes are definitely out.)

2) Outside the home, women should wear the hijab (a veil which covers the hair) so that nothing is visible but the face, hands and feet.

3) Men should not wear flashy clothing — e.g. no silk or gold jewellery.

Some Muslims say this is out of date, especially in western countries, but others stick to it because it was the custom of Muhammad's own wives.

Food laws — no pork, no blood

1) The basic rules are no pork, no blood at all, and no animals that eat meat.

2) This means it's very important how an animal is killed — it must be done by slitting the neck and allowing all the blood to drain out. Meat from animals killed like this is halal, i.e. allowed.

3) Food preparation is also important — no animal fat can be used (but vegetable oil is okay).

4) Fish and vegetables are fine, but they must be cooked without animal fat.

Alcohol and gambling are definitely out

Alcohol is definitely not allowed (see page 53), and neither is gambling. This is due to the damage they can cause to yourself and others — and it's a basic principle of Shari'ah that a Muslim should not harm others.

i) The thinking is that people do stupid things when they're drunk, and don't think about obeying Allah. They also hurt others with behaviour like drink-driving.

ii) And if you win money by gambling, it is only because someone else has lost it.

No charging interest on loans

Charging high rates of interest on loans is called usury — in Arabic this is called riba.

Shari'ah also forbids any financial deals involving interest. This is to prevent rich people making more money at the expense of poorer people, and to make sure wealth is spread more fairly. This means Muslims can't use most Western bank accounts. Also, Muslim businesses must be run differently from others, because the Western economic system depends on lending money and charging interest. So Muslims really need a separate banking system.

There are two kinds of Jihad

Jihad in Arabic means 'striving', and is often misunderstood by non-Muslims. Most Muslims believe there are two kinds of Jihad.

THE GREATER JIHAD

This is every Muslim's personal struggle to obey Allah, follow Shari'ah and become a better Muslim. It's a tough spiritual struggle, lasts a lifetime, and affects every aspect of life. But winning this struggle gets you to Paradise.

THE LESSER JIHAD

This is the struggle to make the world a better place. Part of this means struggling against evils like poverty and injustice, and part of it is the struggle to defend Islam against its enemies. However, both the Qur'an and the Shari'ah teach that this should only be in self-defence. There's a big debate over where terrorism fits in, but most Muslims stick with the simple rule that killing is wrong (haram) except in personal self-defence.

See also page 52.

The Mosque

A <u>mosque</u> (or <u>masjid</u>) is more than a place of worship — it's also a centre of the community for Muslims. Masjid literally means 'place of prostration' (i.e. lying with the face down) — an act of <u>submission</u> to Allah (God).

A mosque (*masjid*) is the Muslim *house of prayer*

1) The Prophet Muhammad said that any <u>clean</u> place could be used for worship.

2) Some mosques are extremely <u>simple</u>, others are very grand, but all have a <u>dome</u> representing the universe.

3) All mosques will have at least one <u>minaret</u>. This is a tall tower from where the <u>muezzin</u> (<u>mu'adhin</u> in Arabic) calls the <u>adhan</u> (<u>call to prayer</u>).

"Muhammad"

"Allah"

Inside the mosque

1) Beautiful coloured <u>mosaic</u> tiles, or richly coloured Arabic <u>calligraphy</u> (writing) often decorate both the outside and inside of a mosque.

2) <u>Shoes</u> must be left at the door, and every mosque must have somewhere for Muslims to <u>wash</u> before prayer.

3) There are no <u>pictures</u> of Muhammad or Allah, since no one is allowed to draw them.

4) There are no <u>seats</u>, but the whole floor is usually covered with rich carpet.

5) There is little in the way of furniture, but you will see a pulpit (called a <u>minbar</u>), where the <u>imam</u> (a respected person) will lead prayers from — especially on Fridays.

6) Muslims face Makkah when they pray, and a special niche (called the <u>mihrab</u>) in the 'direction-wall' shows the direction in which Makkah lies.

MEN, WOMEN AND THE MOSQUE
The main service in the Mosque is on <u>Friday</u>, and all males are expected to attend unless they're ill or travelling. <u>Women</u> don't have to attend the mosque, but if they do they must pray <u>separately</u> from men. Also, women do not lead prayers in a mosque if a man is available, but they may lead other women and children.

Apart from prayer, a mosque is used as a <u>Madrassah</u> (a Mosque school), where Muslims learn the general <u>principles</u> of Islam, as well as how to carry out Muslim <u>practices</u> and recite the <u>Qur'an</u>.

Sunni imams are different from Shi'ite imams

1) In the <u>Sunni</u> Muslim tradition (about 90% of all Muslims are Sunni), the imam is sometimes a paid member of the community. However, any person who has a good knowledge of Islam and is of good character can act as imam, and anyone who knows the prayer can lead it.

2) The imam teaches about the Qur'an, and leads the prayers, but he is <u>not</u> a '<u>holy man</u>'. He may also <u>visit</u> the sick, and <u>care</u> for those who have had a death in the family.

3) In the minority <u>Shi'ite</u> Muslim tradition, the imam is <u>different</u> — he is a successor of Muhammad, and is considered <u>semi-divine</u>.

You need to learn about mosques — inside and out...

The <u>mosque</u> is central to an Islamic community — and is much more than just a place to go and <u>pray</u>. This business of praying <u>in the direction of Makkah</u> is also taken seriously — some Muslims carry a special <u>compass</u> to enable them to pray in the right direction, even when they're nowhere near a mosque.

Worship and Prayer

To a Muslim <u>all life</u> is worship. Every part of life is lived in a way that will please Allah and show obedience to him. If it's done with Allah in mind, then it's <u>worship</u>. It all comes down to the <u>Five Pillars</u> of Islam.

Muslim worship is all about the Five Pillars

Shahadah — the First Pillar of Islam

'*There is no God but Allah, and Muhammad is the Prophet of Allah.*'
This leads to <u>obligations</u> — if Allah's the <u>only</u> God, then Muslims should <u>pray</u> to Allah, and <u>only</u> to Allah.

Salah (prayer) — the Second Pillar

You can't be a Muslim without <u>praying</u> in the way Muhammad did. Regular prayer keeps Allah in a Muslim's mind. It also keeps Muslims aware of their <u>duty</u> to obey Allah.

1) Muslims should pray <u>five times</u> a day — at sunrise, early afternoon, late afternoon, after sunset, and late at night.

2) The <u>muezzin</u> makes the call to prayer (<u>adhan</u>) from the <u>minaret</u> of a <u>mosque</u>. (The words of the call to prayer are on page 121.)

3) Ideally prayer should take place in a <u>mosque</u>. If this isn't possible, a <u>prayer mat</u> should be used to make a prayer place.

4) <u>Wudu</u> (washing before prayer) is important (see page 108). This is because a Muslim must be <u>pure</u> and <u>clean</u> when approaching Allah.

Women and men pray separately — so people keep their mind on Allah rather than on the opposite sex.

5) A Muslim should face <u>Makkah</u> (Muhammad's place of birth) when praying. The direction of Makkah is called the <u>qiblah</u>. A compass can be used to find the qiblah (which in England is roughly southeast).

Salah is <u>compulsory</u> prayer. Extra prayers are called <u>Du'a</u>, and Muslims can do these at <u>any time</u>. In Du'a prayers, <u>beads</u> can be used — 99 beads for the 99 names of Allah.

6) There is a set <u>ritual</u> for prayer — this is known as the <u>rak'ah</u> (and the rak'ah may be repeated <u>several</u> times at each prayer session). Each rak'ah involves <u>standing</u>, then <u>kneeling</u>, then putting your <u>forehead</u> to the ground as a sign of submission. Whilst doing these movements certain words are recited such as 'Allahu Akbar' (God is great).

7) If several Muslims are praying in one place, then they all do the ritual <u>together</u> as a sign of <u>unity</u>.

8) <u>Friday</u> prayers are called <u>Salat-al-Jum'ah</u> (or just <u>Jum'ah</u>) — it's a community occasion, and at least 40 people should be there, all praying together.

Benefits of Prayer
1) Keeps you in close <u>contact</u> with Allah and stops you <u>forgetting</u> him.
2) Expression of <u>solidarity</u> — doing exactly the <u>same</u> as all other Muslims.
3) Moral and spiritual <u>discipline</u>.

Problems with Praying in 'non-Muslim' countries

In <u>non-Muslim</u> countries it can often be hard to pray at the right time, e.g. when you have to go to <u>school</u> or <u>work</u>. This is one of the ways in which life is more <u>complicated</u> for Muslims if they live in a country where Islam is <u>not</u> the way of life of most people.

Zakah — the Third Pillar

This is another <u>practical</u> way of showing obedience — it's a way of <u>redistributing</u> wealth to poorer Muslims.

1) Wealth is <u>given</u> by Allah, so it should be used to <u>serve</u> Allah.

2) The amount donated is usually 2.5% of a person's disposable income. It's given to the <u>mosque</u> and is then <u>redistributed</u> to needy Muslims, or used for religious purposes like Muslim schools.

3) It's a sign of <u>concern</u> for others and encourages <u>unselfishness</u>.

4) A Muslim <u>must</u> pay zakah, but giving extra charity is also okay (see page 45).

Worship and Prayer

The last two pillars of Islam are to do with <u>fasting</u> and <u>pilgrimage</u>.

Sawm — the Fourth Pillar of Islam

1) Muslims must <u>fast</u> between <u>sunrise</u> and <u>sunset</u> during the month of <u>Ramadan</u> in the Muslim calendar.

2) This fasting means no <u>food</u>, no <u>drink</u>, no <u>smoking</u> and no <u>sex</u>.

3) Also, there must be no angry words, no swearing, no gossiping, no lying and no bad behaviour.

4) Ramadan is a time of both physical and moral <u>self-discipline</u>, and a time of <u>total</u> obedience to Allah.

5) It's supposed to help Muslims <u>understand</u> hunger, and so makes them more <u>willing</u> to help others.

6) It's also a time to show publicly that Allah matters more than any <u>physical</u> needs.

There are <u>exceptions</u> to the normal Ramadan rules:

1) <u>Children</u> don't have to fast until they're about 12 years old.

2) People can be excused for <u>medical</u> reasons. Those who are <u>ill</u> (and women having their <u>period</u>) are excused. And it's okay to take <u>medicine</u> which has to be regular, e.g. antibiotics.

3) If you're on a <u>journey</u>, you can be excused. But you have to <u>make up</u> the missed days later.

Thanksgiving for the Qur'an

Ramadan is also the month Muhammad received the first <u>revelation</u> of the <u>Qur'an</u>. So the Ramadan fast is also a period of <u>thanksgiving</u> for the Qur'an, and over the month of Ramadan it's read from beginning to end during prayers at the mosque.

Id-ul-Fitr

<u>Id-ul-Fitr</u> is a joyful day marking the <u>end</u> of Ramadan. Muslims attend the mosque for special prayers to <u>thank</u> Allah for the benefits of Ramadan, and often exchange cards and have family parties. However, the important thing is the fast, <u>not</u> the end of it.

Hajj (pilgrimage to Makkah) — the Fifth Pillar

1) Muslims must make the pilgrimage <u>once</u> in their <u>lifetime</u>, as long as they can <u>afford</u> it and they are <u>strong</u> enough to cope with it.

2) Hajj is a visit to where <u>Muhammad</u> lived and preached, following in his footsteps and in those of the prophets Adam, Ibrahim, and Ismail. It makes stories of the prophets 'come alive' for Muslims.

3) Special pilgrim clothing called <u>ihram</u> is worn by all pilgrims, rich and poor. This clothing is very <u>basic</u>, and shows <u>equality</u> before Allah.

4) Once at Makkah, Muslims must do <u>seven</u> circuits of the <u>Ka'ba</u>, touching the stone if possible — this ritual is called the <u>tawaf</u>.

Muslims believe the Ka'ba was built by Adam, rebuilt by Ibrahim, and purified by Muhammad. It's a <u>giant stone cube</u>, covered with black cloth, and is said to be the <u>first</u> man-made structure dedicated to a <u>single God</u>.

5) Next, a pilgrim must make <u>seven</u> journeys between the hills of <u>Safa</u> and <u>Marwa</u> (where Hagar searched for water for her son Ismail). This part of the pilgrimage is called the <u>Sa'y</u>. Pilgrims then draw water from the Zamzam Well, which Allah made for Hagar.

6) The next stage is a journey to <u>Mount Arafat</u>, where pilgrims stand and pray for Allah's forgiveness. This is where Muslims believe Adam was forgiven after being thrown out of Eden, and also where the <u>Last Judgement</u> will take place.

7) <u>Stones</u> are then thrown at three pillars in <u>Mina</u>, to symbolise driving the Devil away.

8) Near the end comes <u>Id-ul-Adha</u> — a 4-day <u>festival</u>. This consists of <u>prayer</u> at the mosque, then a family <u>gathering</u>, which includes a <u>sacrifice</u> of sheep, goat or chicken, shared with the poor.

9) The title '<u>Hajji</u>' is given to those who complete this pilgrimage.

The Five Pillars are the basis of Muslim worship...

As with many things in Muslim life, the Five Pillars of Islam have their basis in the <u>Qur'an</u> and the <u>life of Muhammad</u>. Make sure you learn this stuff, because the examiner won't be impressed if you don't...

Birth and Death Ceremonies

Every child is born with a 'clean slate', with the chance of becoming a good Muslim, pleasing Allah and reaching Paradise. After death comes judgement, followed by reward or punishment.

'Allah' should be the **first word** a **child hears**

The first word a child should hear is the name of Allah. As soon as it is born the call to prayer (adhan) is whispered in its ear.

> The adhan begins 'Allahu Akbar...' (God is the Greatest...). It continues, 'I bear witness there is no God but Allah, I bear witness that Muhammad is the Messenger of Allah, Rush to Prayer, Rush to Success, God is the Greatest...'

So the first words a child hears are the most central teachings of Islam.

See also page 17 for more on Muslim beliefs about death.

Aqiqa — the **naming** ceremony

1) At seven days old the child's head is shaved, and a donation given to the poor of gold or silver weighing at least as much as the hair. This brings Allah's blessing on the child.

2) It's traditional to make a sacrifice to Allah as a sign of thanksgiving. One sheep or goat for a girl — two for a boy. The meat is shared among the family, after 1/3 of it has been given away to the hungry.

3) The child is then named — there are two traditional kinds of name:
   a) it could be named after one of the Prophet's family or companions,
   b) it could be given a name which shows obedience to Allah. ➡ *For example, Abdullah (servant of Allah) or Abd-ur-Rahman (servant of the Merciful One).*

4) This ceremony generally involves a party and a lot of celebration.

5) For boys, circumcision (removal of the foreskin) is also required. Often it's done in hospital soon after birth, but in some countries it's a separate ceremony at 7 or 8 years old.

'Allah' should be the **last word** a **person hears**

A Muslim hopes not to die alone, but with relatives and friends around, who will:

i) Keep them company and look after them.

ii) Ensure last-minute business is settled, so the dying one is not distracted by things to do with this life.

iii) Pray, and recite 'There is no God but Allah,' so that the person may be helped to concentrate on the name of God. Ideally, just as the name of Allah was the first thing the Muslim heard at birth, it should also be the last at death.

Bodies are **buried facing Makkah**

1) After a person has died, the body is washed, as a sign of respect.

2) The body is then wrapped in a clean white shroud.

3) Funeral prayers (Janazah prayers) are said, praying that the dead person may be judged mercifully and gain a place in Paradise.

It's said that graves are visited by two angels to question the deceased and work out whether they're fit for the next life.

4) The body is buried in a simple grave, lying on its right side with the face towards Makkah.

5) A period of mourning is kept for three days, finishing with Qur'an reading and prayers for the dead person. Some Muslims do this after 40 days as well.

Judgement, then reward or punishment — sounds like Exams...

Islam is a 'total life' thing — with 'Allah' being the first and last word that a person hears. Muhammad's actions at the death of his son are even taken as a guide to the right way to behave at the death of a loved one — Muhammad cried, meaning that Muslims aren't ashamed to cry at the death of a friend or relative.

Warm-Up and Worked Exam Questions

Warm-up Questions

1) What do the words Halal and Haram mean?
2) Why must a Muslim undertake Wudu before prayer?
3) What are Salat–al–Jum'ah?
4) What is the festival at the end of the month of Ramadan called?
5) Describe what a Muslim does when on Hajj.

Worked Exam Questions

You won't get worked answers in the exam — so make the most of them now.

1 a) What is the difference between Greater and Lesser Jihad?

The term Greater Jihad refers to someone's personal striving to become a better Muslim. Lesser Jihad is the struggle to make the world a better place and may involve defending the Muslim faith.

(2 marks)

b) Explain why some Muslims argue that Greater Jihad is the most important part of being a Muslim.

Greater Jihad is extremely important as it is a personal and spiritual struggle to obey Allah and follow Shari'ah. Greater Jihad is something which a Muslim must undertake throughout the whole of his or her life and it affects every aspect of life. Winning this struggle allows you to enter Paradise one day.

(4 marks)

2 a) Why is the Call to Prayer whispered into the ear of a newborn baby?

The Call to Prayer is whispered into the ear of a newborn baby so that the first word the baby hears is the name of Allah. The words the baby hears are central to Muslims belief.

These are rituals carried out at birth — you also need to know the ones carried out at death.

(2 marks)

b) Explain the main events that make up the ceremony of Aqiqa.

The baby's head is shaved — gold or silver weighing as much as the hair is given to the poor. This brings Allah's blessing on the baby. To show thanks to Allah, a sacrifice is made — one sheep or goat for a girl, two for a boy. The baby will be given a name that will either show obedience to Allah or be the name of one of the Phophet's family or companions. Baby boys should be circumcised, but this is not always done at birth.

(5 marks)

Exam Questions

3   Prayer is an essential part of a Muslim's life.

   a)   What is the difference between Salah prayer and Du'a prayer?

(2 marks)

   b)   Describe how and where Muslims carry out Salah prayer.

(6 marks)

4   Describe Zakah and its purposes.

(6 marks)

5   Describe the following in relation to Muslims:

   a)   Fasting

(4 marks)

   b)   Pilgrimage

(4 marks)

6   Explain the differences between imams in the Shi'ite and Sunni traditions.

(6 marks)

7   a)   Mosques are used for worshipping Allah.

      i) Describe the features you would see inside and outside a mosque.

(8 marks)

      ii)Describe another use of the mosque.

(2 marks)

   b)   Explain why it might be difficult for a Muslim to pray, worship and carry out their customs when living in a non-Muslim country.

(5 marks)

   c)   "If you believe in God you should not need to follow rituals."

      Do you agree? Give reasons for your answer, showing that you have thought about more than one point of view. Refer to Islam in your answer.

(5 marks)

Practice Exam

Once you've been through all the questions in this book, you should feel pretty confident about the exam. As final preparation here's a **practice exam** to really get you set for the real thing. There are **four** papers — one for each section in this book. Only do the papers that are relevant to your syllabus, and answer all the questions in the paper. The papers are designed to give you the best possible preparation for the differing question styles of the actual exams, whichever syllabus you're following. You can use the answers provided to work out a rough mark that'll give you an idea how your revision is going.

CGP Practice Exam Paper
GCSE Religious Studies (RS)

General Certificate of Secondary Education

GCSE Religious Studies (RS)

Centre name				
Centre number				
Candidate number				

Paper 1
Perspectives

Surname	
Other names	
Candidate signature	

Time allowed:

2 hours

Instructions to candidates
• Answer **all** of the questions.
• Write your name and other details in the spaces provided above.

Information for candidates
• The marks available are given in brackets at the end of each question or part-question.
• Marks will not be deducted for incorrect answers.
• There are **4** questions in this paper.
• There are no blank pages.

Advice to candidates
• Work steadily through the paper.
• Don't spend too long on one question.
• If you have time at the end, go back and check your answers.

1   The Nature of God

Look at the picture below.

I believe in one God.
I think of God as Father.

(a) (i)   Is the believer above a *monotheist* or *polytheist*?

....

(1 mark)

(ii) Does the believer above think that God is *personal*?
Give **one** reason for your answer.

....

....

....

....

(2 marks)

(b) Explain what religious believers mean when they say that God is *transcendent*.

....

....

....

....

....

....

....

....

(4 marks)

(c) Why do some religious believers find it helpful to think of God as 'one God'?

....

....

....

....

....

....

....

....

(4 marks)

(d) Why do other religious believers find it helpful to think that God has many aspects?

....

....

....

....

....

....

....

....

(4 marks)

(e) "It is impossible to know the nature of God."

Do you agree? Give reasons for your answer, showing that you have thought about more than one point of view.

....

....

....

....

....

....

....

....

....

....

....

....

....

(5 marks)

AQA, 2003

2 (a) Give **ONE** example of racial discrimination. *(2 marks)*

(b) Outline different attitudes to the roles of men and women in *one religion other than Christianity*. *(6 marks)*

(c) Explain how the teachings of Christianity may help to promote racial harmony. *(8 marks)*

(d) "All societies should be multi-faith societies."

Do you agree? Give reasons for your opinion, showing you have considered another point of view. In your answer you should refer to at least one religion. *(4 marks)*

Edexcel, 2003

3   Religious Attitudes to Drug Abuse

    (a) (i)   Why are some drugs **illegal**?   *(3 marks)*

         (ii) Explain why some people take illegal drugs.   *(4 marks)*

    (b) Explain the attitudes of religious believers to caring for their mind and body. Refer
        to the beliefs and teachings of **one** religious tradition in your answer.   *(4 marks)*

    (c) Explain the attitudes of religious believers to drinking alcohol. Refer to the
        beliefs and teachings of a **different** religious tradition in your answer.   *(4 marks)*

    (d) "Smokers and drinkers should be made to pay for their own medical treatment."

        Do you agree? Give reasons for your answer, showing that you have thought about
        more than one point of view. Refer to religious arguments in your answer.   *(5 marks)*

AQA, 2004

4   Human Relationships.

Read the newspaper headlines below.

    (a) What do the **two** religions you have studied teach about contraception?   *(7 marks)*

    (b) How might the beliefs and teachings of these **two** religions help a believer decide
        whether or not to have an abortion?   *(8 marks)*

    (c) "People should **not** use religious teachings to help them make personal decisions about
        contraception and abortion."

        Do you agree? Give reasons for your answer, showing that you have thought about
        different points of view.   *(5 marks)*

AQA, 2004

General Certificate of Secondary Education

GCSE Religious Studies

Paper 2
Christianity

Centre name				
Centre number				
Candidate number				

Time allowed:
2 hours

Surname
Other names
Candidate signature

Instructions to candidates
- Answer **all** of the questions.
- Write your name and other details in the spaces provided above.

Information for candidates
- The marks available are given in brackets at the end of each question or part-question.
- Marks will not be deducted for incorrect answers.
- There are **7** questions in this paper.
- There are no blank pages.

Advice to candidates
- Work steadily through the paper.
- Don't spend too long on one question.
- If you have time at the end, go back and check your answers.

130

1   Baptism

(a) Give **one** reason why some churches will not baptise infants.

....

....

(1 mark)

(b) What is the link between infant baptism and confirmation?

....

....

....

....

(2 marks)

AQA, 2003

2   The Pope and the Magisterium

(a) What is meant by the magisterium?

....

....

....

....

(2 marks)

(b) Why is the Pope important for Roman Catholics?

....

....

....

....

(2 marks)

AQA, 2004

3   The Gospels

  (a) What does the word gospel mean?

....

(1 mark)

  (b) Matthew, Mark and Luke are known as the synoptic gospels. What does the word synoptic mean?

....

....

(2 marks)

AQA, 2003

4   Sources of Authority

  (a) (i) What is a Creed?

....

....

(1 mark)

      (ii) Explain **one** reason why many Christians regard creeds as important.

....

....

....

....

(2 marks)

  (b) Describe **two** different ways in which Christians believe the Bible may be understood.

1..

....

....

2..

....

....

(4 marks)

AQA, 2004

5   Worship and Prayer

    (a) Choose a Christian denomination/tradition. Describe a typical act of Sunday worship in that denomination/tradition. *(7 marks)*

    (b) Describe and explain the use made by Christians of the following in their private prayer.

          (i) An icon

          (ii) The rosary.

(8 marks)

    (c) "You can be a Christian without praying."

        Do you agree? Give reasons for your answer, showing that you have thought about more than one point of view. *(5 marks)*

AQA, 2003

6   Religion: Wealth and Poverty

    (a) Outline the causes of world poverty. *(4 marks)*

    (b) Explain why Christians should try to relieve poverty and suffering in the United Kingdom. *(8 marks)*

    (c) *"All Christians living in the developed world should give 10% of their income to end poverty."*

        Do you agree? Give reasons for your opinion, showing you have considered another point of view. *(8 marks)*

Edexcel, 2004

7   Christianity

    (a) Describe Christian attitudes towards fertility treatment. *(8 marks)*

    (b) Explain Christian beliefs about the use of animals in medical research. *(7 marks)*

    (c) 'Every woman has the right to have a baby.'

        Do you agree? Give reasons to support your answer and show that you have thought about different points of view. You must refer to Christianity in your answer. *(5 marks)*

OCR, 2004

CGP | Practice Exam Paper
GCSE Religious Studies (RS)

General Certificate of Secondary Education

GCSE Religious Studies

Paper 3
Judaism

Centre name				
Centre number				
Candidate number				

Time allowed:
1 hour 45 minutes

Surname
Other names
Candidate signature

Instructions to candidates
- Answer **all** of the questions.
- Write your name and other details in the spaces provided above.

Information for candidates
- The marks available are given in brackets at the end of each question or part-question.
- Marks will not be deducted for incorrect answers.
- There are **4** questions in this paper.
- There are no blank pages.

Advice to candidates
- Work steadily through the paper.
- Don't spend too long on one question.
- If you have time at the end, go back and check your answers.

1   **Tenakh, Talmud and Halakhah**

(a)   Name the **three** parts of the Tenakh.

1...

....

2...

....

3...

....

(3 marks)

(b)   (i)   What is the Mishnah?

....

....

....

....

(2 marks)

(ii)   What is the Gemara?

....

....

....

....

(2 marks)

AQA, 2003

2   (a)   Describe what happened to the Jews during the Twentieth-Century Holocaust.

(8 marks)

(b)   Explain how Jews have responded to the Twentieth-Century Holocaust.   *(7 marks)*

(c)   'The Twentieth-Century Holocaust proves that G-d does not exist.'

Do you agree? Give reasons to support you answer and show that you have thought
about different points of view. You must refer to Judaism in your answer.   *(5 marks)*

OCR, 2004

3   Judaism

(a)   Which Jewish leader led the Israelites out of Egypt?   *(1 mark)*

(b)   What is a covenant?   *(1 mark)*

(c)   What is the Shema?   *(1 mark)*

(d)   Give **two** things that the Jews believe about God.   *(2 marks)*

(e)   Give **two** of the kashrut regulations about meat.   *(2 marks)*

(f)   Describe **three** practices observed during Yom Kippur.   *(3 marks)*

(g)   Explain why the Jews believe that the Torah is important.   *(5 marks)*

(h)   "Keeping Shabbat (the Sabbath Day) holy is the most important part of Judaism."

Do you agree? Give reasons for your answer, showing that you have thought about
more than one point of view.   *(5 marks)*

AQA, 2003

4   The Synagogue

(a)   Outline the main features of a synagogue.   *(4 marks)*

(b)   Explain why the rabbi is important in the Jewish community.   *(8 marks)*

(c)   "All Jewish people should worship in the same way."
Do you agree? Give reasons for your opinion, showing you have considered another
point of view.   *(8 marks)*

Edexcel, 2003

CGP   Practice Exam Paper
      GCSE Religious Studies (RS)

General Certificate of Secondary Education

GCSE Religious Studies

Paper 4
Islam

Centre name					
Centre number					
Candidate number					

Time allowed:
1 hour 45 minutes

Surname	
Other names	
Candidate signature	

Instructions to candidates
- Answer **all** of the questions.
- Write your name and other details in the spaces provided above.

Information for candidates
- The marks available are given in brackets at the end of each question or part-question.
- Marks will not be deducted for incorrect answers.
- There are **5** questions in this paper.
- There are no blank pages.

Advice to candidates
- Work steadily through the paper.
- Don't spend too long on one question.
- If you have time at the end, go back and check your answers.

1   The Family

(a) In Islam, what is an arranged marriage?

....

....

(1 mark)

(b) What is the Muslim attitude to divorce?

....

....

....

....

(2 marks)

(c) What does the Qur'an teach about the way Muslims should dress?

....

....

(1 mark)

AQA, 2003

2   The Pillars

Shahadah, Salah and Hajj are three pillars of Islam.
Explain the meaning of each one.

Shahadah

....

....

Salah

....

....

Hajj

....

....

(3 marks)

AQA, 2004

3 (a) Describe the main features of a mosque. *(8 marks)*

(b) Explain the role of the imam in Muslim life and worship. *(7 marks)*

(c) 'You must attend the mosque every Friday to be a true Muslim.'

Do you agree? Give reasons to support your answer and show that you have thought about different points of view. *(5 marks)*

OCR, 2004

4 (a) Describe the main differences between Sunni and Shi'ah Muslims. *(8 marks)*

(b) Explain the importance of Jihad for Muslims. *(7 marks)*

(c) 'Islam values and encourages peace.'

Do you agree? Give reasons to support your answer and show that you have thought about different points of view. *(5 marks)*

OCR, 2004

5 (a) What was *hijrah*? *(2 marks)*

(b) Outline the events celebrated by Shi'ah Muslims on 10 Muharram. *(6 marks)*

(c) Explain why the Qur'an is important for Muslims. *(8 marks)*

(d) "Muhammad is the prophet for everyone."

Do you agree? Give reasons for your opinion, showing you have considered another point of view. *(4 marks)*

Edexcel, 2003

ANSWERS

Section One — Perspectives
Page 6 (Warm-Up Questions)

1) This is the belief that God is everywhere at once.

2) An agnostic is someone who believes it is impossible to know whether or not there is a God.

3) Any two of, for example: thinking about questions such as "Why am I here?"; volunteering to help the homeless; creating works of beauty and meaning through art, literature or music.

4) Sacred writings, religious leaders, conscience

5) Any two of, for example: Judaism, Christianity, Islam

Page 7 (Exam Questions)

2 a) A personal God is a God that is a "person" *(1 mark)*. A personal God would have human emotions/be someone with whom we could have an individual relationship with *(1 mark)*.

b) The incarnation of Jesus on Earth is an example of an immanent God *(1 mark)*. An immanent God is a God who is in the world with us, taking an active role in history *(1 mark)*.
The opposite of an immanent God is a transcendent God. This is a God who is outside the world. No one knows the exact truth, but many people believe that God is a blend of the two.

3 a) Scientific truth is found by doing experiments and observing things to prove or disprove theories. A theory is said to be true if the experiment or observation to test it has been repeated many times by many people who have all got the same result. However, a more accurate or sophisticated measurement might one day give another result, which disproves the theory. Also, a piece of evidence might have been interpreted wrongly. *(1 mark for each valid point, up to a maximum of 4 marks)*

b) Evidence in favour of a theory makes you think it is likely to be true. However evidence can be misinterpreted, or counter-evidence can come along *(2 marks)*. When something is proved it means that there is no doubt that it is true *(1 mark)*.

c) Religious faith involves going beyond the ordinary world. You are not dealing with things you can test or measure. Religious faith is more like having faith in a friend or family member. *(Other answers are possible. 1 mark for each valid point, up to a maximum of 3 marks)*

4 Any one of:
- William Paley. He thought that if you found an intricate watch you wouldn't think it was made by chance — so you should not believe the world, which is far more intricate, was made by chance.
- Isaac Newton. He thought that the fact that every thumbprint is so intricate and unique shows there must be a God.

(Other answers are possible, such as various quotes from Einstein or Aquinas. 1 mark for the name; 1 mark for the correct example (e.g. watch); final mark for correct theory)
Surely sticky-toffee pudding isn't here just by accident.

5 a) In general revelation God shows himself in experiences that are available to everyone such as acts of nature, conscience and morality, scripture and the work of religious leaders *(1 mark)*. In a special revelation God reveals himself to individuals or small groups in visions, dreams or prophecies *(1 mark)*.

b) To experience a sense of awe and wonder *(1 mark)* that suggests the presence of God *(1 mark)*.

c) Any three of: miracles; answers to prayers; feeling the presence of God while at prayer or in meditation; scripture; charismatic phenomena; the sacraments. *(1 mark for each. 3 marks maximum.)*

Page 13 (Warm-Up Questions)

1) Six days

2) Shahadah (a statement of belief), Salah (prayer), Zakah (charitable duty), Sawm (fasting), Hajj (pilgrimage)

3) Christians

4) Shaytan

5) Possible examples of natural evil: flood, draught, famine, tsunamis, earthquakes, hurricanes...
Possible examples of man-made evil: theft, murder, rape, war...

6) The Shema

Page 14 (Exam Questions)

2 a) *To gain the full 8 marks on this question, you need to give a clear, well-structured description of all the significant relevant teachings of your chosen religion, with examples where appropriate.*
Good answers for Judaism could include:
- suffering occurs because we have free will and some people choose to do evil
- we need to accept that God has a plan, although we do not know what it is
- suffering can bring people closer to each other and to God
- the joys of the next life compensate for suffering in this life
- a reference to the Book of Job, in which Job's sufferings were a test of his faith
- those who are suffering should be treated with compassion

Good answers for Christianity could include:
- all the comments that apply to Judaism (see above)
- the Christian belief that the Son of God himself suffered and died undeservedly in order to pay for sin

Good answers for Islam could include:
- suffering occurs because we have free will and some people choose to do evil
- Islam teaches that we must submit to what God wants for us
- suffering is a test (Surah 2:155-6)
- those who are suffering should be treated with compassion
- suffering should be accepted. The joys of the next life will compensate for suffering in this life as Allah is compassionate

b) *To gain the full 5 marks on this question, you need to give a clear, balanced discussion using religious or moral arguments. You must also reach a personal conclusion.*
Your arguments could include:
- we need to know what evil is to be able to appreciate good
- if every choice we made led to good, moral choices would not matter (even the choice not to love would not matter)
- the purpose of life is a test, and experiencing bad things is more of a test
- the idea of a test is all very well for the person who does evil, but why should innocent victims suffer for someone else's test?
- God himself is meant to be perfectly good, yet he is not meaningless
- if God is good and omnipotent he ought to be able to give a sense of meaning in some less cruel way

There's no right or wrong answer to this question — you've got to argue both sides and then say what you personally believe.

3 a) C *(1 mark)*

b) Those Christians who take the account of creation in the book of Genesis literally cannot believe in evolution *(1 mark)* because it contradicts the idea of God creating the world in six days and all humans descending from Adam and Eve *(1 mark)*. Those Christians who view the Genesis story as a symbolic account of evolution, or as a moral story *(1 mark)* showing that God caused the world to exist and that the world is good, can accept evolution *(1 mark)*.

c) Possible reasons to agree:
- if you keep on asking "what caused that?" eventually you must get back to something that had no cause

Possible reasons to disagree:
- it's a mistake to assume that things have to have a cause — the Universe just happened
- you could disagree with Tara's argument, or not believe in the Big Bang at all, but still believe in God because of scripture or personal experience

(2 marks for any one reason)

4 a) The Holy Spirit *(1 mark)*

b) The Nicene Creed *(2 marks. Allow 1 mark for "creed")*

c) The Shema states that "the Lord is one" *(1 mark)*, in contrast to the Christian belief that God is three persons in one, i.e. a Trinity *(1 mark)*.
Don't get muddled up here — there's only one God in Christianity (so it's monotheistic), it's just that He can exist in three forms — God the Father, God the Son and God the Holy Spirit. The Muslim and Jewish views of God are much more straightforward.

d) Tawhid is the fundamental principle of Islam that states that Allah is one *(1 mark)*. Islam is much more similar to Judaism than Christianity in this respect *(1 mark)*.

140

Page 18 (Warm-Up Questions)

1) Yawmuddin
2) All the souls in heaven
3) We know we will die.
   That's a nice cheery thought isn't it?
4) Purgatory is where sins are punished before our souls can enter heaven. Roman Catholics believe in this.
5) E.g. ghosts, communicating beyond the grave.
6) The physical body will be resurrected.

Page 19 (Exam Questions)

2 a) Life after death *(1 mark)*
  b) Earthly life is a test. God will judge us on how we lived our lives on earth *(1 mark)*.
  c) Paradise *(1 mark)*
     "Take me home to the paradise city where the grass is green and the girls are pretty."
  d) Islam teaches that the dead stay in the grave until the Day of Judgement (Yawmuddin) *(1 mark)*.
  e) On Yawmuddin the soul is judged by Allah *(1 mark)*. It is judged on your character, reactions to events during your life, and your way of life *(1 mark)*. Those who have followed Allah will be rewarded by entry into Paradise *(1 mark)*. Those who do not believe in Allah, or who have committed bad deeds, are rewarded by entry into Jahannam (Hell) *(1 mark)*.

3 a) To reaffirm the belief that death is not the end *(1 mark)*, and the body will be resurrected *(1 mark)*.
  b) In the earliest Jewish scriptures it was believed that everyone, good or bad, went to Sheol after death *(1 mark)*. Sheol was seen as a dark, damp place where the dead lived as shadows *(1 mark)*.
  c) Those who have lived a good life will go to heaven and be in the presence of God *(1 mark)* and those who have rejected God will go to Hell, a place of punishment *(1 mark)*.
  d) In the early days, Jews believed that you would be punished by God for the sins of your parents and grandparents *(1 mark)*. In later centuries most Jews came to believe that God judges you only on your own behaviour *(1 mark)*.
     It's no wonder Jewish ideas have changed on this one. It's a bit harsh if you're condemned to eternal torture just because your granny was a naughty girl.
  e) Reform Jews do not have a firm view on what, if anything, happens after death *(1 mark)*. Rather than worry about the reward they think that you should serve God for the love of him, rather than for the hope of Heaven *(2 marks)*.

4 Catholics believe everyone has an immortal soul that survives death *(1 mark)*. They believe that God will judge us all *(1 mark)* as to whether we have lived a good life in accordance with Jesus' teaching *(1 mark)*. The righteous will go to live in joy with God in heaven *(1 mark)*. Those who have denied God or rejected him by sin will be forever separated from God in Hell *(1 mark)*. Some sinners are sent to Purgatory to be punished before they can move on to heaven *(1 mark)*.
  Remember it's only Roman Catholics who believe in Purgatory. Protestants reject the idea as it's not in the Bible.

Page 25 (Warm-Up Questions)

1) They would save the woman's life, as it is more valuable than the life of the unborn child.
2) Possible answers: If there's a threat to the mother's health, if it could help a woman who already has children, if there is a greater than average chance the child could be born with disabilities, or if the family is too poor to raise a child.
3) At conception
4) You shall not murder
5) Yes, as it allows parents to plan their family in a more responsible way.
6) Voluntary euthanasia is where a person actively requests assistance to die. Involuntary euthanasia is when someone is unable to make such a request, and the decision is made by someone else.

Page 26 (Exam Questions)

2 a) Any two of :
  • Artificial Insemination by the Husband (AIH) in which sperm from the husband is injected into the wife's ovum.
  • Artificial Insemination by Donor (AID) in which sperm from a donor is injected into the wife's ovum.
  • In Vitro Fertilisation (IVF) where eggs fertilised in a test tube are implanted in the mother's womb.
  • Egg donation in which eggs from another woman are implanted in the mother's womb.
  (Allow 2 marks for each correctly named technique and description, maximum 4 marks.)
  b) Either AIH or In Vitro Fertilisation (IVF) *(1 mark)*.
  c) Because in AID, unlike AIH, the woman becomes pregnant via sperm that is not the husband's *(1 mark)*. This makes it equivalent to adultery *(1 mark)*.
  d) Because the "spare" embryos are destroyed or used in experimentation *(1 mark)*. Roman Catholics in particular believe that the embryos are human beings with rights *(1 mark)*.

3 a) Because she believes a woman has the right to <u>choose</u> what to do with her own body *(1 mark)*.
  b) Because she believes a foetus has the right to <u>life</u> *(1 mark)*.
  c) *To gain the full 8 marks on this question, you need to give a clear, balanced discussion using moral and religious evidence. You must also reach a personal conclusion.*
     Your arguments could include:
     • Even if a foetus can't survive outside the womb, it still has the potential for independent life.
     • According to the Roman Catholic Church life begins at conception.
     • It is hard to see a minute bundle of cells as a human being.
     • At the other end of pregnancy, many people are horrified at the idea of a foetus which could survive outside the womb being killed just because the parents don't want it, when in the next ward a premature baby of the same age is lovingly cared for. So the law tries to forbid abortion once the foetus is developed enough to survive on its own.
     • It is an arbitrary limit. But people often have to just draw a line somewhere in order to make decisions without endless argument. For instance the law says you are an adult at eighteen, even though someone of seventeen might be just as sensible.
     Abortion is a very controversial topic. Even if you have very strong views about it, you must be able to describe the other arguments, and know what the different religions say about it.

4 a) Anything which prevents the conception of children from sexual intercourse *(1 mark)*.
  b) *To gain the full 6 marks on this question, you need to give a clear discussion using religious evidence to support Melanie's statement. The views of two different religions must be included.*
     Any two of:
     • Orthodox Jews believe that it in the Book of Genesis they are commanded to be fruitful and multiply, and to fill the earth. Preventing the birth of children breaks this commandment. Furthermore in the book of Deuteronomy it states that God puts to death and he brings to life, which can be taken to mean that human beings should leave the decision of whether life is created to God.
     • The Book of Genesis commands humans to be fruitful and multiply, and to fill the earth, and therefore some Christians, particularly Roman Catholics, believe contraception is wrong. Also they believe that using artificial means of contraception to make it impossible to have children is refusing to be open to God's gift of life, and hence is against natural law.
     • Surah 42 states that God bestows male and female children, and that God makes barren whom he wills. In other words whether or not conception occurs is the will of Allah and humans should not try to interfere.
  c) *To gain the full 6 marks on this question, you need to give a clear, balanced discussion using moral and religious evidence. You must also reach a personal conclusion.*
     Your arguments could include:
     • Unwanted children often are abandoned, live in poverty, or suffer from lack of love.
     • Too many children in a family may mean all of them grow up in poverty.
     • Contraception is not killing a life already started, it is preventing life in

the first place.
- The parents may not have wanted the child but that doesn't mean they won't love him or her when born.
- Babies could be given up for adoption. Many couples are desperate to adopt.

Page 33 (Warm-Up Questions)

1) Monogamy means having only one partner (husband or wife)
And polygamy is having more than one. You can remember which is which by thinking of polygons from maths — these are many sided shapes.
(So, does that make a circle a monogon?)

2) Christianity teaches that the purpose of marriage is for two people to offer mutual support, and to raise children.

3) The ketubah is the Jewish marriage contract.

4) Jews believe that if your mother is Jewish, you are Jewish, whether you like it or not. However, you cannot be born a Christian. You have to choose Christianity for yourself.

5) If a marriage is annulled, it means it is recognised that it was never a true marriage in the first place.

6) Divorce

Page 34 (Exam Questions)

2 a) Homosexual activity is legal among consenting adults in private *(1 mark)*. The age of consent is the same as for heterosexual couples (16 in England, Scotland and Wales and 17 in N. Ireland) *(1 mark)*.

b) *To gain the full 6 marks on this question, you need to give a clear, balanced discussion using moral and religious evidence. You must also reach a personal conclusion.*
Your arguments could include:
- homosexual activity is forbidden by the scriptures of Christianity, Judaism and Islam. E.g. from the Bible, "... males committed indecent acts with other men, and received in themselves the due penalty for their perversion..." (Romans 1:26-27)
- sex is not everything — there are many other joys in life
- it may be difficult, but God does not ask anything that is beyond human strength
- there is no God, so there is no point in following the rule
- those rules were written in very different cultural conditions, and they do not apply now
- God made homosexuals and gave them their nature, so why should they not act accordingly?

3 a) That by marrying, the husband and wife become like one person *(1 mark)*. Nothing should separate them *(1 mark)*.

b) For example:
- Many more marriages end in divorce than previously.
- It is more acceptable to live together before/instead of getting married.
- There are many more single-parent families.
- There are many more reconstituted families, where one or both parents have remarried.
- There are many more children born to women who have never been married.
(1 mark for each valid point. 4 marks maximum)

c) The Roman Catholic Church holds that divorce (the ending of a marriage) cannot happen *(1 mark)*, since marriage is a sacrament that cannot be undone *(1 mark)*. Marriages can be annulled under certain circumstances when it is ruled by the Church that no true marriage ever took place *(1 mark)*.

d) Yes *(1 mark)*.
You could support your answer in several ways, for example:
- when a woman was caught in adultery, Jesus saved her from being stoned but afterwards he said, "Go and do not sin again." This shows that he regarded adultery as a sin.
- "You shall not commit adultery" is one of the Ten Commandments (religious laws). Jesus said he came to fulfil the Law, not overturn it.
- Jesus said that a man looking lustfully at a woman committed adultery in his heart. Clearly, he thought adultery was wrong.
(1 mark for "yes". A further 2 marks for an explanation supported by an example from the Bible.)

4 a) The Fifth Commandment. "Honour your father and your mother." *(2 marks)*

b) i) kiddushin is the Jewish marriage ceremony *(1 mark)*.

ii) ketubah is the Jewish marriage contract *(1 mark)*.

iii) The huppah is a canopy beneath which the couple are married *(1 mark)*.
Watch out — religious terms can often be spelt in more than one way. Chuppah is exactly the same as huppah.

c) Because children of mixed marriages are less likely to be raised as observant Jews. Jews fear for the future of their religion. *(2 marks)*

d) If the baby has a Jewish mother, he or she is a Jew. *(1 mark)*

Page 42 (Warm-Up Questions)

1) Any of:
Men and women usually have separate areas for prayer. It is usually ten men who are required for a service and men who read from the Torah. In divorce, only men are allowed to initiate it.

2) People who are imprisoned for acting or speaking out against government policy.

3) It tries to create unity amongst the different Christian traditions.

4) Prejudice is judging something or someone with no good reason, or without full knowledge of a situation.

5) A German Christian who struggled against injustice. He spoke out against the Nazis' treatment of Jews, and was later hung for it.

6) The Good Samaritan
A very nice chap.

Page 43 (Exam Questions)

2 a) It means that Allah does not care what colour skin or physical appearance a person has *(1 mark)*. Instead he judges what the person is like morally and whether the person does good or evil *(1 mark)*.

b) The ummah is the worldwide community of Muslims *(1 mark)*.

c) All pilgrims wear simple white garments *(1 mark)*, showing that the race of the pilgrim does not matter *(1 mark)*.

3 a) That women and men are equal in status *(1 mark)* but have different roles *(1 mark)*.

b) No. The difference is because under Islamic law, men must provide for women but not vice versa *(2 marks)*.

c) That it is acceptable for women to do respectable work, as Khadijah is considered a model wife *(2 marks)*.

d) It allows them to go about their business without being seen as sex objects *(2 marks)*.

4 a) A person who spreads the Christian message *(1 mark)* with the aim of winning converts *(1 mark)*.
And then there's missionaries who also spread the message of Christianity in the hope of converting people.

b) Pete *(1 mark)*

c) Disagreement does not have to mean hostility *(1 mark)*.

d) "I am the way and the truth and the life. No one comes to the Father except through me." (John 14:6) *(3 marks)*

Page 48 (Warm-Up Questions)

1) He should share his tunics with someone who doesn't have one.

2) "Khalifah" means "trustee" or "Vice-Regent" — it is the idea that we are responsible for taking care of the Earth.

3) Interdependence means that everything depends on everything else.

4) Quakers

5) The Jewish term is Tzedaka, and the Muslim term is Zakah.

Page 49 (Exam Questions)

2 a) Answers could include: population growth, war, low prices of raw materials, economic failure, climate change, corruption, debt, etc.
(1 mark for each cause. 4 marks maximum)

b) *To gain the full 6 marks on this question, you need to give a clear, well-structured description of the views of your chosen religions. You must refer to two different religions in your answer.*
Your answer could include, for Christianity:
- Jesus said that you should love your neighbour as yourself

- Jesus taught that people should help the poor — for instance he told a rich man to sell all he had and give it to the poor, and he said that the man with two tunics should share with him that has none
- All denominations teach that it is a Christian duty to help the poor (However, Jesus also said, "the poor will always be with you.")

For Judaism:
- Jews are instructed in Deuteronomy not to be hardhearted or tightfisted
- Tzedaka is the duty of Jews to contribute 10% of their wealth
- Gemilut Hasadim refers to kind actions beyond Tzedaka
- Maimonides said it was most blessed to give in such a way as to help the recipient become self-sufficient

For Islam:
- Zakah is one of the Five Pillars of Islam — Zakah means 2.5% of your savings should be donated to the needy
- In addition to Zakah, Muslims also practise voluntary additional giving called Sadaqah
- Deals involving interest are forbidden. This means that wealth (which all belongs to Allah) is more fairly distributed.

Basically, all three of these religions say you should help the poor and not be stingy. It's the finer points that you need to concentrate on learning.

c) After natural disasters such as earthquakes or floods, these charities provide immediate short-term aid such as food, tents, medicine and clothing. *(3 marks)*
Another part of CAFOD's work is to provide long-term aid with the aim of helping the recipients to become self-sufficient. This includes teaching agricultural techniques or giving training in other skills, providing tools for agriculture or starting businesses, and building infrastructure such as wells. *(3 marks)*

3 a) Any four of: global warming, greenhouse effect, deforestation, extinction, pollution, scarcity of natural resources. *(1 mark for each. 4 marks maximum)*

b) *To gain the full 6 marks on this question, you need to give a clear, balanced discussion using moral and religious evidence. You must also reach a personal conclusion.*
Your arguments could include:
- it is people that have rights — the environment is just a thing
- we can be certain that some measures that help the environment harm people right now (e.g., restricting businesses) but the future environmental benefits are just guesses
- strict environmental regulations slow down the development of poor countries
- we have a duty to take care of God's creation
- due to interdependence, when the environment is harmed people are harmed
- failing to take care of the environment may make natural disasters more likely. These can kill or injure people.
- human convenience or wealth is less important than animal extinction

4 a) That your generosity is not measured by the absolute amount you give *(1 mark)* but by what proportion it is of your wealth *(1 mark)*.
So, if Richard Branson gave a few quid to charity, it wouldn't be a patch on someone a lot poorer giving a few pence.

b) Possible answers:
- The poor, hungry and those who weep are blessed. (Luke 6:19-21)
- You cannot serve both God and Money. (Mark 6:1-18)
- Lay up treasure in Heaven not on Earth. (Matthew 6:19-21)
- It is easier for a camel to go through the eye of a needle, than for a rich man to enter the Kingdom of God. (Mark 10:23-27)
- The man with two tunics should give away one. (Luke 3:11)
- Go, sell everything you have and give to the poor, and you will have treasure in heaven. (Mark 10:21)
- You could also describe the story of the rich man and Lazarus, the beggar at his gate (Luke 16:19-31); or the story of the rich man who asked, "What must I do to gain eternal life?" (Matthew 19:16-21 or Mark 10:21-22).

(2 marks for each example. 4 marks maximum)
Make sure you've got lots of Bible quotes up your sleeve for questions like this.

c) *To gain the full 6 marks on this question, you need to give a clear, balanced discussion using moral and religious evidence. You must also reach a personal conclusion.*
Your arguments could include:
- following Jesus' teachings is not impractical — just difficult
- it is very practical to be more concerned with eternal life than money now — you can't take it with you
- people often find that if they trust in God, he looks after them
- if you give away everything you will just be destitute yourself, which means other people will be responsible for you

- what about people who depend on you?
- money can be used for good purposes (such as investing in ethical businesses) without giving it all away

Page 56 (Warm-Up Questions)

1) A sin is when <u>religious</u> law is broken.
A crime is when the <u>state</u> laws are broken.

2) a) Pacifists believe that war and physical violence are always wrong.
b) Martyrs are people who have died for their faith.

3) False. It depends on the religion. Islam teaches that drinking alcohol is always wrong. Judaism and Christianity allow the consumption of alcohol but disapprove of drinking it to excess. Some Christian denominations disapprove of alcohol more than others.

4) The term 'mass media' refers to any form of communication to lots of people at once. E.g. TV, radio, newspapers, magazines, film, the Internet.

5) Film classification refers to the giving of official certificates to films. Films are officially classified to warn people of their content. Film classification exists so that people know what age-groups a film is considered suitable for.

Page 57 (Exam Questions)

3 a) A just war must:
- be declared by a proper authority (e.g. elected government, president or monarch)
- have a just cause
- have a just aim
- be waged with discrimination (i.e. without endangering civilians)
- be waged without undue force (i.e. with a sense of proportion)

(1 mark for each)
Of course, exactly what a "just cause" is can be a matter of great debate.

b) *To gain the full 5 marks on this question, you need to give a clear, balanced discussion using moral and religious evidence. You must also reach a personal conclusion.*
Arguments could include:
- modern weaponry often does more damage to God's creation than ancient warfare
- war may lead to more innocent people losing their lives
- war may be necessary to protect people from oppression
- war may be necessary for self-defence

4 a) Terrorism *(1 mark)* and nuclear warfare *(1 mark)*.

b) Unilateral disarmament is when just one country gives up its weapons *(1 mark)*; multilateral disarmament is when many countries give up their weapons at the same time *(1 mark)*.

c) It would leave that country vulnerable to attack from other countries *(1 mark)*.

d) The Church of England is against nuclear weapons, as these weapons don't discriminate between civilians and people fighting the war *(1 mark)*. It wants countries to reduce the number of their nuclear weapons *(1 mark)*. It recognises that unilateral disarmament is hard for governments to do, so it calls for countries to work together towards multilateral disarmament *(1 mark)*.

5 a) Possible answers include:
- TV or radio services allow people who cannot get to church (or who would prefer to worship in private) to take part in an act of worship
- broadcasts can also communicate religious messages to people in their own homes and raise money for religious groups
- the media can educate people about particular faiths
- TV programs, films and soaps can also be used to explore a variety of moral issues

(One mark for each example, up to a maximum of 3 marks.)

b) Possible answers include:
- the media may sideline or misrepresent some faiths
- some media content may be offensive to followers of a specific faith
- there are concerns that scenes containing sex, drugs or violence may adversely influence the young

(One mark for each, up to a maximum of 3 marks.)

c) *To gain the full 5 marks on this question, you need to give a clear, balanced discussion using moral and religious evidence. You must also reach a personal conclusion.*
Arguments could include:
- viewers don't live their own lives, but try to live through others
- soap characters (and actors) are often bad role models

- watching them wastes time which could be put to a more religious use, such as helping others
- soaps deal with important moral or spiritual issues, such as racism and abortion
- they allow us to see how a variety of characters deal with issues that we may all face one day

Now you can claim that avidly watching Neighbours and Hollyoaks is just a spot of research.

Section Two — Christianity
Page 65 (Warm-Up Questions)

1) 1st Century CE

2) Father, Son and Holy Spirit

3)   i) Being sorry for sin
  ii) The act by which God became a man
  iii) Christian love/charity

4) He meant that you should not seek revenge when someone does something to hurt you.

Page 66 (Exam Questions)

2 a) Greek *(1 mark)*

  b) Because God is just, our sins have to be paid for *(1 mark)*. By dying, Jesus paid that price for mankind *(1 mark)*.

  c) It is a Liberal interpretation *(1 mark)*. The Liberal view is that the miraculous events described in the Bible did not really happen *(1 mark)* — they are symbolic stories intended to explain spiritual truths *(1 mark)*.

3 a) Any two of: you shall have no other Gods before me; you shall not bow down before idols; you shall not misuse the name of the Lord; observe the Sabbath and keep it holy; honour your father and mother; you shall not murder; you shall not commit adultery; you shall not steal; you shall not give false testimony; you shall not covet. *(1 mark each, 2 marks maximum)*

  b) "Do to others what you would have them do to you." *(1 mark)*

  c) *To gain the full 6 marks on this question, you need to give a clear, balanced discussion using moral and religious evidence. You must also reach a personal conclusion.*
Your arguments could include:
- it is wrong for people to impose their morals on others — Christians should not act as a "moral police force"
- when an adulteress was about to be stoned, Jesus called for mercy, saying "If any of you is without sin... let him be the first to throw a stone at her."
- Jesus tells Christians not to judge. This should be left to God.
- adultery is wrong, so it should be illegal
- Christians ought to challenge unchristian behaviour rather than sit back and "let society go down the drain."

4 a) Certain things are always right and certain things are always wrong *(1 mark)*, whatever the circumstances *(1 mark)*.
Absolute morality means everything's black and white — there's no grey at all.

  b) • Through speech or writing, e.g. to non-Christians in Alpha courses.
- Through living a Christian life based on love for God and other people.
- Through full-time work in a vocation, e.g. as a monk/nun.
(1 mark for each or any other sensible answer. 3 marks maximum).

  c) *To gain the full 8 marks on this question, you need to give details of several possible Christian views, each supported by religious or moral arguments.*
Your arguments could include:
- reformed criminals can go on to make valuable contributions to society
- Jesus tells Christians not to judge, lest they be judged
- Christianity teaches forgiveness
- strict punishments can help deter potential criminals
- society needs protecting when reform is impossible
- terrorists and cold-blooded murderers have given up their right to reform
- Jesus replaced the Old Testament "eye for eye" principle with the idea of encouraging reform through constructive punishment

Page 74 (Warm-Up Questions)

1) Teaching and preaching from the Bible.

2) Orthodox and Roman Catholic

3) Any four of, for example: altar, sanctuary, font, pulpit, lectern, nave, pews, aisle, stained glass window

4) "High Church" Anglicanism is more like Roman Catholicism. "Low Church" Anglicanism is more like Methodism / more Protestant.
I went to a high church once. It was up a really big hill.

5) Latin America

Page 75 (Exam Questions)

2 a) Ordination is the ceremony by which a person is made a member of the clergy (a priest or deacon). *(1 mark)*

  b) For example: daily services; services on Christian festivals such as Easter and Christmas; baptisms; weddings; funerals *(1 mark for each example, 3 marks maximum — accept any other valid examples)*

  c) For example: leading regular worship; performing services such as baptisms, weddings and funerals; providing Christian teaching; ministering to the sick, needy or troubled; supporting good works within the community *(1 mark for each valid point, 4 marks maximum)*.
So vicars and priests don't just work on Sundays.

  d) "The Church" refers to the whole community of Christian believers *(1 mark)*. St Paul taught that the Church was the body of Christ on Earth *(1 mark)*. *(Allow one further mark for relevant developments, e.g. "Christ is the head of the Church," or "the Church includes Christians who have died".)*

3 a) For example: hymns sung by choirs and/or the congregation, music to accompany dancing in charismatic churches, sacred music composed for sung masses etc. *(1 mark for any sensible point)*

  b)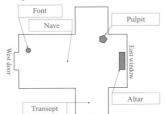

(3 marks for all correct — lose one mark for each mistake)

  c) For example, any two of:
- In a Baptist church the focus of attention is on the pulpit, but in an Anglican church the focus is on the altar.
- A Baptist church would have a baptistry, whereas an Anglican church would have a font.
- A Baptist church would be decorated simply, but an Anglican church would be more ornate with statues and pictures.
(2 marks for each difference, 4 marks maximum. Allow up to 2 marks for relevant comments about only one type of church building without comparison with the other.)

  d) For example, any one of:
- Baptists believe the Bible is most important, hence the focus is on the pulpit. However Anglicans place central importance on Communion, hence the focus is on the altar.
- Baptist churches have a baptistry because they believe in adult baptism by total immersion. The Anglicans have a font as they believe in infant baptism and do not practice total immersion.
- Baptist churches are kept simple in order not to break the commandment forbidding worship of images. Anglicans believe religious images / statues are allowed as visual aids so long as they are not worshipped.
(No marks for restating an answer to c). Allow up to 2 marks for an answer explaining an effect of the beliefs of one denomination on the design of its churches without comparison to the other. 3 marks maximum.)

4 a) The highest rank of bishop next to the Pope *(1 mark)*. Cardinals advise the Pope and appoint a new Pope when the old one dies *(1 mark)*.

  b) i) Papal infallibility is the doctrine that the Pope cannot make a mistake on questions of faith and morals. *(1 mark)*
So the Pope would be pretty much guaranteed to get 100% on his RS exam.

ii) The Immaculate Conception is the doctrine that Mary was born without original sin *(1 mark)*.

iii) The Magisterium is the authority of the Roman Catholic Church to teach doctrine *(1 mark)*.

c) Most Protestants think that the bread and wine are symbolic of the body and blood of Christ *(1 mark)*. However, Roman Catholics believe that the bread and wine become the body and blood of Christ (transubstantiation) *(1 mark)*.
(1 further mark for an appropriate development, such as a discussion of the words spoken by Jesus at the Last Supper, or for correct use of specialised vocabulary, e.g. transubstantiation.
Another further mark for a personal opinion, e.g. "I believe that the bread and wine are symbolic as I think it is impossible for the chemical structure of bread and wine to change through consecration."
4 marks maximum.)

Page 81 (Warm-Up Questions)

1) During meditation, the believer clears his or her mind of distracting thoughts and focuses on an image of God's creation or a specific prayer.

2) Any one of: The Lord's Supper, Mass, Eucharist, the Lord's Table, the Breaking of Bread etc.

3) a) Epiphany celebrates Jesus being shown to the wise men, his baptism and his first miracle.
And it's also the day you have to put your Christmas decorations away by if you don't want bad luck.

b) Ascension marks the day when Jesus returned to Heaven.

c) Pentecost celebrates the coming of the Holy Spirit upon the disciples.

4) Advent

5) The coffin is carried into the Church. There are hymns, Bible readings and prayers. There is often a sermon read about the Christian belief in life after death, and someone may talk about the life of the person who has died (give a eulogy). The body may be buried or cremated, and there is usually another short service at the graveside.

Page 82 (Exam Questions)

2 a) Maundy Thursday. *(2 marks. Allow 1 mark for "Thursday")*

b) During a mass or Eucharist *(1 mark)* many Christians eat a piece of bread or communion wafer representing Christ's body *(1 mark)*, and drink some wine representing his blood *(1 mark)*, in memory of Jesus' words at the Last Supper *(1 mark)*.

c) *To gain the full 6 marks on this question, you need to give an explanation of what each event means to Christians and why each event is important in its own way. You must also reach a personal conclusion.*
Your arguments could include:
• Christmas celebrates the Incarnation — the birth of Jesus
• Christ's birth is a very happy occasion, and shows God's love for his people
• if there had been no Incarnation, there could be no Easter
• Easter is about Jesus' crucifixion and the resurrection
• Christians believe that Jesus died to save them from their sins, so his death was the most important event in Jesus' life
• Christ's resurrection offered hope of life after death

3 a) The service is held on a Sunday morning and includes:
- confession and absolution *(1 mark)*
- the liturgy, (which includes set readings, a sermon, the creed and prayers) *(1 mark)*
- the priest consecrates the bread and wine *(1 mark)*
- the Lord's Prayer is recited and the bread and wine are distributed *(1 mark)*

b) Roman Catholic, Orthodox, and most Anglican churches have structured and liturgical services, meaning that they follow a set pattern of prayers, readings and a sermon. Their Sunday services usually include Holy Communion (Mass). *(2 marks)*
On the other hand, Methodists and other nonconformists have a form of worship that does not follow a strictly set-down pattern. Often hymns are alternated with readings and a sermon, and they only celebrate communion occasionally or not at all. *(2 marks)*
The most spontaneous services are in Pentecostal Churches and other independent Christian fellowships, where worship is unstructured and is often charismatic. *(2 marks)*

c) Any two of, for example:
• "Quiet Time" — time spent alone with God, perhaps reading the Bible and praying
• meditation — the believer clears his or her mind of distracting thoughts (often by repeating a prayer over and over again) and concentrates on God's nature or works
• contemplation — intimate, wordless prayer in which the believer feels the presence of God strongly
• the Rosary — a string of beads use by Catholics. As the beads are passed through the fingers, prayers are said
• icons — pictures of saints are used by Orthodox Christians to help them focus on God. They will often light candles in front of the icons and kiss them.

(Allow 1 mark for the name of the method and a second mark for a correct description. 4 marks maximum)

4 a) A sacrament is a direct communication *(1 mark)* of God's grace *(1 mark)*.

b) Roman Catholics and Orthodox Christians believe in seven sacraments: Baptism, Confirmation, Reconciliation, Eucharist, Ordination, Marriage, Anointing of the sick. *(4 marks for all correct. Lose 1 of the 4 marks for each incorrect or missing answer)*
Only two of these, Baptism *(1 mark)* and Eucharist *(1 mark)*, are accepted by most Protestants.

Page 89 (Warm-Up Questions)

1) Scripture means holy writings inspired or dictated by God.

2) For example:
The sower: seed only grows in good soil. Similarly, the word of God will only flourish in a person who lives a "Kingdom of God" lifestyle.
The growing seed: the Kingdom of God is like a seed — it grows gradually but there is no stopping it.
Don't get parables muddled up with miracles. Jesus tended to have a starring role in his miracles, whereas he just told the parables.

3) The Pharisees were a group of influential Jews who applied the rules of their religion very strictly. Jesus challenged them by, for example, picking corn on the Sabbath and questioning the practice of ritual washing.

4) Jesus' disciples recognise him as the Christ.
Jesus tells his disciples not to tell anyone about him.

5) Jesus was betrayed by Judas in the Garden of Gethsemane. He was arrested and tried by the Sanhedrin. Priests and elders testified falsely against him. At the end of the trial, Jesus was condemned for claiming to be the Christ, and was turned over to the governor, Pilate.
Pilate was to release a prisoner for Passover and let the crowd choose who he released. They had been primed by the priests to shout for a murderer named Barabbas, so Jesus was flogged and handed over for crucifixion. The Roman guards mocked Jesus and made him wear a crown of thorns. Simon of Cyrene carried Jesus' cross to Golgotha, where Jesus was crucified and died. As he died, the curtain in the temple tore in two.

Page 90 (Exam Questions)

3 a) A man leaves his vineyard in the hands of tenants *(1 mark)*. When he sends messengers to collect the rent, they are beaten or killed *(1 mark)*. The tenants kill the owner's son, thinking that they would then get the vineyard *(1 mark)*. The tenants are thrown out by the owner *(1 mark)*.

b) The chief priests and the Pharisees *(1 mark)*.

c) The vineyard owner represents God *(1 mark)*. The priests and the Pharisees are the tenants, who would kill God's Son for their own ends *(1 mark)*.
It's no good just learning the parables — you've got to know what they mean. It's the whole point of them.

d) Jesus told parables because, for example: they were simple stories which were easy to remember. People could also relate to them; story-telling was a big part of Palestinian culture; parables made people think *(Accept any two valid reasons for 1 mark each)*

4 a) Any three of:
• to love children: *"Whoever welcomes one of these little children in my name welcomes me..."*
• to be faithful in marriage: Jesus taught that anyone who divorced and remarried was committing adultery
• to be the servant of all: *"...whoever wants to be first must be slave of all."*

- to make sacrifices: the widow at the treasury gave all she had.
- to preach the Gospel: the Commission given to the disciples after Jesus' resurrection
(2 marks for each of 3 developed points. 6 marks maximum)

b) Jesus promised that whatever the disciples gave up, they would get back a hundred times over, both now and in the future *(1 mark)*.
Being a disciple isn't all a big bed of roses. But it sounds like it'll be worth it in the end.

5 a) i) Judas betrayed Jesus in the Garden of Gethsemane *(1 mark)*

ii) The Sanhedrin was the Jewish court that found Jesus guilty of blasphemy *(1 mark)*

iii) Pilate, the Roman governor, wanted to set Jesus free, but in the end let the crowd choose between Jesus and Barabbas *(1 mark)*

iv) Simon of Cyrene carried Jesus' cross *(1 mark)*

b) *To gain the full 8 marks on this question, you need to give a clear, balanced discussion using moral and religious evidence or examples — particularly from Mark's Gospel. You must also reach a personal conclusion.*
Your arguments could include:
- many people played a part in Jesus' death — no one was fully responsible.
- Pilate could have freed Jesus, but instead let the crowd make his decision for him
- Judas was the one who betrayed Jesus
- the chief priests primed the crowd to shout for Barabbas rather than Jesus
- the Sanhedrin condemned Jesus for blasphemy — which was punishable by death
- Jesus would not deny that he was the Christ, or defend himself in front of Pilate
- God let Jesus die

Section Three — Judaism
Page 98 (Warm-Up Questions)

1) After a rebellion in 70 CE.

2) Torah

3) Towards Jerusalem
The layout of a synagogue is based on the ancient Temple — It faces Jerusalem because that's where the Temple stood.

4) Mount Sinai

5) Ritual mitzvot are about Jews' relationships with God. Moral mitzvot are about Jews' dealing with others.

6) 27 Nisan

Page 99 (Exam Questions)

2 a) Abraham *(1 mark)*

b) The Covenant is the promise made between the Jews and God *(1 mark)*. Jews believe that God promised Abraham that he would have many descendants *(1 mark)*, and God would never abandon them *(1 mark)*. In return they would be circumcised to show they were God's chosen people *(1 mark)*.

c) Your answer could include:
- The Holocaust caused some Jews to doubt the goodness (or existence) of God.
- Some Jews said that the undeserved suffering during the Holocaust was testing them as Job had been tested.
(1 mark for each simple point of view about the Holocaust, or 2 marks for each elaborated point of view. 4 marks maximum.)
- Some said that the founding of the State of Israel showed God's continuing faithfulness to the Covenant.
- Some Jews thought they should have waited for the state of Israel to be established by the Messiah, rather than by politicians.
- Some Jews were concerned that the displacement of the Palestinians was not in accordance with Jewish teaching.
(1 mark for each simple point of view about the founding of the State of Israel, or 2 marks for each elaborated point of view. 4 marks maximum.)

3 a) The Shema *(1 mark)*.

b) That God is a person. That God created the world. That God sustains the world. That God is holy, omnipotent, omniscient, and omnipresent. That God gives us laws to live by and will judge us. That God is merciful. That God has a special relationship with the people of Israel.
(Allow one mark for each point, maximum 6 marks.)

c) Zionism is the belief that Jews should have a homeland of their own *(1 mark)*. *(1 further mark for a relevant elaboration, e.g. "For many Jews the establishment of the State of Israel in 1948 was the Zionist dream.")*

4 a) For example, any three of the following:
- Orthodox Jews live strictly according to the Torah and Jewish ritual and traditional rules. Progressive Jews also believe that the moral commandments in the Torah are eternal, but they believe that some of the ritual commandments can be adapted or abandoned in modern conditions.
- Orthodox Jews believe that the Messiah will come. Progressive Jews hope for a Messianic age of peace, rather than believing in the physical coming of the Messiah.
- In Orthodox Judaism only Hebrew is used in worship. In Progressive Judaism a mixture of Hebrew and the local language is used in worship.
- In Orthodox Judaism, men and women worship in separate parts of the synagogue and women do not take an active role. In Progressive Judaism, women and men worship together and women can be rabbis.
(Up to 3 marks for each difference, up to a maximum of 9 marks. Only allow 1 mark for a point about a type of Judaism which is not compared to the other type of Judaism.)
This is good to remember for questions on male and female equality too. Orthodox Jews uphold old traditions with the women remaining at home, whilst in Progressive Judaism men and women have more equal roles.

b) Any two of:
- The ancestors of Sephardic Jews (or the "Sephardim") came from countries such as Spain, Portugal or North Africa (countries that were Muslim).
- The ancestors of Ashkenazi Jews ("Ashkenazim") came from the 'Christian' countries of central or eastern Europe.
- The Falasha are Jews whose ancestors lived in Ethiopia.
(1 mark for each name and 1 mark for a correct part of the world. Up to a maximum of 4 marks.)

c) *To gain the full 6 marks on this question, you need to give a clear, balanced discussion using moral and religious evidence. You must also reach a personal conclusion.*
Your arguments could include:
- There are many benefits of customs and traditions, including reminding us of important parts of the religion's history.
- Whether or not Jews live strictly by the Torah is a matter of personal choice. Orthodox Jews should not be criticised for their beliefs.
- Following customs provides a sense of belonging to a community.
- Orthodox Jews believe the Torah is the word of God, therefore should not be betrayed by changing customs and beliefs.
- Orthodox Jews may find it difficult to accept new scientific discoveries, such as evolution, as it directly contradicts what they are taught.
- Progressive Jews believe the Torah is an interpretation of the word of God and therefore can be adapted to suit modern life.
- Ritual laws can be adapted or abandoned in response to changes in society, according to Progressive Jews.
- It's possible to follow the moral commandments without performing old-fashioned rituals.

Page 106 (Warm-Up Questions)

1) Treifah

2) The mother of the family

3) On the front door and every other door of the house, except the bathroom and toilet doors.

4) The Israelites' trek through the dessert with Moses and the shelters they camped in.

5) A prayer

6) a) 13 years old

b) 12 years old
The difference is because Judaism recognises that girls mature earlier than boys.

Page 107 (Exam Questions)

2 a) The mezuzah is a scroll containing a prayer from the Torah *(1 mark)* that is placed in a case on the doors of every Jewish house *(1 mark)*.

b) The challah (plural chalot) is a plaited loaf *(1 mark)*. Two are eaten in the Sabbath meal *(1 mark)*.

c) The tefillin or phylacteries are two leather boxes containing Torah passages *(1 mark)*. During most morning prayers one is worn on the head and one on the upper arm next to the heart *(1 mark)*.

3 a) Some Jews believe that the souls of the dead go to a place called sheol *(1 mark)*. It is usually pictured as a shadowy, gloomy underworld *(1 mark)*. Jews believe that when the Messiah comes the physical bodies of the dead will be resurrected *(1 mark)*, and body and soul will be judged by God *(1 mark)*.

b) Not leaving the body alone, washing the body in a mikveh (ritual bath), wrapping it in a plain linen shroud, placing it in a plain wooden coffin, burial within 24 hours, burial not cremation. *(1 mark each, maximum of 4 marks.)*

4 a) The seventh day of creation, when God rested after making the world *(1 mark)*.

b) Because cooking, like many other forms of work, is forbidden on the day of rest *(1 mark)*.

c) It begins at sunset on Friday *(1 mark)* and ends on Saturday night when stars begin to appear *(1 mark)*.

d) There are three Shabbat services *(1 mark)*. On Friday evening the Shabbat is welcomed as a queen with singing led by a cantor or chazan *(1 mark)*. On the main service on Saturday morning *(1 mark)* the rabbi reads from the Torah and gives a sermon *(1 mark)*. Seven men read blessings and one man reads a portion from the Nevi'im *(1 mark)*. On Saturday afternoon there is a reading from the Torah and prayers *(1 mark)*.
Don't get confused between the Jewish officials — the rabbi leads the prayers and services, whilst the chazan is involved in leading the congregation in singing.

e) At dusk on Friday the mother of the family *(1 mark)* begins the celebration by lighting two candles and saying a blessing *(1 mark)*. To begin the family Shabbat meal the father performs a ceremony called the kiddush *(1 mark)*. Wine is used in this *(1 mark)*. Two chalot (plaited loaves) are eaten *(1 mark)* after being blessed and dipped in salt *(1 mark)*. When the Shabbat ends on Saturday evening the father performs the havdalah ceremony *(1 mark)*, which separates the Shabbat from the rest of the week *(1 mark)*. He says a blessing over a special plaited candle and everyone smells sweet-smelling spices *(1 mark)*. *(Maximum 6 marks.)*

5 *To gain the full **6 marks** on this question, you need to give a clear, balanced discussion using moral and religious evidence. You must make a direct reference to Judaism and reach a personal conclusion.* Your arguments could include:
- Jews believe that if your mother is Jewish then you are a Jew. It is important for children to learn about their ancestral heritage.
- Religious beliefs can provide meaning and comfort. It is only natural for parents to want to pass on their beliefs to their children.
- Sharing the same beliefs and customs is important for family unity.
- Children cannot become true followers of a religion until they can understand all the issues.
- It doesn't harm a child born into a religion to be taught about rituals and the holy book. When they are older they can then decide whether to continue to practise it or not.
- Many religions follow the same morals, e.g. it is wrong to kill. Bringing a child up following any religion helps to teach them right from wrong.
- Children are not able to make informed choices about religion and so should not be expected to take part in the rituals of worship of a specific religion.

Section Four — Islam
Page 115 (Warm-Up Questions)

1) It is the Muslim idea of Allah's complete and final control over all events and destiny.

2) Nuh (Noah), Ibrahim (Abraham), Musa (Moses), Isa (Jesus), Muhammad.

3) The Sunnah is a text about the actions and way of life of Muhammad — Muslims look to it for guidance.

4) The Hijrah is the journey to Madinah.

5) Makkah (or Mecca)

6) The Shari'ah law is a code for extra day-to-day guidance.

Page 116 (Exam Questions)

3 Tawhid is the belief that nothing compares to the oneness of Allah *(1 mark)*. Shirk is the belief that Allah is not supreme and is a great sin in Islam *(1 mark)*.

4 Khalifah is the idea that humans are 'custodians' or 'trustees' of the Earth. Humans therefore have a responsibility to Allah's creation — we should look after the Earth *(1 mark)*. Humans should strive to make the world the place that Allah wants it to be *(1 mark)*. Muslims believe humans were given free will — we will answer for our actions on the Day of Judgement *(1 mark)*.

5 Your points could include:
- The Shi'ites followed Ali's descendants, whilst the Sunnis follow the next caliph (successor).
- Some Shi'ites believe the Qur'an has been altered by the Sunnis and the Sunnis believe it is complete and unaltered.
- The Sunnis believe that only Muhammad received special knowledge from God, whilst the Shi'ites believe Ali and Imams also have special knowledge.
- The Sunnis are guided by the consensus of the community, and the Shi'ites are guided from the Hadith of Ali and those of Muhammad.
- The Shi'ites commemorate the martyrdom of Ali and his sons Hasan and Husayn, whilst the Sunnis believe it is wrong to pay them special attention as it takes attention away from Allah and Muhammad. *(2 marks for each valid point referencing both types of Muslims, maximum 10 marks.)*
The question asks you to compare the Shi'ites and the Sunni, so you must show you've directly contrasted the two. Don't be tempted just to write about the Shi'ites and then the Sunnis — you won't get full marks.

6 a) Via the angel (1 mark) Jibrail (Gabriel) *(1 mark)*. Allah is so great that he doesn't communicate directly with humans *(1 mark)*.

b) Muhammad told the people of Makkah that they had to worship one God — Allah *(1 mark)*, and that they should listen to him, because he was Allah's Prophet *(1 mark)*. He also said they should conduct their business honestly and look after the poor *(1 mark)*. If they did not do this they would burn in Hell *(1 mark)*.

c) People laughed at him or said he was mad *(1 mark)*. Life for his followers was hard — some were killed *(1 mark)*. He was not allowed to preach within the city limits *(1 mark)*.
The story had a happy ending though. Muhammad and his followers went to Madinah where people were lots nicer to them.

7 a) i) Muslims believe that the Qur'an is a guidebook for life *(1 mark)*. Its contents tell Muslims what they should believe and how they should live *(2 marks)*. Islam teaches that it is a completely accurate and unchanged record of the exact word of Allah *(1 mark)*. Because the Qur'an was given to Muhammad in Arabic, its true meaning can only be understood if it is read in Arabic *(1 mark)*.

ii) Muslims may keep their Qur'an wrapped up to keep it clean *(1 mark)*. They wash their hands before touching it *(1 mark)*. They keep it on a higher shelf than other books *(1 mark)*. They may place it on a special stand when they read it *(1 mark)*.

b) Extra day-to-day guidance is found in the Shari'ah *(1 mark)*. This is based on the Qur'an *(1 mark)*, and is influenced by the Hadith and Sunnah of Muhammad *(1 mark)*. It also looks at the customs and practice of the Muslim community *(1 mark)*. Scholars use their knowledge of the Qur'an and of Islamic tradition to reach a consensus on how to act *(1 mark)*. Alternatively they look for guidance on a similar issue *(1 mark)*.
So whatever your question, Islam can find an answer.

c) *To gain the full **8 marks** on this question, you need to give a clear, balanced discussion using moral and religious evidence. You must include a direct reference to Islam and reach a personal conclusion.* Your arguments could include:
- Muslims would argue that the Qur'an provides a set of guidelines which help them lead their lives in an honourable and caring way.
- Others may suggest that we have free will and should choose to live the right way instead of being told what to do by books.
- Holy books were written a very long time ago and therefore they may be outdated and not relevant to modern-day life.
- If a Muslim follows the rules in the Qur'an they will lead a good life and please Allah too. This will mean they go to Paradise after they die.
- Muslims believe that everyone owes their creation to Allah so we should do what he asks in the Qur'an.
- Sufis believe it is not enough to follow the rules written in the Qur'an, and that their relationship with God is more important.

Page 122 (Warm-Up Questions)

1) Halah means allowed. Haram means forbidden.
2) To be clean and pure when approaching Allah.
3) Friday prayers
4) Id-ul-Fitr
5) Tawaf ritual – seven circuits of the Ka'ba, touching the stone if possible.
Sa'y – seven journeys between the hills of Safa and Marwa.
Journey to Mount Arafat to stand and pray.
Throw stones at three pillars in Mina.
Id-ul-Adha – a 4-day festival of prayer and sacrifice.

Page 123 (Exam Questions)

3 a) Salah prayers are compulsory prayers that a Muslim should offer 5 times each day *(1 mark)*. Du'a prayers are extra personal prayers that a Muslim can offer at any time *(1 mark)*.

   b) Muslim prayer has a set of rituals or sequences called the rak'ah. These include standing then kneeling, and putting their forehead to the ground. Before praying Muslims must wash in a certain way so that they are clean and pure before Allah. When praying a Muslim must face towards Makkah. Whilst carrying out these moves, certain words should be recited – an example is Allahu Akbar which means 'God is great'. Prayers can take place in any clean place. Ideally this should be a mosque, but if this is not possible a prayer mat should be used.
   (1 mark for each relevant point. Maximum 6 marks.)

4 Zakah is the third pillar of Islam. It involves Muslims donating 2.5% of their disposable income. The money is given to the mosque and is used to help the poor, sick and needy. Also, it may be used for religious purposes such as Muslim schools. It's a practical way to show their obedience to Allah, whilst redistributing wealth to poorer Muslims. It also shows concern for others and encourages unselfishness.
(1 mark for each relevant point. Maximum 6 marks.)
Remember — its 2.5% of their disposable income.

5 a) Fasting occurs during the month of Ramadan, between sunrise and sunset. During Ramadan, Muslims must not eat, drink, smoke or have sex. It is a time of physical and moral self-discipline. It shows complete obedience to Allah. It aims to help Muslims understand hunger and make them more willing to help others. It is a time to show that Allah matters more than physical needs. They celebrate the end of Ramadan with the Id-ul-Fitr festival.
   (Allow 1 mark for each valid point, maximum 4 marks.)
   That's no eating in daylight hours for a month — you've got to have fantastic will-power for that.

   b) Muslims must make the pilgrimage once in their lifetime, as long as they can afford it and are strong enough. They visit Makkah, where Muhammad lived and preached. They wear special clothing called ihram. They do several different rituals once at Makkah. There is a four-day festival near the end called Id-ul-Adha.
   (Allow 1 mark for each valid point, maximum 4 marks.)

6 A Sunni imam can be any person of good character who has good knowledge of the Qur'an. He teaches about the Qur'an and leads the prayers. The name is given as a title of respect. In the Shi'ite tradition, the imam is a successor of Muhammad and semi-divine. Shi'ites believe imams have special knowledge given by God. Some Shi'ite Muslims believe that the last imam is in hiding.
   (Allow 1 mark for each valid point, maximum 3 marks for each tradition. 6 marks available in total.)

7 a) i) Possible answers include:
      • All mosques have a dome representing the universe.
      • They have at least one minaret, which is a tall tower from where the muezzin calls the adhan.
      • Often there are coloured mosaic tiles or richly coloured Arabic calligraphy decoration inside and outside the mosque.
      • There is somewhere for a Muslim to wash before prayer.
      • There are no seats, but usually a carpeted floor.
      • There is a minbar, which is a pulpit.
      • There is a mihrab, which is a special niche that shows the direction in which Makkah lies.
      (2 marks for each described feature. Maximum 8 marks.

      ii) For example:
      Mosques can be used as a school, where Muslims learn about Islamic practices and recite the Qur'an.
      (2 marks for any valid answer.)

   b) A Muslim must pray five times a day and some of these prayers fall during the time when a Muslim may be at school or at work. Also, all Muslim men are expected to go to the Mosque for Friday prayers and this, again, may be a problem in a non-Muslim country where they are expected to be working. There are dress laws including wearing the hijab for women, so that nothing is visible but the face, hands and feet. This could conflict with the school/work uniform. Animals for food need to be killed in a particular way, and it may be difficult to obtain and find out how the meat was prepared. A Muslim business must be run differently as financial deals involving interest are forbidden. This also means that Muslims need to use a separate banking system.
   (1 mark for each valid point. Maximum 5 marks. Other answers possible.)

   c) *To gain the full 5 marks on this question, you need to give a clear, balanced discussion using moral and religious evidence. You must include a direct reference to Islam and reach a personal conclusion.*
   Your arguments could include:
   • Some people might argue that rituals in religion help keep believers focused on God by doing things in certain ways.
   • They also give people a sense of belonging and security.
   • Some people might suggest that you don't need rituals to worship God, and that having a personal relationship with God is more important.
   • Sufis believe Islam is about the bond between each person and God. They do not think just obeying rules is enough. They do make use of ritual practices to get closer to Allah though.
   • Obedience is an important part of Islam. By carrying out rituals Muslims are showing their obedience to Allah.
   • Some people feel that religious rituals are outdated and should be changed or abandoned to suit the times.

EXAM PAPER ANSWERS

Please note: The answers to the past exam questions have not been provided or approved by the examining bodies (AQA, OCR and London Qualifications Ltd - Edexcel). As such, AQA, OCR and London Qualifications Ltd do not accept any responsibility for the answers given. CGP has provided suggested solutions — other possible solutions may be equally correct.

See page 153 for how to work out your grade.

Paper One — Perspectives

1 a) i) a monotheist *(1 mark)*
      ii) Yes *(1 mark)*. A reason, e.g. because they call God 'Father' *(1 mark)*.

   b) Your answer could include:
      • God is outside the material world.
      • He does not act in human lives.
      • He is not limited by time or space;
      • He is the almighty creator of the universe and is therefore separate from it.
      1 mark: A relevant statement.
      2 marks: Two relevant points, or one elaborated point.
      3 marks: Two points covered clearly and well.
      4 marks: A full answer, showing the application of religious ideas.

   c) Your answer could include:
      • So that believers don't get confused.
      • So that believers don't worship images other than God.
      • If there were more than one God with independent wills, there would be chaos.
      • God is perfect and greater than anything humans can imagine. He can have no rivals, so He must be One.'
      1 mark: A relevant statement.
      2 marks: Two relevant points, or one point with elaboration.
      3 marks: An explanation, covering at least two points well.
      4 marks: A full answer, showing the application of religious ideas.

   d) Your answer could include:
      • To help them understand the full nature of God. For example, as creator, judge and provider.
      • So that believers can draw on different aspects of God for different occasions. For example, to personalise God for prayer.
      • Muslims find the 99 names for Allah in the Qu'ran useful for understanding what Allah is like. E.g. The Merciful, The Just.
      • Christians believe that God exists in three forms — the Father, the Son and the Holy Spirit. These show different aspects of God, for example, as a person with human emotions, or as God's influence in the world.
      1 mark: A relevant statement.
      2 marks: Two relevant points, or one point with elaboration.
      3 marks: An explanation, covering at least two points well.
      4 marks: A full answer, showing the application of religious ideas.

148

e) You need to say whether you agree or not with the statement and discuss different points of view. You could include the following points —
in agreement with the statement:
- The nature of God is beyond human understanding/concepts/language.
- Humans can only 'know' things they can sense. God is invisible to us, so we can't know him in the same way we know other people.
- Some of God's qualities (e.g. all-loving) go against experience (i.e. suffering).

in disagreement with the statement:
- God's qualities or nature can be know in a variety of ways through religious experience/revelation. E.g. prayer, texts, nature, miracles. Therefore God's nature can be described.
- Many religious traditions describe God's nature (loving, powerful, just, merciful, etc.)

1 mark: An opinion supported by a simple reason.
2 marks: An opinion supported by a two reasons, or one elaborated reason.
3 marks: An opinion supported by a two elaborated reasons, or one well-developed reason.
4 marks: An opinion with reasoned consideration of two viewpoints.
5 marks: An opinion with coherent, reasoned consideration of two points of view.
Think carefully about what's being asked. This question isn't about whether God exists or not, it's about whether it's possible to know what He's like.

2 a) Not giving someone a job because of their race or skin colour, or other sensible answer. *(1 mark for a partially correct answer. 2 marks for a correct answer)*

  b) Possible answers include:

  In Islam the traditional view is that men and women have an equal role in religion but that men have the role of providing for the family while women should stay at home and look after the children. However, the modern view is that men and women are equal in religion and life and that women can have careers.

  OR

  Most Orthodox Jews believe men and women have different roles. For example, they believe that men should attend the synagogue for prayers three times a day, whereas women are responsible for taking care of the home and are trusted to pray there. When women do attend an orthodox synagogue, they must sit separately from the men. However, Progressive Jews believe in completely equal roles for men and women. Men and women worship together and they have women rabbis.
1-2 marks: One relevant statement.
3-4 marks: A few examples showing basic relevant knowledge.
5-6 marks: An organised description, showing relevant knowledge of two different views. Specialist vocabulary is used when appropriate.

  c) Possible teachings that you could refer to include:
- The Parable of the Good Samaritan: A Samaritan (considered an enemy by the Jews) helps a robbery victim, whereas a priest and a Levite just carried on walking. Jesus used this parable to teach that people should treat everyone as neighbours, regardless of their race.
- Simon Peter is told by God not to consider impure anything that God has made. So when a Roman soldier sends for Peter, Peter goes willingly, even though it is against the law for Jews to associate with non-Jews. This teaches that we are all God's people, and people should not dislike certain races.
- The Old Testament says, "When an alien lives with you in your land, do not ill-treat him... Love him as yourself" (Leviticus 19:33-34). This tells us that everyone should be treated equally, whatever their race.
- Jesus taught us that we should do to others what we would have them do to us. This tells us that if we wouldn't want to be treated badly because of our race, we shouldn't treat others badly because of theirs.
1-2 marks: One simple, relevant idea.
3-4 marks: A basic explanation showing understanding of an idea.
5-6 marks: A developed explanation, showing understanding of the main ideas.
7-8 marks: A full explanation, showing good understanding of the main ideas. At least two Christian teachings must be explained.
'Explain' is a key word here. If you just describe a teaching, without saying how it promotes racial harmony, you won't get more than one mark for it.

  d) You need to say whether you agree or not with the statement and discuss different points of view. You could include the following points —
in agreement with the statement:
- In a multi-faith society, people have more chance to learn about other religions. This helps improve understanding and tolerance.
- In a mono-faith society people are likely to be more ignorant of other faiths and may fear them, leading to hostility.
- People have a legal right to follow a religion of their choice.
- Diversity makes societies much more interesting.
- People should be exposed to different faiths so that they can make an informed decision about which to follow.

in disagreement with the statement:
- Multi-faith societies confuse people. Not everyone can be right.
- Different societies have different religious traditions. If societies become multi-faith, their traditional identities will be diluted or lost.
- Christians believe that it's only by following the teachings of Jesus Christ that people can reach God. If they care about other people they should try to convert them.
1 mark: An opinion supported by one relevant reason.
2 marks: A reason for and a reason against, or an opinion well-supported by religious or moral arguments.
3 marks: An opinion supported by religious or moral arguments. Two points of view must be referred to.
4 marks: An opinion, supported by a coherent, balanced discussion of religious or moral arguments. Two different points of view must be discussed.
Remember to give your opinion. Without it you won't get more than two marks.

3 a) (i) Possible answers include:
    Some drugs are harmful for a person's body/mind; some drugs are illegal as they are very strong or dangerous; in some Muslim countries alcohol is illegal as it is against their religion; they might be sold, which damages other people; some drugs are unacceptable to society; people can become addicted to them, which may lead to crime to get money to buy them. *(1 mark for each reason, or elaboration of a reason. 3 marks available in total.)*

    (ii) Possible answers include:
    Escapism; peer pressure; enjoy taking the drug; enjoy the risk; want to try it to see what it's like; it is the culture they live in; because it's forbidden; they are addicted to it; pain relief. *(1 mark for each reason, or elaboration of a reason. 4 marks available in total.)*

  b) You need to talk about **one** religion in your answer. You could include:
For Judaism:
- Life is regarded as sacred. You shouldn't do anything that will harm it.
- The mind and the body are gifts from God — we don't have the right to abuse them.
- We were created in God's image. It's disrespectful to damage that.
- If you damage your mind or body it will become harder to follow God.
- There is compassion and support for people who have damaged their body or mind, such as drug users.

For Christianity:
As for Judaism, plus:
- The Bible says that "Your body is a temple of the Holy Spirit...".

For Islam:
- The mind and the body are gifts from Allah — we don't have the right to abuse them.
- Muslims have a duty to pray and must have a clear mind for this. This might not be possible if they've used drugs or alcohol.
- It's a basic principle of Shari'ah that a Muslim should not harm the bodies or minds of others. While under the influence of drugs you might hurt other people.
- It's forbidden to be involved in the production or sale of alcohol/drugs as this may harm others.
1 mark: A relevant statement.
2 marks: Two relevant points, or one point with elaboration.
3 marks: An explanation, covering at least two points well.
4 marks: A full answer, showing the application of religious ideas.

  c) You need to talk about **one** religion in your answer — it must be different from the one you discussed in part (b). You could include:
For both Judaism and Christianity:
- Drinking alcohol in moderation is allowed. Drinking it to excess is disapproved of.
- Abusing alcohol can lead to death, and life is regarded as sacred.
- The mind and the body are gifts from God — we don't have the right to abuse them.
- We were created in God's image. It's disrespectful to damage that.
- Abusing alcohol leads to irresponsible behaviour, such as neglecting your family.
- Alcohol abuse prevents us from following God.

For Judaism:
- Wine is used at meals and festivals.
- There are support services for addicts within Judaism.

For Christianity:
- It's used in Holy Communion, so it must be acceptable.
- Some denominations disapprove more than others, e.g. Salvation Army. However, Salvation Army works to help alcoholics.
- Alcohol distorts perceptions, so abuse of it can be seen as breaking Jesus' principles of love.

For Islam:
- Any form of drug taking (including alcohol) is forbidden.
- Prophet Muhammad said that intoxicants are the mother of all vices.
- Drugs take away all self-control and lead to wrongful behaviour.
- Muslims have a duty to pray and must have a clear mind for this.
- It's a basic principle of Shari'ah that a Muslim should not harm others. While under the influence of alcohol you might hurt other people.
- It's forbidden to be involved in the production or sale of alcohol as this may harm others.
- Users should be helped.

1 mark: A relevant statement.
2 marks: Two relevant points, or one point with elaboration.
3 marks: An explanation, covering at least two points well.
4 marks: A full answer, showing the application of religious ideas.
If you write about the same religion for parts (b) and (c), you're going to throw away a heap of marks. It all comes back to reading the question carefully.

d) You need to say whether you agree or not with the statement and discuss different points of view. You could include the following points —
in agreement with the statement:
- It's their choice to harm themselves, why should others pay?
- There are limited resources, so we should prioritise. Smokers and drinkers shouldn't be priorities. For example, donated organs should be given to more deserving people first.
- There are enough warnings about what will happen — they shouldn't have ignored them.
- They have disobeyed God, and should be punished.

in disagreement with the statement:
- They have paid for the service through taxes and are entitled to it.
- Why pick those people out? Others deliberately hurt themselves and get treated for free.
- God created us all equally, and we should all be treated equally.
- Jesus taught us that we should not judge others.
- The New Testament said we should "Love our neighbour".

1 mark: An opinion supported by one simple reason.
2 marks: An opinion supported by one elaborated reason, or two simple reasons (for the same view or for different points of view).
3 marks: An opinion supported by one well-developed reason, or two elaborated reasons (for the same view or for different points of view).
4 marks: An opinion supported by reasoned consideration of two points of view.
5 marks: An opinion supported by reasoned consideration of two points of view expressed clearly.

4 a) You need to talk about **two** religions in your answer. You could include:

For all three religions:
- Contraception helps promote promiscuity, so is wrong.
- Certain forms of contraception help prevent the spread of disease.

For Judaism:
- Contraception interferes with God's plan.
- Preserving life is of supreme importance, so if the mother's health is at risk by pregnancy, contraception is permitted.
- Some Jews are happy with the use of contraception for family planning, but many Orthodox Jews aren't.

For Christianity:
- Most denominations allow the use of birth control for family planning.
- Roman Catholics do not permit artificial contraception, as it is against 'natural law'. It teaches that humans have an obligation to 'be fruitful and increase in number'.
- Procreation is one of the main purposes of marriage.

For Islam:
- Only Allah should decide when a new life begins, so contraception is unwelcome. Surah 42:49-50 says, "He bestows male and female children... and He makes barren whom he wills."
- It's permitted if:
  - there is a threat to the mother's health
  - there is a greater than average risk that the child will be disabled
  - it could help a woman who already has children
  - if the family is too poor to raise a child.

You get 1 mark for showing you know what contraception is, and up to 3 marks for each religion.

For each religion:
1 mark: One relevant piece of information.
2 marks: Two relevant pieces of information, or good development of one piece of information.
3 marks: Three relevant pieces of information, or at least two pieces of information with development.

b) You need to talk about the **same** two religions as you did in part (a). You could include:

For Judaism:
- The sixth Commandment is do not kill. Knowing this may deter a believer from having an abortion, as she is likely to consider it a sin.
- Judaism allows abortion if the mother's life is threatened, if the child will be severely disabled, or if the pregnancy is a product of rape. If the believer is in one of these situations, they may feel that an abortion is the best thing.

For Christianity:
- A believer might be influenced differently, depending on which denomination she belongs to. Most denominations allow abortion if the mother's life is threatened, if the child will be severely disabled, or if the pregnancy is a product of rape. However, Roman Catholics are strongly against it, whereas Free churches, such as the Quakers, leave it to individuals to decide.
- The Bible teaches us to love our neighbours. A compassionate view should be taken towards the woman and the foetus. A woman may feel that she is making a decision which is compassionate for her foetus. Alternatively, she may find it easier to have an abortion if she feels that the church will not condemn her.
- The sixth Commandment is do not kill. Knowing this may deter a believer from having an abortion, as she is likely to consider it a sin.

For Islam:
- Abortion is permitted if the mother's life is in danger. The potential life in the womb is not as important as the actual life of the mother. This may lead a believer in this situation to have an abortion, as she may feel that it is what Allah would prefer.
- Only Allah can decide when a life begins or ends. Surah 17:31 said "Slay not your children... the slaying of them is a great sin". If the believer did not want to sin, she would be likely to decide not to have an abortion.

1-3 marks: Relevant statement, with no link to religious teaching.
4-5 marks: More understanding shown of how beliefs may affect the decision whether or not to have an abortion. Includes specific religious teachings from at least one religion.
6-8 marks: Good understanding of how beliefs may affect the decision. Teachings from both religions are included.
Don't just quote a bunch of religious teachings here — you've got to say how the teachings may help a believer decide whether or not to have an abortion.

c) You need to say whether you agree or not with the statement and discuss different points of view. You could include the following points —
in agreement with the statement:
- It's a woman's choice what she does with her body.
- It's possible to make a moral decision without using religious teachings. From a human rights perspective, people may believe that unborn babies have rights.
- Today, many women want to have small families or pursue a career. Religious teachings may date back to times when this was not the case.
- The social effects of bringing unwanted children into the world are more important than obeying religious teachings.
- Christians are taught to love their neighbour. People should not be judged if their decisions go against religious teachings.
- If people aren't religious they shouldn't care about religious teachings.

in disagreement with the statement:
- If someone truly believes in a religion, they should want to do what their religion considers right.
- Many of the religious teachings are based on morals and what is ethically correct. Using them helps us avoid being selfish.
- On Judgement Day God will decide if they have led good lives. They should follow religious teachings in order to be judged favourably.

1 mark: An opinion supported by one simple reason.
2 marks: An opinion supported by one elaborated reason, or two simple reasons (for the same view or for different points of view).
3 marks: An opinion supported by one well-developed reason, or two elaborated reasons (for the same view or for different points of view).
4 marks: An opinion supported by reasoned consideration of two points of view.
5 marks: An opinion supported by reasoned consideration of two points of view expressed clearly.

Paper Two — Christianity

1 a) Infants cannot choose whether they want to be baptised or not *(1 mark)*.

 b) Confirmation is when a Christian renews the promises made on their behalf at baptism *(2 marks for a full answer, 1 mark for a simple answer)*.

2 a) The teaching authority of the Roman Catholic Church *(1 mark)*, and the Pope and bishops' decisions on matters of faith or morals *(1 mark for this or another relevant point)*.

 b) He is believed to be a successor of St Peter (the first Pope). He is infallible on matters of faith and morals. Other answers are possible. *(1 mark for each point, up to a maximum of 2 marks)*.

3 a) Good news *(1 mark)*

 b) Portraying things in a similar way/from a common viewpoint *(1 mark)*.

4 a) (i) A summary of Christian beliefs *(1 mark)*.

 (ii) As a guide, reminding them of the main beliefs of Christianity. Other answers are possible. *(2 marks for a clear answer, 1 mark for an incomplete answer)*

 b) Any two of:
 • That everything in the Bible must be taken literally.
 • That the Bible was dictated by God, so it cannot contain errors. Therefore, it is wrong to question anything in it.
 • That the Bible was inspired by God, but was not dictated by Him — it is not a scientific text.
 • That the Bible contains spiritual truth, rather than historical truth — almost everything in it can be interpreted symbolically.
 (2 marks for each clear, complete answer. 1 mark for an incomplete answer. 4 marks available in total.)

5 a) You can use any act of Sunday Worship from any Christian denomination. For example, in the Roman Catholic tradition Mass remembers the Last Supper. It consists of the following:
 - Penitential Rite: participants confess their sins and ask for forgiveness.
 - The Liturgy of the Word: readings, sermons and the creed.
 - The Eucharistic Prayers: the priest consecrates the bread and wine using the words of the Last Supper. Catholics believe that the bread and wine become the body and blood of Jesus (transubstantiation).
 - The Rite of Communion: The Lord's Prayer is recited and the bread and wine is distributed.
 1-2 marks: A simple statement concerning an act of Sunday worship.
 3-4 marks: A simple description of the main aspects of the act.
 5-7 marks: A clear description with some elaboration about the events.
 It's a good idea to pick an act of worship that you've got lots to say about. Don't forget to say which denomination you're referring to.

 b) (i) Icons are paintings of Jesus, Mary and the saints. To Orthodox Christians they represent the presence of the person in the picture. They are used to focus thoughts during prayer.

 (ii) The rosary is a string of beads used by Roman Catholics to focus attention during prayer. As the beads are moved through the fingers prayers, such as the Lord's Prayer, Hail Mary and Gloria, are said. (There are other points you could mention about the rosary.)

 There are 4 marks available for each part.
 1 mark: One simple fact.
 2 marks: A basic outline, with some confusion.
 3 marks: An account covering most of the main points.
 4 marks: An accurate, clear account.

 c) You need to say whether you agree or not with the statement and discuss different points of view. You could include the following points —
 in agreement with the statement:
 • If you believe in the Christian faith you're a Christian.
 • How you live determines whether or not you are a Christian.
 • Religion is a private matter — no one has the right to tell others how to be a Christian.

 in disagreement with the statement:
 • Prayer is communicating with God, which is important to Christians.
 • Prayer is an important part of public worship. Public worship is fellowship with God and other Christians.
 • Prayer is important to ask for forgiveness for sins.
 • Prayer is an important aspect of Christianity. If people do not pray then they shouldn't consider themselves true Christians.

1 mark: An opinion supported by one simple reason.
2 marks: An opinion supported by one elaborated reason, or two simple reasons (for the same view or for different points of view).
3 marks: An opinion supported by one well-developed reason, or two elaborated reasons (for the same view or for different points of view).
4 marks: An opinion supported by reasoned consideration of two points of view.
5 marks: An opinion supported by reasoned consideration of two points of view expressed clearly.

6 a) Your answer may include:
 • natural disasters, such as tsunamis or earthquakes — these destroy buildings and roads, and prevent the distribution of electricity and water, meaning industry and businesses can't function.
 • debt — many poor countries are struggling to repay money they have borrowed from other countries (with interest).
 • wars — money is spent on the military rather than on other matters.
 • population growth — if population is growing quickly there are large numbers of children that can't contribute to the economy.
 • unfair trade — raw materials from poor countries only fetch low prices.
 1 mark: One or two causes named.
 2 marks: Three or four causes named, or two causes outlined.
 3 marks: Three causes are outlined (not just named).
 4 marks: Four causes are clearly outlined (not just named).

 b) You could include the following points in your answer:
 • Jesus always helped to relieve suffering, for example when he healed people. In following his example, we should try to relieve suffering to the best of our ability.
 • The church teaches that Christians should help to relieve poverty and suffering. For example, the Catechism of the Roman Catholic Church says, "Rich nations have a grave moral responsibility towards those which are unable to ensure the means of their development by themselves".
 • The parable of the Good Samaritan teaches that we should help others who are suffering. Race or religion doesn't matter — all people are our neighbours.
 • Many Bible passages demonstrate Jesus' compassion and indicate what Christians should do to follow Jesus' ways. For example, "The man with two tunics should share with him that has none, and the one who has food must do the same," Luke 3:11.
 You could also explain the parable of the sheep and the goat (Matthew 25), Amos' teachings (Amos 8:4-6), or the Christian principle of agape.

 1-2 marks: A simple statement of a relevant idea.
 3-4 marks: An explanation showing understanding of a relevant idea.
 5-6 marks: Two relevant ideas, one of which must be a developed explanation. Some specialist vocabulary is used.
 7-8 marks: At least two ideas are well developed. Specialist vocabulary is used appropriately.

 c) You need to say whether you agree or not with the statement and discuss different points of view. You could include the following points —
 in agreement with the statement:
 • Any of the Christian teachings from part (b).
 • All wealth ultimately belongs to God and should be used for the good of everyone.
 • True Christians will want to put their faith into practice and will not be interested in accumulating wealth, but in serving God.

 in disagreement with the statement:
 • It is not up to individuals to help. It is the government's responsibility.
 • People have varying circumstances. Some people, such as the elderly, may not be able to give 10% and still have enough to live on.
 • Giving money to the poor will make them reliant on outside help.
 • Being a Christian is more about your beliefs than your actions.
 • There are other ways to help people, such as giving your time to a voluntary group.
 • The church is a very rich institution; it should do more to help the poor.

 1-2 marks: An opinion supported by one simple reason.
 3-4 marks: Two reasons, one for and one against, or an opinion supported by one elaborated reason.
 5-6 marks: An opinion supported by elaborated points of view, both for and against.
 7-8 marks: An opinion supported by a balanced account of two points of view, expressed clearly.
 To get maximum marks, you need to give a clear, well-organised answer. Before you start scribbling away willy-nilly, have a bit of a think about where you're going with your argument.

7 a) You could include the following points in your answer:
- Christians generally believe that it is OK to use fertility treatment to help couples conceive.
- Christianity teaches compassion, and fertility treatment helps people who desperately want children.
- Christians look less favourably on methods that use donated sperm (AID), as this interferes with the sanctity of marriage.
- The Roman Catholic Church is opposed to IVF, as this creates spare embryos which may be used for experimentation, or just thrown away.
- Some Christians may be against fertility treatment as they believe that it interferes with 'Natural Law' (God's plan).

1-2 marks: One or two simple points.
3-4 marks: At least two elaborated points.
5-6 marks: A description that elaborates on at least three points.
7-8 marks: A clear description that covers almost all of the points above in a reasonable amount of detail.

b) You could include the following points in your answer:
- Many Christians believe that we are superior to animals because we are created in God's image.
- It said in Genesis 1:26 that humans will have power over animals. This may be interpreted to imply that animals are here for our use.
- Most Christians think that animals don't have souls. This is another argument for using them to benefit mankind.
- Animals are part of God's creation, so should be cared for. If they are used in research they should be treated kindly.
- The use of animals in medical research is justifiable as it reduces human suffering.
- The use of animals in medical research is acceptable, whereas other uses, such as research into cosmetics, is not.
- Animals used in medical research should be treated humanely.

1-2 marks: One or two simple points.
3-5 marks: At least two elaborated points.
6-7 marks: A clear explanation, covering all of the main issues.

c) You need to say whether you agree or not with the statement and discuss different points of view. You have to refer to Christianity.
You could include the following points —
in agreement with the statement:
- Christianity teaches that one of the main purposes of marriage is to have children. Women should be able to fulfil this purpose.
- A woman's purpose is to have children. It is the right of every woman to fulfil this purpose.
- If a woman is desperate to have a baby, she should be helped to have one. This is the compassionate thing to do and compassion is a Christian teaching.

in disagreement with the statement:
- Christians believe that sex should be kept within marriage. Therefore, single women do not have the right to have a baby.
- If a woman is unable to conceive, then this is God's will and shouldn't be interfered with.
- A baby is a gift from God, rather than every woman's right.
- Whether or not a woman conceives is partly due to chance. Therefore, this cannot be a right.
- A woman should only have a baby if she can care for it sufficiently.

1 mark: One simple relevant statement.
2 marks: An opinion, well supported by a reason.
3 marks: An opinion supported by two reasons, one for and one against.
4 marks: An opinion supported by reasoned consideration of two points of view.
5 marks: An opinion supported by reasoned consideration of two points of view expressed clearly.

Paper 3 — Judaism

1 a) Torah, Nevi'im, Ketuvim OR Law, Prophets, Writings *(1 mark for each).*

b) Oral Torah, written down by Rabbi Judah the Prince about 200 CE. Means learning or repetition. *(1 mark for basic fact, 1 mark for development.)*

c) An extended commentary on the Mishnah. Means completion. *(1 mark for basic fact, 1 mark for development.)*

2 a) You could include the following points —
- During the 1920s the Nazi party started to pin the blame for their country's economic problems on the Jews.
- Laws were passed depriving the Jews of their citizenship rights.
- From 1933, Jews became under increasingly severe oppression by the Nazis.
- Hitler introduced a plan to wipe out all the Jews completely.

- During World War II concentration camps and extermination camps were built, where Jews were killed in gas chambers.
- 6 million Jews died.

1–2 marks: One or two brief relevant statements.
3–4 marks: A basic description, covering some of the main events.
5–6 marks: A developed description, showing understanding of the main events.
7–8 marks: A comprehensive description, showing a clear understanding of the main events.

b) You could include the following points —
- A lot of Jews were forced to question their beliefs in God.
- Some Jews believed that all the suffering was a test of faith.
- The State of Israel was established after the Holocaust, to which many Jews have devoted their energy.
- A memorial was built called Yad Vashem, which has all the names of the concentration camps engraved in the floor of a candlelit hall. It is visited by pilgrims.

1–2 marks: A simple, appropriate idea.
3–4 marks: A basic explanation, showing understanding of the main ideas.
5–6 marks: A developed explanation, showing understanding of the main ideas and using specialised vocabulary when appropriate.
7 marks: A comprehensive explanation, showing a clear understanding of the main ideas and using specialised vocabulary when appropriate.

c) You need to say whether you agree or not with the statement and discuss different points of view. You could include the following points —
in agreement with the statement:
- If God does exist, and is all-powerful (omnipotent), he would have been able to intervene.
- Jews believe they are God's chosen people. If God does exist, he would not have let six million of them be killed.

in disagreement with the statement:
- God could intervene but chose not to. He gave us free will which we abused, so he refused to override it.
- God does exist, but he is not omnipotent, as is generally thought.
- God does exist, and all the suffering was a test of faith.

1 mark: An opinion supported by a relevant reason.
2 marks: An opinion supported by one elaborated reason or two or more simple reasons.
3 marks: An opinion supported by one well-developed reason or two elaborated reasons (for the same view or different points of view.)
4 marks: An opinion supported by reasoned consideration of two different points of view.
5 marks: An opinion supported by reasoned consideration of two points of view expressed coherently.

3 a) Moses *(1 mark)*

b) An agreement between two parties (e.g. God and the Jews)/a two-way promise *(1 mark)*.

c) The opening of a very important Jewish prayer *(1 mark)*.

d) Two of the following —
- There is only one god.
- He is the creator.
- He is omnipotent (all powerful).
- He is omniscient (knows everything).
- He is omnipresent (present throughout the universe).
- He is the true judge.
- He is the sustainer (his energy keeps the world going).
(1 mark each, maximum 2 marks. Other answers possible.)

e) Two of the following —
- A mammal must have cloven (split) hooves.
- A mammal must chew cud.
- Fish must have fins and scales.
- All blood must be removed.
- Meat and dairy cannot be eaten together.
(1 mark each, maximum 2 marks. Other answers possible.)

f) Three of the following —
- A visit to the mikveh the previous evening.
- A fast lasting 25 hours.
- Wearing the kittel (white smock).
- Chanting the Kol Nidre (annulment of vows).
- Attending the Neilah (closing service).
(1 mark each, maximum 3 marks. Other answers possible.)

g) You could include the following points —
- It contains the first five books of the Bible (Genesis to Deuteronomy) — the creation stories.

- It contains commandments (mitzvot) that Jews are to live by.
- It is regarded as the holiest part of the Tenakh, because it was given to Moses directly by God.
- It is read every Shabbat in the synagogue.
1 mark: One relevant statement.
2 marks: One elaborated statement, showing some understanding of the main ideas.
3 marks: A reasonable outline of at least two of the main ideas.
4 marks: An outline of at least three points showing clear understanding of the main ideas.
5 marks: A developed explanation of the main ideas, including the Torah's use in worship.

h) You need to say whether you agree or not with the statement and discuss different points of view. You could include the following points —
in agreement with the statement:
- It is a day of rest to commemorate the 7th day of creation.
- The fourth commandment instructs them to observe the Sabbath.
- It's a day of calm, rest and peace. It is a chance to focus on worship.
- It is celebrated at home as well as in the synagogue, with the kiddush ceremony, including food and drink.
- It helps to keep Judaism alive.
in disagreement with the statement:
- Prayer is important every day of the week, compared with the Sabbath which is only once a week.
- There are many festivals which are very important as they celebrate various occasions in the Jewish history. For example, Pesach celebrates the exodus from Egypt.
- Being a good person and believing in God is more important.
- Keeping Shabbat holy is an outdated teaching which is no longer relevant and should be abandoned.
- Keeping Jewish traditions, such as food and dress laws, are more important as these should be followed every day.
1 mark: An opinion supported by a relevant reason.
2 marks: An opinion supported by one elaborated reason or two or more simple reasons.
3 marks: An opinion supported by one well-developed reason or two elaborated reasons (for the same view or different points of view.)
4 marks: An opinion supported by reasoned consideration of two different points of view.
5 marks: An opinion supported by reasoned consideration of two points of view expressed clearly.

4 a) You could include the following points —
- A menorah (a seven-branched candlestick) on the outside.
- A magen David (a six-pointed star/shield of David) on the outside.
- Aron Hakodesh (the ark), which is a large cupboard or alcove set on the wall facing Jerusalem.
- Ner Tamid (everlasting light), above the ark, representing the menorah that was kept alight in the Temple.
- Sefer Torah (scrolls of the Torah), handwritten, and usually decorated.
- Bimah or Almemar, a raised platform with a reading desk.
1 mark: One relevant feature mentioned.
2 marks: Three features mentioned, or two features described.
3 marks: A description of at least three features. Some use of specialised vocabulary.
4 marks: A clear description of at least four features. Specialised vocabulary is used.

b) You could include the following points:
- Rabbis are central figures during worship in the synagogue. They lead the worship, read from the Torah and give sermons on Shabbat.
- Rabbis are important as they conduct ceremonies such as weddings and funerals.
- They provide comfort and compassion to the sick and elderly.
- Rabbis are respected figures and often give advice to members of the community. They also educate people about religion and morals.
- Rabbis are respected as they have studied for many years and have undergone practical training.
1–2 marks: A simple relevant idea.
3–4 marks: A basic explanation of a relevant idea.
5–6 marks: A developed explanation showing understanding of some of the main ideas, using some specialist vocabulary.
7–8 marks: A clear explanation showing a good understanding of the main ideas, using specialist language appropriately.

c) You need to say whether you agree or not with the statement and discuss different points of view. You could include the following points —
in agreement with the statement:
- The words of the Torah should be followed strictly — it tells the Jews how they should live and worship.

- All beliefs and practices are still important today, and so worship should be the same as it always has been.
in disagreement with the statement:
- Orthodox and Progressive Jews worship in different ways.
- Some rules can be adapted or abandoned in response to the changes in society.
- The moral commandments are considered open to interpretation, and consequently there will be differences in how individuals worship.
1–2 marks: An opinion supported by a single relevant reason.
3–4 marks: A reason for and a reason against, or an opinion supported by a developed reason.
5–6 marks: An opinion, supported by reference to two points of view.
7–8 marks: A clear, balanced account, referring to two points of view. A personal conclusion must be reached.

Paper 4 — Islam

1 a) A marriage where the parents have found a suitable partner for their son or daughter *(1 mark)*.
b) Divorce is allowed but only as a last resort. If a marriage begins to go wrong, it is the parents' responsibility to help.
1 mark for a partial answer, and 2 marks for the complete answer.
c) People should wear modest clothing *(1 mark)*.

2 Shahadah: The Muslim statement/declaration of faith *(1 mark)*.
Salah: Praying to Allah five times a day (keeps Allah in mind) *(1 mark)*.
Hajj: The pilgrimage to Makkah (reminds them of Islam's origins) *(1 mark)*.

3 a) You could include the following points —
- A dome representing the universe.
- At least one minaret (a tall tower) from which the muezzin calls the adhan.
- Inside, there is a place for the Muslims to wash before prayer (wudu).
- A minbar (pulpit) from which the imam leads prayers.
- A special niche in the direction-wall called the mihrab that shows the direction of Makkah.
1–2 marks: One or two relevant features mentioned.
3–4 marks: A basic description of one or two main features.
5–6 marks: A developed description, showing good understanding of most of the main features.
7–8 marks: A full, coherent description, showing good understanding of all the main features.
You've been asked to describe the features, so don't just name them.

b) You could include the following points —
- Muslims do not have a 'priest'; instead they have an imam, who leads the prayers from the minbar in the mosque.
- Imams teach the Qur'an.
- They may visit the sick and the bereaved.
- An imam may conduct weddings and funerals.
- They have the right to be able to interpret the Qur'an and advise the community on how to live their lives in modern society, and in non-Muslim societies.
- In the Shi'ite tradition, the imam is a successor of Muhammad and considered a 'holy man'.
1–2 marks: A simple relevant idea.
3–4 marks: A basic explanation of a relevant idea.
5–6 marks: A developed explanation showing understanding of some of the main ideas, using some specialist vocabulary.
7 marks: A clear explanation showing a good understanding of the main ideas, using specialist language appropriately.

c) You could include the following points —
in agreement with the statement:
- Salat-al-Jum'ah are Friday prayers and are an important community occasion; it creates a sense of unity and provides a focal point.
- For Muslims, you have got to act on your beliefs, and this includes attending the mosque on Friday as part of Salah.
- It keeps Allah foremost in the minds of the community.
in disagreement with the statement:
- Not all true Muslims will be able to attend the mosque every Friday, especially those who live in non-Muslim communities and are expected to be at work at the time of the services.
- Muhammad said that a Muslim can pray anywhere that's clean, so if an individual is unable to get to the mosque they are still able to pray and worship Allah, and be a true Muslim.
- Going to a mosque every Friday is not as important as other Muslim beliefs, such as the declaration of faith.

1 mark: An opinion supported by one relevant reason.
2 marks: An opinion supported by one elaborated reason, or two simple reasons (for the same view or for different points of view).
3 marks: An opinion supported by one well-developed reason, or two elaborated reasons (for the same or for different points of view).
4 marks: An opinion supported by reasoned religious or moral arguments. Two points of view must be considered.
5 marks: An opinion supported by a coherent, balanced discussion of religious or moral arguments. Two different points of view must be discussed.

4 a) You could include the following points —
- Sunnis and Shi'ahs split after the death of Ali.
- Some Shi'ahs believe the Qur'an has been altered by the Sunnis, but the Sunnis believe it is complete and unaltered.
- The Shi'ah Muslims believe that Ali was the first true leader after Muhammad, and all leaders should be descended from Muhammad, whilst the Sunnis follow the next successor (caliph), who is selected by the community.
- The Sunnis believe that only Muhammad received special knowledge from God, whilst the Shi'ahs believe Ali and imams also have special knowledge.
- The Sunnis are guided by the consensus of the community, and the Shi'ahs are guided from the Hadith of Ali and those of Muhammad.
- The Shi'ahs commemorate the martyrdom of Ali and his sons Hasan and Husayn, whilst the Sunnis believe it is wrong to pay them special attention as it takes attention away from Allah and Muhammad.

1–2 marks: One relevant difference
3–4 marks: A basic description of one or two differences.
5–6 marks: A description of at least three differences, using some specialist vocabulary when appropriate.
7–8 marks: A full description of most of the main differences, using specialist vocabulary when appropriate.
Shi'ah Muslims are the same as Shi'ite Muslims.

b) You could include the following points —
- Jihad means 'striving' to resist evil.
- There are two types of Jihad — Greater Jihad which is a personal struggle against a person's own selfish desires, and Lesser Jihad which is a struggle to make the world a better place.
- Greater Jihad is an individual's effort to obey Allah and to become a better Muslim. It is a spiritual quest.
- Lesser Jihad is fighting against wider issues like poverty, injustice and defence against enemies.
- War is an example of Lesser Jihad. Muslims must only fight as a last resort and war is only justified if it brings or restores peace.

1–2 marks: A simple, relevant idea.
3–4 marks: A basic explanation, showing understanding of the main ideas.
5–6 marks: A developed explanation, showing understanding of the main ideas and referring to both Greater and Lesser Jihad.
7 marks: A clear explanation, showing a good understanding of the main ideas of both Greater and Lesser Jihad.

c) You could include the following points —
in agreement with the statement:
- In Islam, war is only justified if it will bring peace.
- War is a very last resort, must involve minimum suffering, and be led by a spiritual leader.
- The Qur'an teaches love and forgiveness.
- Daily prayers promote peace.
- A Hadith says, "Hate your enemy mildly; he may be your friend one day".
in disagreement with the statement:
- Holy war is an example of Lesser Jihad. It's allowed to defend the faith.
- The concept of Jihad has been interpreted by some Muslims as a justification for terrorism.
- Dying in the service of Allah turns Muslims into martyrs, who will go to Paradise immediately. This encourages violence claimed to be in the name of Allah.

1 mark: An opinion supported by one relevant reason.
2 marks: An opinion supported by one elaborated reason, or two simple reasons (for the same view or for different points of view).
3 marks: An opinion supported by one well-developed reason, or two elaborated reasons (for the same or different points of view).
4 marks: An opinion supported by reasoned religious or moral arguments. Two points of view must be considered.
5 marks: A coherent, balanced discussion of religious or moral arguments. Two different points of view must be discussed and a personal conclusion reached.

5 a) Hijrah was the emigration of Muhammad and his follows, from Makkah to Madinah, in 622 CE.
(You get 1 mark for a partially correct answer, and 2 marks for the correct answer.)

b) You could include the following points —
- The festival of Ashura is celebrated on 10 Muharram.
- It's the celebration of the martyrdom of Husayn, who was one of Ali's sons.
- Husayn was killed at Karbala.
- On this day, the Shi'ah Muslims perform rituals re-enacting the event, and some may injure themselves to share in his suffering.

1–2 marks: One relevant example.
3–4 marks: A few points showing basic relevant knowledge.
5–6 marks: An organised description, showing relevant knowledge. Specialist vocabulary is used when appropriate.
Shi'ah Muslims are the same as Shi'ite Muslims.

c) You could include the following points —
- The Qur'an is the most important book for Muslims as it records all of Allah's revelations.
- The Qur'an is sacred as it is a completely accurate and unchanged record of Allah's words, which were revealed to Muhammad. It can be trusted completely.
- The Qur'an is important as it is a complete guide to Islamic life. It tells Muslims what to believe and how they should live so that they can get to Paradise.

1–2 marks: One simple, relevant idea.
3–4 marks: A basic explanation, showing understanding of a main idea.
5–6 marks: A developed explanation, showing understanding of the main ideas and using specialised vocabulary when appropriate.
7–8 marks: A comprehensive explanation, showing a clear understanding of the main ideas and using specialised vocabulary when appropriate.
'Explain' is the important word in the question. If you only describe the Qur'an you cannot get more than a couple of marks.

d) You could include the following points —
in agreement with the statement:
- According to Islam, Muhammad was the last prophet to be spoken to by God. God is important to Jews and Christians, so Muhammad is relevant to them too.
- The moral messages Allah gave to Muhammad are relevant to everyone, regardless of their chosen religion.
- After the death of Ali, there was a split in the Muslim religion, but both religions agree that Muhammad was very important, and therefore he is the prophet for all Muslims.
in disagreement with the statement:
- Muhammad is very specific to the Islam religion, therefore he is only important for Muslims.
- The Qur'an teaches that all good people will be rewarded, regardless of what religion they follow, therefore it does not matter if people pay particular attention to Muhammad or not.
- Followers of other religions believe that their religion is the one true religion. Therefore, they will not pay any attention to Muhammad.

1 mark: An opinion supported by one relevant reason.
2 marks: A reason for and against, or a reasoned opinion supported by religious or moral evidence.
3 marks: An opinion supported by a reference to two points of view.
4 marks: A clear, balanced account. Two points of view must be referred to, and a personal conclusion reached.

Working out your Grade

It's not easy to mark your own Religious Studies answers to give a reliable grade. However, as a guide, 76% is an A*, 66% is an A, 56% is a B, 47% is a C, 39% is a D, 32% is an E, 24% is an F and 17% is a G.
Paper 1 has a total of 80 marks.
Paper 2 has a total of 77 marks.
Paper 3 and Paper 4 have a total of 67 marks each.

Index

Index

Make sure you're not missing out on another superb CGP revision book that might just save your life...

...order your **free** catalogue today.

CGP customer service is second to none

We work very hard to despatch all orders the **same day** we receive them, and our success rate is currently 99.9%. We send all orders by **overnight courier** or **First Class** post.
If you ring us today you should get your catalogue or book tomorrow. Irresistible, surely?

- Phone: 0870 750 1252   (Mon-Fri, 8.30am to 5.30pm)
- Fax: 0870 750 1292
- e-mail: orders@cgpbooks.co.uk
- Post: CGP, Kirkby in Furness, Cumbria, LA17 7WZ
- Website: www.cgpbooks.co.uk

...or you can ask at any good bookshop.